P9-DWY-489

# The New
# Artisan Bread
## in Five Minutes a Day

Also by Jeff Hertzberg, M.D., and Zoë François

*Healthy Bread in Five Minutes a Day: 100 New Recipes Featuring Whole Grains, Fruits, Vegetables, and Gluten-Free Ingredients*

*Artisan Pizza and Flatbread in Five Minutes a Day: The Homemade Bread Revolution Continues*

# The New ARTISAN BREAD in Five Minutes a Day

## The Discovery That Revolutionizes Home Baking

**REVISED EDITION**

JEFF HERTZBERG, M.D. and ZOË FRANÇOIS

Photography by STEPHEN SCOTT GROSS

THOMAS DUNNE BOOKS
ST. MARTIN'S PRESS NEW YORK

THOMAS DUNNE BOOKS.
An imprint of St. Martin's Press.



www.thomasdunnebooks.com
www.stmartins.com

Design by Phil Mazzone



Library of Congress Cataloging-in-Publication Data

Hertzberg, Jeff.
Artisan bread in five minutes a day / Jeff Hertzberg and Zoë François.—1st ed.
p. cm.
ISBN 978-1-250-01828-1 (hardcover)
ISBN 978-1-250-01829-8 (e-book)
1. Bread. I. François, Zoë. II. Title.
TX769.H474 2013
641.81'5—dc23

2013026648

St. Martin's Press Books books may be purchased for educational, business, or promotional use. For information on bulk purchases, please contact Macmillan Corporate and Premium Sales Department at 1-800-221-7945, extension 5442, or write specialmarkets@macmillan.com.

First Edition: October 2013

20 19 18 17 16 15 14

With love to Laura, Rachel, and Julia, who fear nothing and love to bake.

J.H.

To Graham, Henri, and Charlie, my inspiration in the kitchen and in life.

Z.F.

# CONTENTS

# ACKNOWLEDGMENTS

Cookbook deals for unknown authors without TV shows were a long shot when we started this adventure in 2007—and they still are. On top of that, we knew bread baking, but we didn't know publishing. So we needed some luck, and some generous people to help us. Our most heartfelt thanks go to our first editor at Thomas Dunne Books, the late Ruth Cavin. She liked our idea and decided to publish us. Decisive is good. We are grateful to the folks at St. Martin's Press who took over for Ruth and helped us make this revision an even stronger book: Peter Wolverton, Matthew Baldacci, Amelie Littell, Leah Stewart, Anne Brewer, Kymberlee Giacoppe, Nadea Mina, and Judy Hunt, who created another brilliant index. Lynne Rossetto Kasper took Jeff's call on her radio show, which gave us the opportunity to meet Ruth in the first place. Lynne also gave great advice and connected us with our top-notch literary agent, Jane Dystel, and Jane's fantastic team, Miriam Goderich and Lauren Abramo.

We also had great friends and family to act as recipe testers. They baked endlessly and offered us their criticism and praise. Once they started using our recipes, we understood that this would be a book for everyone—avid bakers and non-bakers alike. That was a revelation. So we owe our book to them: Allison Campbell Jensen, Alex Cohn, Ralph Cohn, Shelly Fling and Mark Luinenburg, Leslie Held, Paul Gates (whose home was the first proving ground), Kathy Kosnoff and Lyonel Norris, Danny Sager and Brian McCarthy, Joy Estelle Summers (who baked nearly every bread in the book), Ralph Gualtieri and Debora Villa (who carried our dough across international borders), Jim and Theresa Murray, Lorraine Neal, Sally Simmons, Jennifer Sommerness, and David Van de Sande. Thank you to Jeff Lin of BustOutSolutions.com, for maintaining our website. Graham (Zoë's husband) gave immeasurable moral support and created our website, BreadIn5.com, and Laura Silver (Jeff's wife) made sure that Thomas Dunne Books got manuscripts that were already vetted by an experienced editor. Thanks to Brett Bannon, Leslie Bazzett, Jay, Tracey, Gavin, and Megan Berkowitz, Sarah Berkowitz, Marion and John Callahan, Fran Davis, Barb Davis, Anna and Ewart François, Alec Neal, Kristin Neal, Carey and Heather Neal, Craig and Patricia Neal, and Lindy Wolverton for all of their support.

Gratitude to colleagues in our baking and culinary worlds past and present: Shauna James Ahern of GlutenFreeGirl.com; Steven Brown of Tilia; Robert Dircks and Briana Falk at Gold Medal; Stephen Durfee of the Culinary Institute of America; Barbara Fenzl of Les Gourmettes Cooking School; Thomas Gumpel of Panera Bread; Bill Hanes and Kelly Olson of Red Star Yeast; Michelle Gayer of The Salty Tart; Brenda Langton of Spoonriver restaurant and the Minneapolis Bread Festival; Silvana Nardone of EasyEats.com; Raghavan Iyer; Karl Benson and the team at Cooks of Crocus Hill; Peter Reinhart; Suvir Saran and Charlie Burd of American Masala; Tara Steffen of Emile Henry, and Andrew Zimmern, Dusti Kugler, and Molly Mogren of Food Works; and Dorie Greenspan.

It was a joy to work with photographer Stephen Scott Gross, whose sense of style, passion for getting the shots just right, and wicked sense of humor made the intense week of our photo shoot a total success. His creative assistant, Kayla Pieper, kept the whole operation running smoothly. Veronica Smith's talent for finding props made our breads shine. Sarah Kieffer helped us bake hundreds of beautiful loaves of bread and her humor made the time pass with ease, and the magic of Andrea Horton's makeup made us look like we were well rested for our portraits, after a very long week of no sleep.

Most of all we are thankful for the love and support of our families: Zoë's husband, Graham, and her two boys, Henri and Charlie, and Jeff's wife, Laura, and his girls, Rachel and Julia. They're our best taste testers and most honest critics.

# THE SECRET

## Mix Enough Dough for Several Loaves and Store It in the Refrigerator

It is so easy to have freshly baked bread when you want it, with only five minutes a day of active effort. First, mix the ingredients into a container all at once, and then let them sit for two hours. Now you are ready to shape and bake the bread, or you can refrigerate the dough and use it over the next couple of weeks. Yes, weeks! Each recipe makes enough dough for many loaves. When you want fresh-baked bread, take a piece of the dough from the container and shape it into a loaf. Let it rest for twenty minutes or more and then bake. Your house will smell like a bakery and your family and friends will love you for it.

# PREFACE TO THE REVISED EDITION: WHAT'S NEW?

Welcome to the Revised Edition of ***Artisan Bread in Five Minutes a Day***. This astonishing, crazy adventure—one that started as nothing more than a little project between friends but has become one of **the bestselling bread cookbooks of all time**—began in our kids' music class in 2003. It was an unlikely place for coauthors to meet, but in the swirl of toddlers, musical chairs, and xylophones, there was time for the grown-ups to talk. Zoë mentioned she was a pastry chef and baker who'd been trained at the Culinary Institute of America (CIA). What a fortuitous coincidence. Jeff wasn't a food professional at all, but he'd been tinkering for years with an easy, fast method for making homemade bread. He begged her to try a secret recipe he'd been developing. The secret? Mix a big batch of dough and store it in the refrigerator. It was promising, but it needed work.

Zoë was skeptical. Jeff had been trained as a scientist, not as a chef. On the other hand, that might be an advantage when it came to experimenting with new approaches to homemade bread. So we did a taste test—and luckily, Zoë loved it. Better yet, she was willing to develop a book with an amateur. Our approach produces fantastic homemade loaves without the enormous time investment required in the traditional artisanal method.

This had been an opportunity that was just waiting for the right moment. In 2000, Jeff had called in to Lynne Rossetto Kasper's National Public Radio

show, *The Splendid Table,* to get advice on getting a cookbook idea into print. Lynne was supportive and helpful on the air, but more important, a St. Martin's Press editor named Ruth Cavin, who'd been listening to Lynne's show, phoned *The Splendid Table* and asked for a book proposal. The rest, as they say, is history.

We were first-time authors, with a great idea but no track record. Worse, we were far from being celebrity chefs, which was fast becoming a requirement for cookbook success. But we knew that if people got their hands on this method they would use it. The only problem was proving that to the publisher. St. Martin's Press gave us a small budget for photographs, which meant only eight color pictures, plus a smattering of black-and-white how-to shots. We'd have loved to have had more, but were thrilled to have any. We may have the lack of photos to thank for the birth of our website.

We knew that people would need guidance to bake bread, and having a lot of pictures would help more than just about anything. We hoped that we had a winner: the book *plus* our new website (BreadIn5.com), chock-full of pictures and with its two authors eager to answer reader questions themselves. Our website exceeded our wildest hopes—it's become the center of a five-minute-a-day bread-baking community, with over a quarter-million page views per month. We're on duty every day—to answer questions, respond to comments, and post about what we're baking and working on. It's become part of our daily lives and our creative process. Through the questions and comments from readers, we've learned what works well, what could have been easier, what needs more explanation, and what new breads people want. So our next books, ***Healthy Bread in Five Minutes a Day*** (2009) and ***Artisan Pizza and Flatbread in Five Minutes a Day*** (2011), were based on requests that came from our readers, who reached us through our website, our Facebook page (Facebook.com/BreadIn5), or our Twitter identity (@ArtisanBreadIn5). We've met thousands of bakers just like us—busy people who love fresh bread but don't necessarily have all day to make it. It's been a joy.

Our book became a best seller and we traveled the country, meeting our readers, teaching classes, and making the regional television morning-show circuit. Everyone loves great bread, and here was a way to make it that was fast, super easy, and *cheap* (under fifty cents a loaf). Our method caught the eye of General Mills—we became the official bread cookbook of Gold Medal Flour (our standard testing flour from day one). After two more books and more than half a million copies sold, we're back with this Revised Edition of our first and most popular book. It was co-created with the help of our readers, from whom we've learned so much. In this new edition, we'll share the fruits of a six-year conversation.

First off, people asked for more recipes. This revision contains over thirty brand-new recipes and variations. So even if you already have a first-edition copy of ***Artisan Bread in Five Minutes a Day***, you'll want to add this one to your cookbook library. You'll find new recipes, like Wisconsin Beer-Cheese Bread, Pullman Loaf, lots of rolls, Sauerkraut Rye, Crock Pot Bread, Swiss Twisted Wurzelbrot, Panini, Pretzel Buns, Apple-Stuffed French Toast, and lots more.

We had an overwhelming response when we rolled out a few gluten-free recipes on BreadIn5.com and in our other books. We'd thought that the gluten-free chapters in ***Healthy Bread*** and in ***Artisan Pizza and Flatbread*** would be used by people who could eat wheat themselves but just wanted a few gluten-free recipes to bake for others when they needed to. But it's gone further than that—some of our readers who are completely gluten-free tell us that they bought ***Healthy Bread*** or ***Artisan Pizza and Flatbread*** for the gluten-free chapters alone. So we've written a gluten-free chapter for this edition—check it out on page 267.

More recipes means more pictures, and this time our publisher has obliged. Our breads come to life in forty color shots and one hundred black-and-white how-to photos. We're thrilled with our new photos, and we hope they'll inspire you to bake every day.

When we wrote ***Healthy Bread*** and ***Artisan Pizza and Flatbread***, we had a chance to reconsider things we'd left out of ***Artisan Bread***. So "Tips and Techniques" (Chapter 4), and "Ingredients" (Chapter 2) are bigger and better than ever before. We include some of our readers' "Frequently Asked Questions" that kept popping up on the website (page 40). Another major addition has been to provide weight equivalents for our dough recipes in addition to our usual cup-measures for flour and other ingredients. The new electronic scales have really simplified the weighing of ingredients. It's a timesaver, with more consistent results, and no need to wash measuring cups. And the dough recipes are now set up so readers can customize the salt to their own palates. We've also decreased the amount of yeast in our doughs, because you can get the same result with less. We include a discussion on how to go even lower if you like (page 14). Finally, people loved the whole-wheat recipes in ***Healthy Bread***, but they asked whether we could include a high–whole wheat loaf in ***Artisan Bread*** that wouldn't require the addition of vital wheat gluten, which we call for in ***Healthy Bread***. The answer is yes (see our variation on Light Whole Wheat Bread, page 131). And, of course, we still include our original recipe for a hearty 100% Whole Wheat Sandwich Bread, page 134, that doesn't require additional gluten.

And this may sound geeky, but we are so excited about our new index (we are, after all, bread geeks). In *The Way to Cook* (1993), Julia Child wrote that ". . . a book is only as good as its index." Today we're proud to say that we have a great index—bigger and more intuitive than before.

Our goal in ***Artisan Bread in Five Minutes a Day*** has been to help home bakers make great daily breads and sweets but still have a life outside the kitchen. To all of you who helped us make this series happen, thank you. Together we've started a revolution—opening up hundreds of thousands of homes to the satisfaction and delights of homemade bread. And most important, we've had fun.

So please, you have fun too. If you worry about the bread, it won't taste as good.

1

# INTRODUCTION

## Making Artisan Bread in Five Minutes a Day: Refrigerating Pre-Mixed Homemade Dough

Like most kids, Jeff and his brother loved sweets, so dessert was their favorite time of day. They'd sit in the kitchen, devouring frosted supermarket doughnuts.

"Those are too sweet," Grandmother would say. "Me, I'd rather have a piece of good rye bread, with cheese on it."

*Munch, munch, munch.* Their mouths were full; the boys could not respond.

"It's better than cake," she'd say.

There's a certain solidarity among kids gorging on sweets, but secretly, Jeff knew she was right. He could finish half a loaf of very fresh, very crisp rye bread by himself, with or without butter (unlike Grandma, Jeff considered cheese to be a distraction from perfect rye bread). The right stuff came from a little bakery on Horace Harding Boulevard in Queens. The shop itself was nondescript, but the breads were Eastern European masterpieces. The crusts were crisp, thin, and caramelized brown. The interior crumb was moist and chewy, but never gummy, and bursting with tangy yeast, rye, and wheat flavors. It made great toast, too—and yes, it was better than cake.

The handmade bread was available all over New York City, and it wasn't a rarefied delicacy. Everyone knew what it was and took it for granted. It was not a stylish addition to affluent lifestyles; it was a simple comfort food brought here by modest immigrants.

But over the years people lost interest in making a second stop just for bread, and the shops mostly faded away. Great breads, handmade by artisans, were still available, but they'd become part of the serious (and seriously expensive) food phenomenon that had swept the country. The bread bakery was no longer on every corner—now it was a destination. And nobody's grandmother would ever have paid six dollars for a loaf of bread.

So we decided to do something about it. ***Artisan Bread in Five Minutes a Day*** is our attempt to help people re-create the great ethnic and American breads of years past, in their own homes, *without investing serious time in the process*. Using our straightforward, fast, and easy recipes, anyone will be able to create artisan bread and pastries at home with minimal equipment. *But who has time to make bread every day?*

After years of experimentation, it turns out that *we* do, and with a method as fast as ours, you can, too. We solved the time problem *and* produced top-quality artisan loaves without a bread machine. We worked out the master recipes during busy years of career transition and starting families (our kids now delight in the pleasures of home-baked bread). Our lightning-fast method lets us find the time to bake great bread every day. We developed this method to recapture the daily artisan-bread experience without further crunching our limited time—and it works.

Traditional breads made the old-fashioned way need a lot of attention, especially if you want to use a "starter" for that natural, tangy taste. Starters need to be cared for, with water and flour replenished on a schedule. Dough must be kneaded until resilient, set to rise, punched down, allowed to rise again. There are boards and pans and utensils galore to be washed, some of which can't go into the dishwasher. Very few busy people can go through this every day, if ever. Even if your friends are all food fanatics, when was the last time you had homemade bread at a dinner party?

What about bread machines? The machines solved the time problem and turn out uniformly decent loaves, but unfortunately, the crust is soft and dull flavored, and without tangy flavor in the crumb (the bread's soft interior), unless you use and maintain time-consuming sourdough starter.

So we went to work. Over the years, we figured out how to subtract the various steps that make the classic technique so time-consuming, and identified a few that couldn't be omitted. It all came down to one fortuitous discovery:

**Pre-mixed, pre-risen, high-moisture dough keeps well in the refrigerator.**

This is the linchpin of ***Artisan Bread in Five Minutes a Day***. By premixing high-moisture dough (without kneading) and then storing it, daily bread baking becomes an easy activity; the only steps you do every day are shaping and baking. Other books have considered refrigerating dough, but only for a few days. Still others have omitted the kneading step. But none has tested the capacity of wet dough to be long-lived in your refrigerator. As our high-moisture dough ages, it takes on sourdough notes reminiscent of the great European and American natural starters. When dough is mixed with adequate water (this dough is wetter than most you may have worked with), it can be stored in the refrigerator for up to two weeks (enriched or heavy doughs can't go that long but can be frozen instead). And kneading this kind of dough adds little to the overall product; you just don't have to do it. In fact, overhandling stored dough can limit the volume and rise that you get with our method. That, in a nutshell, is how you make artisan breads with only five minutes a day of active effort.

**Wetter is better:** The wetter dough, as you'll see, is fairly slack, and offers less resistance to yeast's expanding carbon dioxide bubbles. So, despite not being replenished with fresh flour and water like a proper sourdough starter, there is still adequate rise, especially in the oven.

A one- or two-week supply of dough is made in advance and stored in the refrigerator. Measuring and mixing the large batch of dough takes less than fifteen minutes. Kneading, as we've said, is not necessary. Every day, cut off a hunk of dough from the storage container and briefly shape it without kneading. Allow it to rest briefly on the counter and then toss it in the oven. We don't count the rest time (twenty minutes or more depending on the recipe) or baking time (usually about thirty minutes) in our five-minute-a-day calculation, since you can be doing something else while that's happening. If you bake after dinner, the bread will stay fresh for use the next day (higher-moisture breads stay fresh longer), but the method is so convenient that you probably will find you can cut off some dough and bake a loaf every morning before your day starts (especially if you make flatbreads like pita). **If you want to have one thing you do every day that is simply perfect, this is it.**

Using high-moisture, pre-mixed, pre-risen dough makes most of the difficult, time-consuming, and demanding steps in traditional bread baking completely superfluous:

**1. You don't need to make fresh dough every day to have fresh bread every day:** Stored dough makes wonderful fresh loaves. Only the shaping and baking steps are done daily, the rest has been done in advance.

**2. You don't need a "sponge" or "starter":** Traditional sourdough recipes require that you keep flour-water mixtures bubbling along in your refrigerator, with careful attention and replenishment. By storing the dough over two weeks, a subtle sourdough character gradually develops in our breads without the need to maintain sponges or starters in the refrigerator. With our dough-storage approach, your first loaf is not exactly the same as the last. Its flavor will become more complex as the dough ages. Some of our readers like to stagger their batches so they are always baking with dough that has aged at least a few days—we love that strategy.

**3. It doesn't matter how you mix the dry and wet ingredients together:** So long as the mixture is uniform, without any dry lumps of flour, it makes no difference whether you use a spoon, Danish dough whisk (page 27), a heavy-duty stand mixer, or a high-capacity food processor. Choose based on your own convenience.

**4. You don't need to "proof" yeast:** Traditional recipes require that yeast be dissolved in water with a little sugar and allowed to sit for five minutes to prove that bubbles can form and the yeast is alive. But modern yeast simply doesn't fail if used before its expiration date and the baker remembers to use lukewarm, *not hot water.* The high water content in our doughs further ensures that the yeast will fully hydrate and activate without a proofing step. Further storage gives it plenty of time to ferment the dough—our approach doesn't need the head start.

**5. It isn't kneaded:** The dough can be mixed and stored in the same lidded container. No wooden board is required. There should be only one vessel to wash, plus a spoon (or a mixer). You'll never tell the difference between breads made with kneaded and unkneaded high-moisture dough, so long as you mix to a basically uniform consistency.

**What We *Don't* Have to Do: Steps from Traditional Artisan Baking That We Omitted**

1. Mix a new batch of dough every time we want to make bread
2. "Proof" yeast
3. Knead dough
4. Rest and rise the loaves in a draft-free location—it doesn't matter
5. Fuss over doubling or tripling of dough volume
6. Punch down and re-rise: **Never** punch down stored dough
7. Poke rising loaves to be sure they've "proofed" by leaving indentations

**Now you know why it only takes five minutes a day, not including resting and baking time.**

In our method, a very quick "cloaking and shaping" step substitutes for kneading (see Chapter 5, Step 5, page 57).

**Start a morning batch before work, bake the first loaf before dinner:** Here's a convenient way to get fresh bread on the table for dinner. Mix up a full batch of dough before breakfast and store it in the refrigerator. The lukewarm water you used to mix the dough will provide enough heat to allow the yeast to do its thing over the eight hours until you're home. When you walk in the door, cloak and shape the loaf and give it a quick rest, then bake as usual. Small loaves, and especially flatbreads, can be on the table in twenty minutes or less. You can do the same thing with an after-dinner start on the dough—it's ready the next morning.

**6. It's hard to over-rise high-moisture stored dough:** Remember that you're storing it anyway. Assuming you start with lukewarm (not cold) water, you'll see a brisk initial rise at room temperature over two hours (don't punch down); then the risen dough is refrigerated for use over the next week or two. But rising longer (even as long as eight hours) won't be harmful; there's lots of leeway in the initial rise time. The exception is dough made with eggs or dairy, which should complete its rising in the refrigerator if it goes beyond two hours.

Given these simple principles, anyone can make artisan bread at home. We'll talk about what you'll need in Chapters 2 (Ingredients) and 3 (Equipment). You don't need a professional baker's kitchen. In Chapter 4, you'll learn the tips and techniques that have taken us years to accumulate. Then, in Chapter 5 (The Master Recipe), we'll lay out the basics of our method, applying them to a simple white dough and several delicious variations. Chapter 5's master recipe is the model for the rest of our recipes. We suggest you read it carefully and bake it first before trying anything else. You won't regret it. And if you want more information, we're on the Web at **BreadIn5.com**, where you'll find instructional text, photographs, videos, and a community of other five-minute bakers. Other easy ways to keep in touch: follow us on Twitter at Twitter.com/ArtisanBreadIn5, on Facebook at Facebook.com/BreadIn5, on Pinterest at Pinterest.com/BreadIn5, or on our YouTube channel, YouTube.com/BreadIn5.

2

# INGREDIENTS

Here's a practical guide to the ingredients we use to produce artisan loaves. Great breads really only require four basic ingredients: flour, water, yeast, and salt.

## Flours and Grains

**All-purpose flour:** This is the staple ingredient for most of the recipes in this book. All-purpose flour is our number-one choice for white flour because most households have it in the pantry and its medium- (rather than high-) protein content. Most of the protein in wheat is highly elastic gluten, which allows bread dough to trap the carbon dioxide gas produced by yeast. Without gluten, bread wouldn't rise. That's why flours containing only minimal gluten (like rye) need to be mixed with wheat flour to make a successful loaf. Traditional bread recipes stress the need to develop gluten through kneading, which turns out *not* to be an important factor if you keep the dough wet.

With a protein content of about 10 percent in most national brands, all-purpose flour will have adequate gluten to create a satisfying "chew," but not so much protein as to cause heaviness. Gluten is strengthened when the proteins align themselves into strands after water is added. This creates a network that traps gas bubbles and creates an airy interior crumb. These lined-up strands can be formed in two ways:

- **The dough can be kneaded:** Not the way we like to spend our time. **OR . . .**
- **By using lots of water:** The gluten strands become mobile enough to *align themselves.*

So creating a wet dough is the basis for our no-knead method. It's easy to consistently achieve this moisture level with U.S. all-purpose flour. We tested our recipes with Gold Medal brand all-purpose, but most standard supermarket all-purpose products will give similar results. Here are some adjustments you might want to make for other flours:

***Some all-purpose flours have more protein and need extra water:*** These flours have protein content of about 11½ percent:

- King Arthur Unbleached All-Purpose Flour
- Dakota Maid Unbleached All-Purpose Flour
- Most Canadian all-purpose flours

They work beautifully in our recipes, but if you use them, you need to increase the water a little—in the Master Recipe (page 53), use about ¼ cup extra water—or the dough will be drier than usual and won't store as well. And some flours have *too little* protein to make successful high-moisture dough—stay away from cake flour and pastry flours (around 8 percent protein).

**We prefer unbleached flours for their natural creamy color, not to mention our preference for avoiding unnecessary chemicals.**

**Bread flour:** A white flour with about 12 percent protein. If you prefer extra-chewy bread, you can substitute bread flour for all-purpose by increasing the water by ⅓ cup in the Master Recipe (page 53). For specialty breads that really need to hold their shape (like *pain d'epí,* bagels, and pretzels), we call for bread flour *without* adjusting the water.

**Whole wheat flour:** Whole wheat flour contains both the germ and bran of wheat, both of which are healthful and tasty. Together they add a slightly bitter, nutty flavor to bread that most people enjoy. The naturally occurring oils in wheat germ prevent formation of a crackling crust, so you're going for a different type of loaf when you start increasing the proportion of whole wheat flour. In general, you can use any kind of whole wheat flour that's available to you. Stone-ground whole wheat flour will be a bit coarser, denser, and more rustic, and it may require a little more water than what we call for—we tested with non-stone-ground supermarket whole wheat flour. Whole wheat pastry flour is very low in protein but it works fine when mixed with white flour. But it's too low in protein to be used in our 100% Whole Wheat Sandwich Bread (page 134). That loaf is denser than our whole-grain recipes that include some white flour; if you want 100 percent whole grain with a lighter result, we introduce other techniques and ingredients that give more structure to high–whole-grain loaves in ***Healthy Bread in Five Minutes a Day*** (2009).

**White whole wheat:** White whole wheat flour is 100 percent whole grain, but it's ground from a white wheat berry rather than the usual "red" one. It's relatively new to the U.S. market, but great products are now available from Gold Medal, Bob's Red Mill, and King Arthur. It's pale colored and mild tasting, but it packs the same nutrition as regular whole wheat. It measures like regular whole wheat and can be used as a substitute for it. But don't expect it to taste like white flour and don't try to substitute it 1:1 for all-purpose or you'll get a dry, dense dough that won't store well at all.

**Rye flour:** Specialty catalogs offer a bewildering variety of rye flours. According to our survey, medium or dark rye flours are available, plus the very coarsely ground rye meal (sometimes labeled as pumpernickel or whole-grain rye flour, depending on how coarsely it is ground).

**Storing whole wheat flour:** Oils in whole wheat flour can go rancid if stored for long periods at room temperature. So if you don't use it often, store it in an airtight container in the freezer.

The flours have varying percentages of rye bran, but the labeling generally doesn't make this clear. Be aware, though, that the very coarse-ground high-bran products will produce a coarser, denser loaf. You will not be able to get too particular about this ingredient, because in U.S. supermarkets, choices are usually limited to the high-bran, high-protein varieties like Hodgson Mill Stone-Ground Whole-Grain Rye and Bob's Red Mill Organic Stone-Ground Rye Flour. True "medium" rye, with reduced bran and protein, is available from King Arthur Flour (see Sources, page 367) and it produces a rye loaf that's closer to commercial rye bread. Whichever kind of rye you use, it must be paired with wheat flour because it has just a little gluten and won't rise well on its own. Use the various rye products interchangeably in our recipes, based on your taste.

**Semolina flour:** Semolina is a high-protein white wheat flour that is a major component of some Italian breads, where it lends a beautiful yellow color and spectacular winey-sweet flavor. The best semolina for bread is the finely ground "durum" flour. It is available from Bob's Red Mill (in groceries or online), or from mail-order sources like King Arthur Flour (see Sources, page 367). If you use flour labeled as "semolina" (commonly found in South Asian groceries), you'll usually find that it's a coarser grind and needs to be decreased in the recipes or the result can be an overly dry dough.

**Oats:** Raw oats or oat flour adds a wonderful hearty flavor and contributes to a toothsome texture, but neither one has gluten. Technically, oats are gluten free, but can only be certified as such if they are milled in a gluten-free facility. So, like rye flour, oats need to be paired with flour to produce a loaf that rises. Rolled oat varieties sold as "old-fashioned" (not precooked and dried) are best—the milling process actually rolls the whole kernel flat. Steel-cut oats, often sold as "Scottish" or "Irish" oats, are coarser ground and will yield a coarser result—the kernel is not flattened but rather broken into fragments.

**Organic flours:** We don't detect flavor or texture differences with organic flour, but if you like organic products, by all means use them (we often do). They're not required, and they certainly cost more. One reason some people take up the bread-baking hobby is to be able to eat organic bread every day, as it is usually unavailable commercially or is prohibitively expensive. There are now a number of organic flour brands available in the supermarket, but the best selection remains at your local organic food co-op, where you can buy it in bulk.

## Gluten-free Flours

Double-check with your doctor before consuming any new grain if you have celiac disease or are allergic or intolerant of gluten.

**Coconut flour:** It's just dehydrated coconut, ground into a powder. It has the natural sweetness and richness of coconut and is high in fiber and protein.

**Potato flour:** Cooked and then dehydrated potatoes are ground to a powder to produce flour that helps create bread that has a smooth crumb and stays fresher longer. This flour should not be confused with potato starch, which is a much-whiter powder and has different baking and nutritional properties.

**Rice flours:** Brown rice flour is made from rice with its external bran left in place. It's higher in nutrients and fiber than white rice flour. White rice flour is used in many gluten-free recipes for its fine texture and its flavor. Avoid "glutinous" rice flour, Asian market flours, or "sweet" rice flour.

**Sorghum:** Sorghum is a very popular cooking grain related to sugarcane. It is used around the world but has just recently found its way into American kitchens.

**Tapioca:** Tapioca is made from a root that's known by many names: cassava, manioc, or yucca. It is extracted and ground into a flour that is high in starch, calcium, and vitamin C, but low in protein. It is most often associated with its thickening properties, but it is now frequently used in gluten-free baking. It is sold as both tapioca starch and flour, but they are exactly the same.

**Teff:** An indispensable grain in Ethiopia, teff has been virtually unheard of in the rest of the world until recently. It is a variety of whole-grain millet that is wonderfully sweet but packed with iron and calcium.

**Xanthan gum:** This powdered additive, a naturally derived gum that creates gas-trapping structure in dough, is used in gluten-free breads to replace the stretchiness and chew that breads would otherwise get from gluten in wheat.

**Yeast:** Some yeasts with dough enhancers contain enzymes derived from wheat; just avoid them by reading the label.

## Water

Throughout the book we call for lukewarm water. This means water that feels just a little warm to the touch; if you measured it with a thermometer it would be no higher than 100°F (38°C). The truth is, we never use a thermometer and we've never had a yeast failure due to excessive temperature—but it can happen, so be careful. Cold tap water will work (and you cannot kill yeast with cold water) but the initial rise will take much, much longer (the bread will be just as good, and some tasters even prefer the taste of cold-risen dough). Typically, in our homes, we're in no hurry, so we often use cold water and let it sit for eight hours or more (refrigerate egg-enriched dough to complete its rising after two hours at room temperature).

**About water sources:** We find that the flavors of wheat and yeast overwhelm the contribution of water to bread's flavor, so we use ordinary tap water run through a home water filter, but that's only because it's what we drink at home. Assuming your own tap water tastes good enough to drink, use it filtered or unfiltered; we can't tell the difference in finished bread.

## Yeast: Adjust It to Your Taste

Use whatever yeast is readily available; with our approach you won't be able to tell the difference between the various national brands of yeast (though we tested our recipes with the Red Star brand), nor between packages labeled "granulated," "active dry," "instant," "quick-rise," or "bread-machine." Fresh cake yeast works fine as well (though you will have to increase the yeast volume by 50 percent to achieve the same rising speed). The long storage time of our doughs acts as an equalizer between all of those subtly different yeast products. **One strong recommendation: If you bake frequently, buy yeast in bulk or in 4-ounce jars, rather than in packets (which are much less economical).**

**Using yeast packets instead of jarred or bulk yeast:** Throughout the book, we call for 1 tablespoon of granulated yeast for about 4 pounds of dough. **You can substitute one packet of granulated yeast for a tablespoon, even though, technically speaking, those amounts aren't perfectly equivalent (1 tablespoon is a little more than the 2¼ teaspoons found in one packet).** We've found that this makes little difference in the initial rise time or in the performance of the finished dough.

Food co-ops often sell yeast by the pound, in bulk (usually the Red Star brand). Make sure that bulk-purchased yeast is fresh by chatting with your co-op manager. Freeze yeast after opening to extend its shelf life, and use it straight from the freezer, or store smaller containers in the refrigerator and use within a few months. Between the two of us, we've had only one yeast failure in many years of baking, and it was with an outdated envelope stored at room temperature. **The real key to avoiding yeast failure is to use water that is no warmer than lukewarm (about 100°F). Hot water kills yeast.**

**Will the recipes work with small amounts of yeast?** Some readers prefer less yeast in their dough—finding that a long, slow rise produces a better flavor—but it's really a matter of taste. Less yeast works well for all of our recipes except for the gluten-free dough—but the initial rise will be slower. This book uses less yeast than our very first edition of ***Artisan Bread in Five Minutes a Day*** from 2007—but you can go even lower if you have time to spare. We've had great

**Modern Yeast . . .**

**. . .** almost never fails if used before its expiration date, so you do not need to "proof" the yeast (i.e., test it for freshness by demonstrating that it bubbles in sweetened warm water). And you don't have to wait for yeast to fully dissolve after mixing with water. You can even mix all the dry ingredients first, and then add liquids.

After several days of high-moisture storage, yeasted dough begins to take on a flavor and aroma that's close to the flavor of natural sourdough starters used in many artisan breads. This will deepen the flavor and character of all your doughs. The traditional way to achieve these flavors—pre-ferments, sours, and starters like *biga* (Italian), *levain* (French), and *poolish* (Eastern European)—all require significant time and attention. Our method provides the flavor without all that effort.

results using as little as one-quarter of our standard amount of yeast. If you decrease the yeast, the initial rising time may increase to eight hours, or even longer, depending on how much you decreased it and the temperature in your house.

The other way to slow down the rise is to use cool or even cold water in the initial mix. If you try this, the initial rise time increases dramatically, even more so if you also decreased the yeast, so you'll need more advance planning. **If you're making dough with eggs and you're considering a long, slow rise, do only the first two hours at room temperature,** then transfer to the refrigerator to complete the rise (and expect a long wait). According to the U.S. Department of Agriculture, raw eggs shouldn't be kept at room temperature for longer than two hours.[1]

## Salt: Adjust It to Your Taste

All of our recipes were tested with Morton brand kosher salt, which is coarsely ground. If you measure salt by volume and you're using something finer or coarser, you need to adjust the amount because finer salt packs denser in the spoon. The following measurements are equivalent:

**Weighing yeast and salt:** In the recipes, we provide weight equivalents for yeast and salt, which is a more professional technique—but professionals measure out enormous batches. Be sure your home scale weighs accurately in the lower ranges; otherwise spoon-measure yeast and salt.

- **Table salt (fine):** 2 teaspoons
- **Morton Kosher Salt (coarse):** 1 tablespoon
- **Diamond Kosher Salt (coarsest):** 1 tablespoon plus 1 teaspoon

You can use sea salt, but be sure to adjust for its grind. If it's finely ground, you need to measure it like table salt above, and if it's more coarsely ground than Morton, you'll need to increase the volume accordingly. And reserve the really expensive artisan sea salts for sprinkling on finished products—artisan salts lose their unique flavors when baked. **If you decide to weigh salt to avoid the problem of compensating for fineness-of-grind, do so only for double batches or larger unless you're really confident of your scale's performance at low weights (see page 31).**

In traditional bread recipes, salt is used not only for flavor—it also helps

[1]U.S. Department of Agriculture Fact Sheet. *Egg Products Preparation: Shell Eggs from Farm to Table.* http://www.fsis.usda.gov/wps/portal/fsis/topics/food-safety-education/get-answers/food-safety-fact-sheets/egg-products-preparation/shell-eggs-from-farm-to-table, accessed July 14, 2013.

tighten and strengthen the gluten. Because our dough is slack in the first place, and is stored for so long, the differences between high- and low-salt versions of our doughs are less pronounced. Adjust the salt to suit your palate and your health—we give you a range. We love the taste of salt and don't have any health-related salt restrictions, so we tend to use the higher amounts. Saltier dough can help bring out flavor early in the batch life, but if you like our doughs best after they've been stored awhile, you may find you can decrease the salt. The low end of our salt range will be salty enough for many—and if health conditions require it, you can decrease the salt radically and the recipes will still work. In fact, you can bring the salt all the way down to zero, though the taste and texture will certainly change.

## Seeds and Nuts

Caraway seeds are so central to the flavor of many rye breads that a lot of people think that caraway is actually the flavor of the rye grain. It's not, but for us, something does seem to be missing in unseeded rye bread. The only problem you can run into with caraway, sesame, or poppy seeds (or nuts, for that matter) is that the oil inside seeds or nuts can go rancid if you keep them too long. Taste a few if your jar is older than a year and freeze them if you are storing for longer than three months.

## Chocolate

Some of our enriched breads call for chocolate, either cocoa powder, bar chocolate, or chunks. Use the highest-quality chocolate if you can—it improves the flavor. For cocoa powder, it doesn't matter if it's labeled "Dutch-process" (alkali-treated) or not. The question of Dutch-process is only important for baked goods risen with baking soda or baking powder—yeast doesn't seem to care. If premium chocolate isn't available, try the recipes with your favorite supermarket brands. The premium stuff is not a requirement by any means.

# 3

# EQUIPMENT

In the spirit of our approach, we've tried to keep our list spare, and present items in order of importance. The most helpful items are:

- Equipment for baking with steam: we'll give you four options
- Baking stone, cast-iron pizza pan, cast-iron skillet, or unglazed quarry tiles
- Oven thermometer
- Pizza peel

See Sources (page 367) to locate mail-order and Web-based vendors for harder-to-find items.

## *EQUIPMENT FOR BAKING WITH STEAM (You Only Need One of These)*

**Metal broiler tray to hold boiling water for steam:** This is our first choice for creating the steam needed for lean-dough breads—those made without fat or eggs—to achieve a crispy crust (enriched breads like challah and brioche don't

**Two important warnings: 1. Do not use a glass pan to catch water for steam, or it will shatter on contact with the water. 2. We've gotten rare reports of cracked oven-window glass from accidentally spilled water on its hot surface. If you want extra assurance that this won't happen, cover the window with a towel before pouring water into the tray; remove before closing the oven door.**

benefit from baking with steam because the fat in the dough softens the crust). Pour hot water (or drop a handful of ice cubes) into the preheated metal broiler tray just before closing the oven door.

Some ovens (including most professional-style ones and many that heat with gas) don't have a good seal for holding in steam. ***If your oven allows steam to dissipate and you're not getting a beautiful shiny crust with the broiler-tray method, try one of these three alternatives:***

**1. Food-grade water sprayer:** Spray the loaf with water before closing the oven door, then open it at thirty-second intervals for two more sprayings.

**2. Metal bowl or aluminum-foil roasting pan for covering free-form loaves in the oven:** By trapping steam next to the loaf as it bakes, you

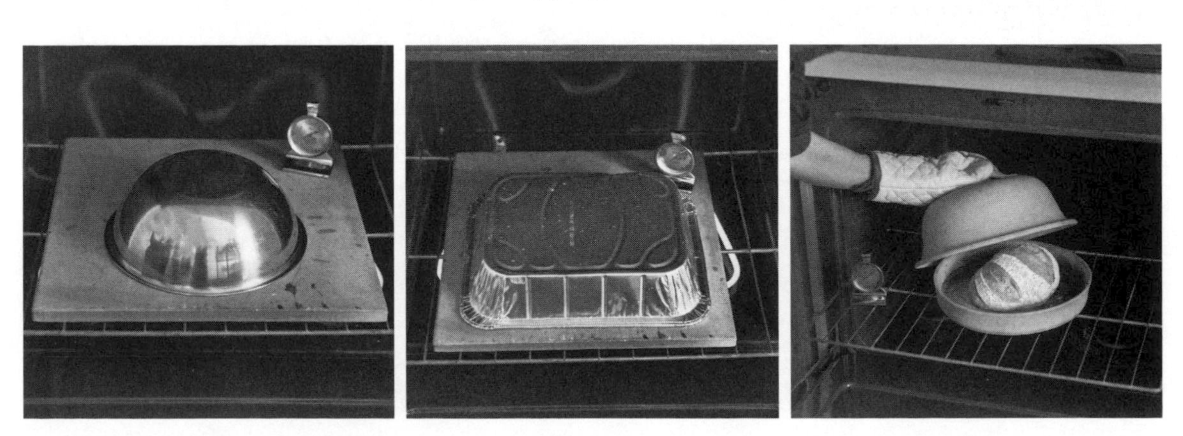

can create the humid environment that produces a crisp crust without using a broiler tray or a sprayer. The bowl or dish needs to be heat-tolerant and tall enough so that the rising loaf won't touch it, but not so large that it hangs beyond the edge of the stone, or it won't trap the steam. This is a great technique for outdoor grills, which don't trap steam even when the lid is down.

**3. Bake inside a clay baker or a covered cast-iron pot:** The clay baker (in French, *la cloche* [la klōsh], meaning "bell," after its distinctive shape) is a time-honored way to bake—the covered, unglazed-clay baking vessel traps steam inside, so the crackling crust forms without the need for a baking stone, broiler tray, water, or sprayer. Crispiest results are obtained with a twenty- to thirty-minute preheat. We don't soak clay bakers in water before use as is sometimes advocated, and unglazed clay shouldn't be greased. It's easiest (but not required) to rest the loaf on parchment paper, and then carefully slide the loaf, paper and all, into the preheated baker when ready to bake. Start the baking with the cover on, but finish baking *uncovered* for the last third of the baking time. **Covered cast-iron pots** also work well when used this same way, though some of them will need a heat-resistant replacement knob—check with the manufacturer.

## *OTHER EQUIPMENT*

**Baking stone, cast-iron pizza pan, cast-iron skillet, or unglazed quarry tiles:** Bread turns out browner, crisper, and tastier when the dough is baked on one of these, especially in combination with a steam environment (see page 19). Products may be labeled "pizza stones" (usually round), or "baking stones" (usually rectangular), but they're both made from the same kinds of materials and perform the same way. The larger ones will keep flour, cornmeal, and other ingredients from falling to the oven floor (the 14 × 16-inch models work well). In our experience, ceramic stones don't last forever. Most are pretty durable, but we

no longer find any manufacturers willing to guarantee them against cracking. Thick stones take longer to preheat compared to thinner ones, or to cast-iron (see below), but in general, they are more durable.

Unglazed quarry tiles, available from home-improvement stores, are inexpensive and work well. The drawbacks: you'll need several of them to line an oven shelf, and stray cornmeal or flour may fall between the tiles onto the oven floor, where it will burn.

Traditionally, professionals have given two reasons to bake right on a ceramic stone. **First,** the stone promotes fast and even heat transfer because of its weight and density (versus, for example, a baking sheet), so it quickly dries and crisps the crust. That massive heat transfer also creates terrific "oven spring," especially in home ovens that don't deliver even heat. ("Oven spring" is the sudden expansion of gases within the bread—it occurs upon contact with the hot air and stone, and it prevents a dense, tough result.) **Second,** it's always been assumed that the stone's porosity allows it to absorb excess moisture from the dough (especially wet dough), encouraging crispness. It turns out that the effect must be mostly due to explanation number one, because we've found that dough baked on preheated cast-iron pizza pans, and even in preheated cast-iron skillets, turns out as well as dough baked on stones, despite the fact that cast-iron isn't porous at all.

Having said all this, we must emphasize that you can make decent bread without a baking stone; just do it right on a heavy-gauge baking sheet (see page 25). The crust won't be as crisp, but the result will be better than most any bread you can buy.

**Oven thermometer:** Home ovens are often off by up to 75 degrees, so this is an important item. You need to know the actual oven temperature to get predictable bread-baking results. An inexpensive oven thermometer (less than twenty dollars) will help you get results just like the ones you see in our photos. Place your oven thermometer right on the stone for best results.

A hot oven drives excess water out of wet dough, but if it's too hot you'll burn the crust before fully baking the crumb (the bread's interior). Too low, and you'll end up with a pale crust and undercooked crumb unless you extend the baking time—but that can give you a thick, tough crust. Without the thermometer, your bread baking will have an annoying element of trial and error. If your oven runs significantly hot or cool, you may want to have it recalibrated by a professional. Otherwise, just compensate by adjusting your heat setting.

When a baking stone is in place, your oven may take longer to reach final temperature than the twenty or thirty-minute preheat that we specify. And digital oven settings are no more accurate than old-fashioned dial displays, so rely on your oven thermometer. If you don't like the result you're getting with a thirty-minute preheat, consider a longer one (forty-five or even sixty minutes).

**Pizza peel:** This is a flat board with a long handle used to slide bread or pizza onto a hot stone. Wood or metal work well, but don't use anything

made of plastic to transfer dough onto a stone—it could melt upon contact. Prepare the peel with cornmeal, flour, or parchment paper before putting dough on it, or everything will stick to it, and possibly to your stone. If you don't have a pizza peel, a flat baking sheet without sides (rimless) will do, but it will be more difficult to handle. A thin wood cutting board also works in a pinch—some have handles that make them almost as easy to work with as peels.

**A bucket, large plastic storage container, or a glass, stainless steel, crockery container or pot with a lid:** You can mix and store the dough in the same vessel—this will save you from washing one more item (it all figures into the five minutes a day). Look for a food-grade container that holds about 6 quarts, to allow for the initial rise. Round containers are easier to mix in than square ones (flour gets caught in corners). Great options are available on our website, or from Tupperware, King Arthur Flour's website, and kitchen-supply specialty stores, as well as discount chains, such as Costco and Target. Some food-storage buckets include a vented lid, which allows gases to escape during the fermentation process. Another vented option is a beer fermentation bucket, which is sold at beer-making (home-brew) stores. You can usually close the vent (or seal the lid) after the first two days because gas production has really slowed by then. If your vessel has a plastic lid, you can poke a tiny hole in the lid to allow gas to escape. Avoid glass or crockery containers that create a truly airtight seal (with a screw top, for example) because trapped gases could shat-

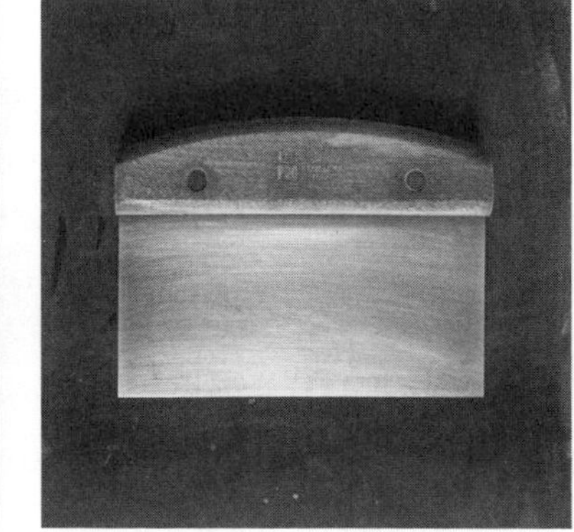

ter them. If you don't have a vented container, just leave the lid open a crack for the first two days of storage.

And of course, you can always use a mixing bowl covered with plastic wrap (don't use a towel—it sticks horribly to high-moisture dough).

**Dough scraper ("bench knife"):** The dough scraper makes it easier to work with wet dough—especially when you're just starting out. It can help lessen the temptation to work in extra flour to prevent things from sticking to the work surface. Just scrape wet dough off the work surface when it sticks—this is particularly useful when working with dough as it's rolled out for pizza or flatbread. The scraper is also handy for scraping excess cornmeal or flour off your hot baking stone. We prefer the rigid steel scrapers over the flexible plastic ones—in part because you can't use plastic to scrape off a hot stone.

**Heavy-gauge baking sheets, jelly-roll pans, and cookie sheets:** The highest-quality baking sheets are made of super-heavyweight aluminum and have short rims (sometimes called jelly-roll pans). When well greased or lined with parchment paper or a silicone mat, they are a decent alternative to the pizza peel/baking stone method and let you avoid sliding dough off a pizza peel onto a stone.

Similar gauge flat, round pans are available specifically for pizza. Avoid "air-insulated" baking sheets—they don't conduct heat well and won't produce a crisp crust. Thin cookie sheets can be used, but like air-insulated bakeware, they won't produce a great crust and can scorch bottom crusts due to their uneven heat delivery.

**Silicone mats:** Nonstick, flexible silicone baking mats are convenient and are reusable thousands of times. They're terrific for lower-temperature recipes (such as sweet brioches and challahs), but we find that pizzas and other lean-dough specialties don't crisp as well on silicone. They're used on top of a baking sheet or dropped onto a hot stone, and don't need to be greased, so cleanup is a breeze. Be sure to get a mat rated to the temperature you need—most brands aren't rated for high-temperature baking.

**Parchment paper:** Parchment paper is an alternative to flour or cornmeal for preventing dough from sticking to the pizza peel as it's slid into the oven. Use a paper that's temperature-rated to withstand what's called for in your recipe. The paper goes along with the loaf, right onto the preheated stone, and can be removed halfway through baking to crisp up the bottom crust. Parchment paper can also be used to line baking sheets, and this can substitute for greasing the sheet. Don't use products labeled as pastry parchment, butcher paper, or waxed paper—they will smoke and stick miserably to baked bread dough.

---

**Baguette pan (metal or silicone):** We usually bake French baguettes right on a stone, but metal or silicone baguette pans work as an alternative. They are a great way to bake several beautifully shaped baguettes at once, without crowding. They also prevent sideways spreading, which can give baguettes an odd shape when using longer-aged or wetter dough. If using the metal pans, you will want to bake the dough on a sheet of parchment, to prevent the bread from sticking.

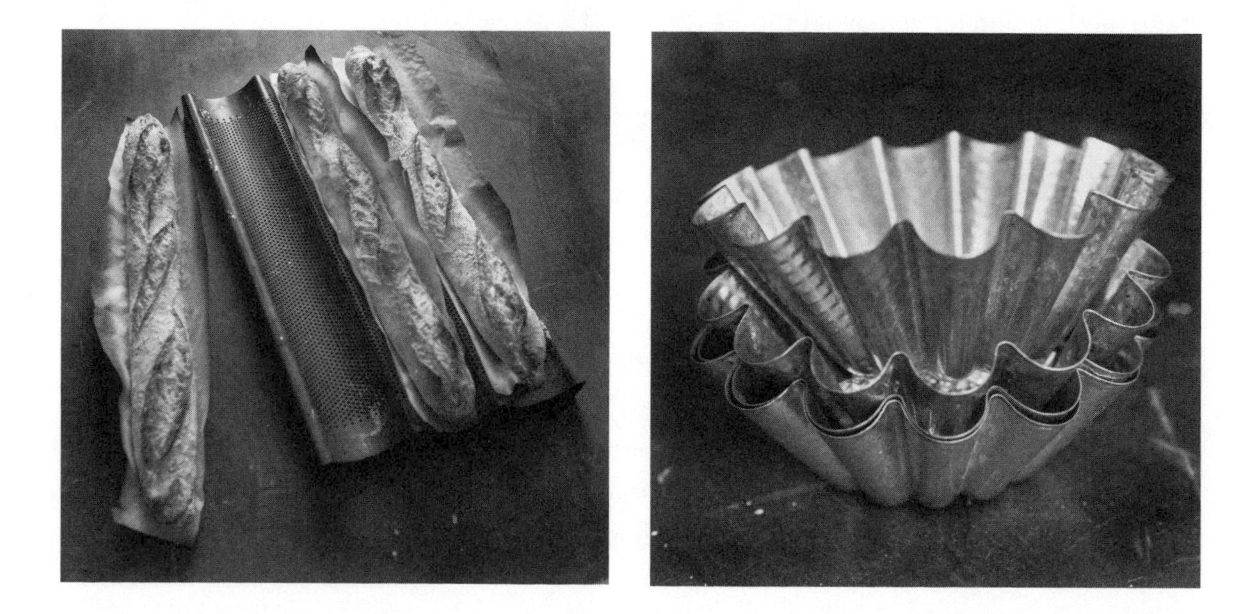

**Loaf pans:** For sandwich loaves, we prefer smaller pans with approximate dimensions of 8½×4½ inches. With high-moisture dough, it can be difficult to get bigger loaves to bake through. This size pan is often labeled as holding 1 pound of dough, but we specify a more generous fill for taller slices—up to 2 pounds when filled three-quarters full.

Like baking sheets and silicone mats, loaf pans work well but don't promote the development of a crisp and beautifully colored crust—wherever the pan touches the bread, it's going to be pale compared to free-form loaves. One word of caution about loaf pans: When you're starting out with our wet doughs, use a pan with a nonstick coating, and even then, grease it. Traditional loaf pans (without the nonstick coating) are more challenging. We've had best success getting loaves to release from traditional uncoated pans when they're made from heavy-gauge aluminum or glazed ceramic—the thin ones don't do as well. Be sure to grease them well with butter or oil.

**Mini loaf pans:** For smaller sandwich breads, and especially when baking with kids, it's fun to use mini loaf pans. They're sometimes labeled "number-1" loaf pans, measure about 6×3 inches, and hold about three-quarters of a pound of dough. The loaves bake faster than those in full-size loaf pans, so check for doneness sooner than the recipe calls for when using them.

**Brioche pans:** Traditionally, brioche is baked either in a fluted brioche mold or in a loaf pan. The fluted mold is easy to find either online or in any baking supply store. They are available in several sizes, with or without a nonstick coating. Flexible silicone brioche molds are now also available.

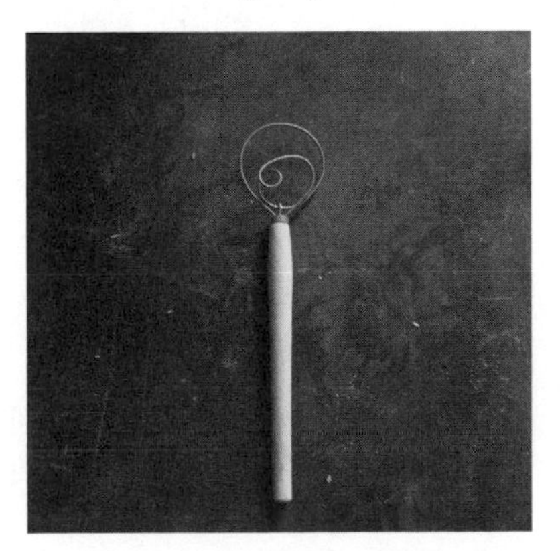

**Panettone molds:** Large ceramic ramekins or ordinary fluted brioche pans work nicely, or you can buy an authentic panettone pan or panettone molds made from paper.

**Dough whisk:** Unlike flimsy egg-beating whisks, Danish-style dough whisks are made from strong nonbendable wire on a wood handle, and they're used to blend liquid and dry ingredients together quickly in the dough bucket. We find that they work faster and offer less resistance than a traditional wooden spoon—though a wooden spoon works fine.

**Rolling pin:** You'll need one if you want to make any of our rolled-out desserts, and using one definitely speeds up the process of flattening dough for pizzas. We love the skinny French rolling pins that look like large dowels, tapered or straight, but traditional American-style pins with handles work well, too. We have tried them all and have determined that wood, marble, and metal all get the job done; we've even rolled out the dough with a bottle of wine in a pinch.

**Bread knife:** A serrated bread knife does a great job cutting through fresh bread without tearing or compressing it. It's also the best implement we've found for slashing high-moisture loaves just before baking. Razor blades and French *lames* (lămm), usually recommended in traditional artisan baking methods, catch and stick in very wet dough—not so for serrated bread knives.

**Cooling rack:** These are fashioned of wire or other thin metal and are usually intended for cake. They are very helpful in preventing the soggy bottom crust that can result when you cool bread on a plate or other nonporous surface.

**Measuring cups:** We have only one piece of advice: Avoid 2-cup measuring cups because they are inaccurate when used with the scoop-and-sweep method specified in our recipes. The 2-cup measures collect too much flour due to excessive packing down into the cup. And be sure to use *dry* measuring cups for flour, which allow you to level the top of the cup by sweeping across with a knife; you can't level off a liquid measuring cup filled with flour.

**Measuring spoons:** Seek out a set that includes a ½-tablespoon measure in addition to the usual suspects. Some of our ingredient lists call for ½ tablespoons. If you can't find a measuring set with a ½-tablespoon measure, just measure out 1½ teaspoons.

**Scale:** We love to weigh our ingredients rather than use measuring cups. It's faster and more accurate, and it's begun to catch on in the United States. Luckily, digital scales are getting cheaper all the time, so we now include weights for ingredients in all our dough recipes. Just press "tare" or "zero" after each ingredient is added to the dough vessel and you can use these scales without slowing down to do the arithmetic.

The scale is also a consistent way to measure out dough for loaves or flatbreads, but it isn't absolutely necessary because we also give you a visual cue for dough weight (for example, a grapefruit-size piece is 1 pound, and an orange-size piece is about ½ pound of dough).

**Serrated steak knife, kitchen shears:** You'll need something to cut dough out of the storage bucket, and either of these works well. Shears are also handy for cutting pita bread, or even pizza, and you'll need a pair to cut the *pain d'epí* before baking (page 75).

**Stand mixers and food processors—these are even easier than hand mixing:** You can use a heavy-duty stand mixer (with paddle) or 14-cup food processor (with dough attachment) instead of a spoon or dough whisk to mix the dough. Be sure your food processor can handle a full batch of our dough, which weighs about 4 pounds and takes around 7 cups of flour. Check with the manufacturer—if your machine doesn't have the capacity, mix a half batch at a time. Some food processors don't make a seal perfectly, so you may need to add the dry ingredients first, then pour in the liquids; otherwise it will leak a bit. Stop the machine as soon as the ingredients are uniformly mixed.

**Immersion blenders** are great for breaking up a lump of old dough, known in French as *pâte fermentée* (pot fair-mon-táy). Pâte fermentée can be used to jump-start the sourdough process for stored dough (see box, page 62, in the Master Recipe). These blenders are also nice for breaking up pieces of whole tomatoes for pizza sauce. Be sure that the immersion blender is fully submerged in any liquid mixture before turning it on; otherwise you'll be spattered with ingredients. **Safety note:** Remember that immersion blenders don't have a protective safety interlock so it's possible to touch the sharp spinning blades while the unit is on.

**Pastry brushes:** These are used to paint cornstarch wash, egg wash, oil, or water onto the surface of the loaf just before baking. We both prefer the natural-bristle style to the silicone, but that's a matter of taste.

**Microplane zester:** Microplane zesters are used for removing the zest from citrus fruit without any of the bitter pith. We use them when we want an assertive citrus flavor that you can't get from the fruit's juice.

**Convection ovens:** These produce a first-rate brown and crispy crust, and speed the baking by circulating hot air around bread in the oven. Some older convection models specify that temperatures should be lowered 25 degrees to prevent overbrowning, while many recent models make the correction automatically, so check your manual. In some, you'll need to turn the loaf around at the halfway point so that each side will brown evenly. Ignore convection-oven instructions that claim you can skip the preheat—the preheat is necessary for our method, especially if you're using a baking stone. As always, use an oven thermometer to check temperature; air circulation in convection ovens can "fool" thermostats in some ovens, sometimes driving the temperature up as much as 75 degrees.

These instructions apply only to range-based convection ovens, not microwaves with convection modes, which we have not tested.

# 4

# TIPS AND TECHNIQUES

This chapter will help you perfect your stored-dough, high-moisture breads. In the discussion that follows, we provide tips and techniques to create breads with a professional-quality crust (exterior) and crumb (interior).

## Measuring Ingredients by Weight Rather than Cup-Measures

Many readers of our first edition, especially those outside the United States, asked us for weight equivalents. Though most American home bakers haven't taken to it yet, this is probably the quickest way to mix up a batch of dough—and based on current trends, it may become standard here. So now we have weight equivalents for all our dough recipes.

**Using digital scales** (see Equipment, page 29): Inexpensive digital scales are a snap to use. Simply press the "tare" (zeroing) button after placing your empty mixing vessel on the scale. Then "tare" again before adding each subsequent ingredient. There's less cleanup, and your measurements won't be affected by different scooping styles, or how tightly or loosely compacted your flour was in its bin.

**Weighing small-quantity ingredients:** Our recipes only require a fraction

of an ounce of some ingredients (like salt and yeast). Since many scales for home use are accurate only to the nearest 1⁄8 of an ounce (3 or 4 grams), measuring small amounts this way can introduce inaccuracy—this becomes less important when measuring larger quantities for doubled recipes. **Unless you're confident of your scale's accuracy for very small amounts, or you're making a double batch or larger, measure salt and yeast with measuring spoons.**

## Storing Dough to Develop Flavor

All of our recipes are based on dough that can be stored for up to fourteen days in the refrigerator, depending on ingredients. That makes our method incredibly convenient. But there's another benefit to storing the dough: Sourdough flavor develops over the lifespan of the batch. That means that your first loaves won't taste the same as your last ones. Some of our readers have taken to mixing staggered batches, so that they're never baking with brand-new dough.

**How much to make and store:** In order to have fresh-baked artisan bread in only five minutes a day of active preparation time, you'll want to make enough dough to last a week or more. Your initial time investment (mixing the dough) is the most significant one, though it generally takes no more than fifteen minutes. By mixing larger batches, you can spread that investment over more days of bread making. So, we recommend mixing enough dough to last at least seven to fourteen days (less for egg-based and some whole-grain doughs). For larger households, that might mean doubling or even tripling the recipes. Don't forget to choose a container large enough to accommodate the rising of the larger batch.

## Conversion Tables for Common Liquid Measures

### Volumes

| U.S. Spoon and Cup-Measures | U.S. Liquid Volume | Metric Volume |
|---|---|---|
| 1 teaspoon | ⅙ ounce | 5 ml |
| 1 tablespoon | ½ ounce | 15 ml |
| ¼ cup | 2 ounces | 60 ml |
| ½ cup | 4 ounces | 120 ml |
| 1 cup | 8 ounces | 240 ml |
| 2 cups | 16 ounces | 475 ml |
| 4 cups | 32 ounces | 950 ml |

### Oven Temperature: Fahrenheit to Celsius Conversion

| Degrees Fahrenheit | Degrees Celsius |
|---|---|
| 350 | 180 |
| 375 | 190 |
| 400 | 200 |
| 425 | 220 |
| 450 | 230 |
| 475 | 240 |
| 500 | 250 |
| 550 | 288 |

## Dough Consistency: How Wet Is Wet Enough?

Our recipes were carefully tested, and we arrived at the ratio of wet to dry ingredients with an eye toward creating a relatively slack and wet dough. But flours can vary in their protein content, the degree to which they're compacted into their containers, and in the amount of water they've absorbed from the environment. And environment changes; in most places, humidity will fluctuate over the course of the year. All of this means that our recipes may produce slightly variable results depending on humidity, compaction, and the flour brand you're using.

If you find that your doughs are too stiff, especially if after storage they don't show good "oven spring" (the sudden rising seen soon after going into a hot oven), decrease the flour by ⅛ cup at a time in subsequent batches (or increase the water by a tablespoon). If they're too loose and wet, and don't hold a shape well for free-form loaves, increase the flour, again by ⅛ cup at a time. If you don't want to wait until your next batch to correct a problem with moisture content, you can work extra flour into a too-wet batch (give it some time to absorb after doing this). For too-dry batches, it can be challenging to mix water into the dough—but it can be done. If all else fails, overly wet dough still works well as flatbread, or in loaf pans. The same is true for dough nearing the end of its storage life.

You can vary the moisture level in our recipes based on your taste. Here's what you can expect:

| **If you modify a recipe, using . . .** | |
|---|---|
| **. . . more liquid or less flour (giving you wetter dough), you'll get . . .** | **. . . less liquid or more flour (giving you drier dough), you'll get . . .** |
| Larger air holes | Smaller air holes |
| Desirable "custard" crumb (page 35); can become gummy if too little flour is used | Difficult to achieve custard interior; crumb (interior) will be drier |

*(continued)*

| If you modify a recipe, using . . . | |
|---|---|
| **. . . more liquid or less flour (giving you wetter dough), you'll get . . .** | **. . . less liquid or more flour (giving you drier dough), you'll get . . .** |
| May be difficult for free-form loaf to hold shape, may spread sideways, but will do well in loaf pans or as flatbread | Free-form loaves will hold shape well and remain high and domed |
| Requires less resting time before baking | Requires more resting time before baking |

## "Custard" Crumb

Perfectly baked high-moisture dough can produce a delightful "custard" crumb (interior). When mixed with water and then baked, wheat flour's protein, mostly gluten, traps the water and creates a chewy and moist texture, with air holes that have shiny walls. As you adjust flour amounts for your favorite recipes, you'll find that this is an effect you can manipulate. Too much flour, and you will lose the "custard" crumb character. Too little, and the dough will be difficult to shape and the crumb may be gummy.

## Resting and Baking Times Are Approximate

All of our resting and baking times are approximate. Since loaves are formed by hand, their size will vary from loaf to loaf, which means their resting and baking time requirements will vary as well. In general, flat or skinny loaves don't need much resting time, and will bake rapidly. High-domed loaves will require longer resting and baking times. So unless you're weighing out exact 1-pound loaves and forming the same shapes each time, your resting and baking times will vary, and our listed times should be seen only as a starting point.

In the 2007 edition of this book, we recommended a resting time of 40 minutes for 1-pound, round loaves made from lean dough (see page 44). We were very sensitive to the beginning baker's time constraints—if it took too long, even for passive resting times, people might not bake the bread. And most of our readers were happy with the result they got with the 40-minute rest. But others said they'd be willing to try a longer rest to get an airier crumb. For those folks, we started recommending a range of rest times for a 1-pounder: 40 to 90 minutes, especially if your kitchen is cool. The longer rest will give you a more open hole structure and a loftier result. This is more important when you are using whole grains in the loaf. If you extend the resting time beyond 40 minutes, or if your environment is particularly dry, cover the loaf with plastic wrap or a roomy overturned bowl—this prevents the surface from drying out and forming a crust that might inhibit rising and oven spring. Skinny loaves (like baguettes, see page 64) or flatbreads (see Chapter 7) do well with the shorter resting times; in fact, pizza and many flatbreads need none at all (for more on pizza and flatbread, see ***Artisan Pizza and Flatbread in Five Minutes a Day,*** 2011). Here are some guidelines for varying resting and baking times:

**Increase resting and/or baking time if any of the following apply:**

- The temperature of your kitchen is low: This only affects rising and resting times, not baking.
- Larger loaf: A 2-pound, free-form, white loaf takes a 90-minute resting time and 45 to 50 minutes to bake. A 3-pound loaf will take about 2 hours resting time and nearly an hour to bake.
- You're using more whole grain than we call for in the recipe.

**Baking temperature is based on dough ingredients:**

- Non-enriched doughs: 450°F
- Egg, honey, or brioche dough: 350°F

**A good rule of thumb for resting time after shaping: if you want loaves to develop maximum rise and air holes, wait until the dough no longer feels dense and cold. A perfectly rested loaf will begin to feel "jiggly" when you shake it on its peel—like set Jell-O.**

## Preparing the Pizza Peel—Grains or Parchment Paper?

Many of our recipes call for sliding the loaf off a pizza peel directly onto a hot baking stone. Cornmeal is the usual "lubricant," but it's only one of many options. We tend to use cornmeal on the peel for the more rustic, full-flavored loaves, and whole wheat flour for the more delicate breads, like the French baguette. White flour serves the same purpose under pita and *ciabatta*. Coarser grains like cornmeal are the most slippery, and fine-ground flours may require a heavier coating to prevent sticking (sometimes you'll have to nudge the loaves off with a spatula or dough scraper). Mostly though, the choice of grain on the pizza peel is a matter of taste. We've used Malt-O-Meal cereal or oatmeal in a pinch, and Zoë's mom once used grits. If you're really having trouble sliding loaves off a pizza peel prepared with grain, you can switch to parchment paper (see Equipment, page 26).

## Underbaking Problems

**The crust is crispy when it emerges from the oven, but it softens as it comes to room temperature:** The bread may be underbaked. This is most often a problem with large breads, but it can happen with any loaf. Internal moisture, so high in wet dough, doesn't dissipate in underbaked bread, so it redistributes to the crust as the bread cools. As you gain experience, you'll be able to judge just how brown the loaf must be to prevent this problem with any given loaf size. We use brownness and crust firmness as our measure of doneness (there will be a few blackened bits on the loaf in non-egg breads).

**The loaf has a soggy or gummy crumb (interior):**

- Check your oven temperature with a thermometer.
- Be sure that you're adequately preheating your stone and oven, and consider a longer preheat (see page 43).
- Make sure you are allowing the dough to rest for the full time period we've recommended.
- Be sure you're measuring your flour and liquids correctly, whether you opt for measuring cups or a scale.
- Your dough may benefit from being a little drier. For the next batch, increase the flour by ⅛ cup (or decrease the liquids a little) and check the result.
- If you're baking a large loaf (more than 1 pound), rest and bake it longer (see page 36).

**Don't slice or eat loaves when they're still warm, unless they're flatbreads, rolls, or very skinny baguettes.** The proteins continue to cook and set as the bread cools. Warm bread has a certain romance, so we know that it's hard to wait for it to cool. But waiting will improve the texture—loaf breads are at their peak of flavor and texture about two hours after they come out of the oven (or whenever they completely cool). Hot or warm bread cuts poorly (the slices collapse and seem gummy) and dries out quickly, and all of these problems are exaggerated with high-moisture dough. Use a sharp serrated bread knife to go right through the crisp crust and soft crumb. Flatbreads, rolls, and skinny baguettes are different—their size makes them easier to bake through despite the high-moisture dough, so you can enjoy them warm.

**Top crust won't crisp and brown:**

- Use a baking stone when called for, and preheat it for at least twenty minutes, in an oven whose temperature has been checked with a thermometer.
- Bake with steam when called for. Use one of the methods described on page 19.
- Try the shelf switcheroo: If you're a crisp-crust fanatic, here's the ultimate approach for baking the perfect crust. Place the stone on the bottom shelf and start the loaf there. Two-thirds of the way through baking, transfer the loaf from the stone directly to the top rack of the oven (leave the stone where it is). Top crusts brown best near the top of the oven, and bottom crusts brown best near the bottom. This approach works beautifully with free-form loaves, but also helps crisp the crust of hard-crusted loaf-pan breads: Just pop the bread out of the pan before transferring to the top shelf—it makes a big difference. With this approach, you can permanently park your baking stone on the very lowest rack, where it will help even out the heat for everything you bake, not just bread. Then there'll be no need to shift around the stone or racks to accommodate your bread-baking habit.

## Overbaking Problems, Dry Patches

**The crust is great, but the crumb (interior) is dry:**

- The bread may be overbaked. Make sure your oven is calibrated properly using an oven thermometer, and double-check your baking time.
- The dough may have been dry to begin with. In traditional recipes, there's usually an instruction that reads something like "knead thoroughly, until the mass of dough is smooth, elastic, and less sticky,

adding flour as needed." This often means too much flour gets added. Be careful not to work in additional flour when shaping.

**Flour blobs in the middle of the loaf:** Be sure to completely mix the initial batch. Using wet hands to incorporate the last bits of flour will often take care of this. The culprit is sometimes the shaping step—extra flour can get tucked up under and inside the loaf as it's formed. Use lots of dusting flour, but allow most of it to fall off.

## Frequently Asked Questions (FAQs) from Readers

### *"WHY DON'T THE LOAVES RISE MUCH DURING THE RESTING PERIOD AFTER SHAPING?"*

Compared with traditional doughs, our breads get more of their total rise from "oven spring" (sudden expansion of gases inside the loaf that occurs on contact with hot oven air and baking stone)—and less from "proofing" (the resting time after a loaf is shaped, before baking). So don't be surprised if you don't see much rising during our resting step. You'll still get a nice rise from oven spring, so long as you didn't overwork the dough while shaping. If you want to coax a little more rise during the resting period, try prolonging it (see Resting and Baking Times Are Approximate, page 35). And make sure your oven's up to temperature by checking with a thermometer (see Equipment, page 23). If the oven is too cool or too hot, you won't get proper oven spring.

### *"MY LOAVES SPREAD SIDEWAYS RATHER THAN RISING VERTICALLY."*

Since our dough is wet, it can be less structured than traditional dough. Even when their loaves expanded well and had good air bubbles before baking, readers sometimes got free-form loaves that didn't hold their shape and spread sideways during baking rather than rising upward. The bread was delicious, but it didn't make tall sandwich slices. The usual cause was insufficient "gluten-cloaking," the stretching of the outside of the dough around itself during the shaping step. See our videos on YouTube.com/BreadIn5, and be sure to use enough dusting flour when you shape loaves. If you continue to find that your loaves spread sideways, you can dry out the dough by increasing the flour (1⁄8 cup per batch).

And if your dough is nearing or exceeding the end of its storage life, consider using it for pizza or flatbread—those don't need much structure—they're flat in the first place and don't need to support the weight of a heavy loaf.

## *"MY LOAVES ARE TOO DENSE AND HEAVY—WHAT AM I DOING WRONG?"*

If your bread is dense, doughy, or heavy, with poor hole structure . . .

**1. Make sure that your dough is not too wet or too dry**; both extremes will result in a dense crumb. Some white flours need a little extra water or you'll get a dry dough—see Ingredients, page 10, for adjustments. If you're measuring flour by volume, make sure you are using the **scoop-and-sweep method** that we describe in Chapter 5, and view our video, "How to Measure Flour," on our YouTube channel (YouTube.com/BreadIn5). And if you're getting inconsistent results, consider weighing the flour rather than measuring it out with measuring cups (see "Tips and Techniques," page 31), using a digital scale.

**2. Be quick and gentle when shaping loaves:** We find that many bakers, especially experienced ones, want to knead the dough—but you can't do that with this kind of dough, or you will knock the gas out of it and the result will be a dense crumb. When shaping our doughs, you're trying to preserve air bubbles as much as possible—these bubbles create the holes in the bread. Shape your loaves in only 20 to 40 seconds.

**3. Try a longer rest after shaping, especially if your kitchen is cool or you're making a large loaf:** See Resting and Baking Times Are Approximate (page 35).

**4. You may prefer longer-stored dough for pizza or flatbread:** If you are using a dough that is nearing the end of its batch life, you may want to stick to pizza, pita, naan, or another option from the flatbread chapter (page 213), or from our third book, ***Artisan Pizza and Flatbread in Five Minutes a Day*** (2011). As the dough ages it produces denser results when you use it for loaves—many of our readers love it a little dense, but others use the older stuff for flatbreads. If you prefer your dough "younger," you can freeze it when it begins to produce denser loaves.

**5. Check your oven temperature:** See Equipment, page 23; if your oven's temperature is off, whether too warm or too cool, you won't get proper "oven spring" and the loaf will be dense, with a pale or burnt crust.

**6. Try the "refrigerator rise" trick:** By using the refrigerator, you can shape your dough and then have it rise in the refrigerator for 8 to 14 hours. **First thing in the morning,** cut off a piece of dough and shape it as normal. Place the dough on a sheet of parchment paper, loosely wrap with plastic or cover it with an overturned bowl, and put it back in the refrigerator. **Right before dinner,** preheat your oven with a stone on a middle rack and take the loaf out of the refrigerator. You may find that it has spread slightly, and may not have risen much, but it will still have lovely oven spring. Because you don't handle the dough at all after the refrigerator rise, the bubbles in the dough should still be intact. A 20 to 30 minute rest on the counter while preheating is all you need. Then slash and bake as usual.

### *"WHAT DO I DO ABOUT CHANGES IN THE DOUGH TOWARD THE END OF ITS STORAGE LIFE? AND WHY DOES MY DOUGH LOOK GRAY?"*

Especially if you don't bake every day, you may find that toward the end of a batch's storage life, its entire surface darkens (or even turns gray) and it develops a more intense sourdough flavor; dark liquid may collect. None of this is mold or spoilage—don't toss it, just pour off the liquid, and work in enough flour to absorb excess moisture in the dough. Then rest the dough for 2 hours at room temperature before using. If you are not using it right away, refrigerate it again; you can keep it until the end of the dough's recommended life.

**Discard any dough that develops mold on its surface, which you can identify as dark or light patches, with or without a fuzzy appearance.**

### *"SHOULD I PREHEAT THE STONE FOR LONGER THAN YOU RECOMMEND?"*

Professionals sometimes suggest preheating the baking stone for an hour to absorb all the heat it possibly can, but we specify a shorter time in our recipes. Many of our readers expressed concern about wasted energy with a long preheat, not to mention the need for more advance planning. So we compromised—we know that some ovens will produce a crisper crust with a longer preheat, but we're pretty happy with the results we get at 20 to 30 minutes (even though many ovens equipped with a stone won't quite achieve target temperature that soon). If you find that the crust isn't as crisp as you like, or baking time is longer than expected, try increasing the preheating time, to 45 or even 60 minutes. It's not essential but it can be useful, especially with a thicker stone.

Cast-iron "stones" (see page 21) and 1/4-inch-thick ceramic stones heat up faster than 1/2-inch-thick ceramic ones, so consider those if you're committed to the shortest possible preheat.

---

### *"WHY DO I GET ODDLY SHAPED LOAVES?"*

If you haven't used enough cornmeal on the pizza peel, a spot of dough may stick to it. As you slide the loaf off the peel, the spot pulls, causing an odd-shaped loaf. Solution: Use more cornmeal or flour on the pizza peel, especially if the dough is particularly sticky, or switch to parchment paper (see Equipment, page 26).

**Other causes of odd-shaped loaves:**

If your loaves are cracking along the bottom or bulging on the sides, it is generally due to these two issues:

- Not slashing deeply enough—be sure to slash ½-inch-deep cuts straight down into the dough.
- Not letting the shaped loaves rest long enough before baking. Consider a longer resting time, especially if your environment is cool (see page 35) or your dough feels dry.

### *"WHAT ARE 'LEAN' AND 'ENRICHED' DOUGHS?"*

"Lean" doughs are those made without significant amounts of eggs, fat, dairy, or sweetener. They bake well without burning or drying out at high temperatures. Doughs "enriched" with lots of eggs, fat, dairy, or sweeteners require a lower baking temperature (and a longer baking time), because eggs and sweetener can burn at high temperature.

### *"WHAT'S THE BEST WAY TO STORE FRESH BREAD?"*

We've found that the best way to keep bread fresh once it has been cut is to store it cut-side down on a flat, nonporous surface like a plate or a clean countertop. Don't store inside foil or plastic, which traps humidity and softens the crust by allowing it to absorb water. An exception is pita bread, which is supposed to have a soft crust and can be stored in a plastic bag or airtight container once cooled.

Breads made with whole-grain flour and those made with dough that has been well aged stay fresh longest. Use day-old bread for making bread crumbs in the food processor, or try one of our recipes like Tuscan Bread Salad (page 97), bread puddings (pages 99 and 359), or *fattoush* (page 252). Or recycle your stale bread into new loaves as "*altus*" (page 123).

### *"CAN I FREEZE THE DOUGH?"*

Our dough can be frozen at any point in its batch-life, so long as the initial rise has been completed. It's best to divide it into loaf-sized portions, then wrap it very well or seal it in airtight containers. Defrost overnight in the fridge when ready to use, then shape, rest, and bake as usual. How long to freeze is partly a matter of taste—our dough loses some rising power when frozen and some people find the results dense if it's frozen for too long. That's especially true for enriched doughs, such as challah and brioche. Here are some basic guidelines for maximum freezing times:

- Lean dough (no eggs and minimal butter or oil): Four weeks
- Challah (see page 296): Three weeks
- Brioche (see page 300): Two weeks
- Gluten-free dough (see page 267): Two weeks

### *"MY DOUGH HAS A STRONG YEAST OR ALCOHOL SMELL. CAN I USE LESS YEAST?"*

Some people detect a yeasty or alcohol aroma or flavor in the dough, and that's no surprise—yeast multiplies in dough, creating alcohol and carbon dioxide gas as it ferments sugars and starches. The alcohol will boil off during baking, but our stored dough develops character from the by-products of yeast fermentation; most people appreciate the flavor and aroma of this mild sourdough. But others want less of that, so here are some things to try:

1. Always vent the rising container as directed, especially in the first two days of storage (see page 24). You can even poke a tiny hole in the lid to allow gas to escape.

2. Consider a low-yeast version of our recipes (see page 14).

3. Store your dough for shorter periods than we specify, freezing the remainder. Or make smaller batches so they're used up more quickly.

### *"CAN I ADD NATURAL SOURDOUGH STARTER TO THE RECIPES?"*

Yes, sourdough starter works in our recipes. Most sourdough starters are about half water and half flour when fully "activated" and ready for use. About 1½ cups of activated sourdough starter works well in our full-batch recipes. This means that you need to decrease the water in the recipes by ¾ cup, and the flour by ¾ cup.

We've found that we still need some added yeast in addition to the natural starter, although you can use less (see page 14).

### *"HOW DO I BAKE AT HIGH ALTITUDE?"*

There can be a big difference in how yeast behaves if you live above 4,000 feet (1,220 meters). With less air pressure constraining the rising dough, it balloons up too quickly, and then collapses abruptly, giving you a dense result. The following adjustments can help you avoid that by slowing down the initial rise (the dough won't be ready for the refrigerator in the usual 2 hours):

- Decrease the yeast by half or even more (see page 14).
- Use bread flour to increase the strength of the dough, but you will also have to increase the water (see Ingredients, page 10).
- Assuming you like the flavor and aren't on a salt-restricted diet, consider a saltier dough—salt inhibits fast yeast growth. If you go this route, use the higher end of our salt range in the ingredient lists. And decrease sugar if there's any in the recipe—it feeds yeast.
- Do the initial dough rise overnight in the refrigerator (see the refrigerator-rise trick, "Tips and Techniques," page 42), and consider mixing the dough using cold liquids.

These techniques allow the dough to rise more slowly, giving it more time to achieve full height without collapsing.

### *"HOW DO I KEEP BAKING IN THE SUMMER?" USING THE GAS GRILL*

For those hot summer days when you want fresh bread but can't stand the idea of turning on the oven, outdoor covered gas grills are one answer (or try crock pot baking on page 83). When baking on a grill, thinner is better. Flatbreads are the easiest, but if you keep them skinny (like baguettes), loaf breads work, too. When you're first starting out with grilled breads, stick with lean doughs—they're more resistant to scorching. Once you get the knack of your grill's hot spots, you can broaden your repertoire.

**1. Form a free-form loaf (make it skinny and long) or an oblong-shaped flatbread with your favorite recipe.** Pay attention to the shape so it will fit between the gas grill burners and bake over *indirect* heat (the flames aren't right underneath the bread). Allow to rest and rise on a pizza peel; parchment paper can be helpful in preventing scorching, but it isn't required. If you keep it really thin, as an elongated flatbread narrow enough to fit mostly between the burner flames (⅛- to ¼-inch thick), you don't need any resting time.

**2. Preheat the grill** with burners set to high, but decrease to low just before placing the loaf right on the grates—between the gas grill burners so it isn't exposed to direct grill flames. Slash if you're doing a loaf bread. **Close the grill cover to retain heat.** You may need to experiment with the heat setting—grill brands differ.

3. Open the grill in 4 to 15 minutes (depending on loaf thickness), **turn the loaf over,** and finish on the second side for another 4 to 15 minutes. You may need to briefly expose the loaf to direct heat in order to achieve browning.

**If your grilled breads are burning, you can experiment with using a baking stone on the grill,** which shields the loaf from scorching grill heat (cast-iron "stones" will be more crack-resistant on the grill). If you opt for a stone, you can achieve nice crust-browning with a moisture-trapping metal bowl or aluminum-foil roasting pan covering the loaf, but you'll probably still need to turn the loaf at the midpoint to get top-browning. Remove the bowl or pan for the last third of the baking time. You can also use covered cast-iron pots or cloches (see page 21) on the grill (preheat the top and bottom before putting in the loaf). If these scorch the bottom crust, line the pot or cloche with crumpled aluminum foil and use parchment paper between the loaf and the foil. Or, put a baking stone on the grill underneath the pot, to shield it from scorching heat. Bake two-thirds of the baking time closed, then uncover for the last third (but keep the grill cover closed).

For instructions on baking pizzas on the outdoor grill, see ***Artisan Pizza and Flatbread in Five Minutes a Day*** (2011).

### *"HOW DO I PARBAKE ARTISAN LOAVES?"*

Parbaking means partially baking your loaves and finishing the baking later. Parbaked bread can even be frozen. The perfect opportunity for this approach? You are invited to your friends' home for dinner. Parbake the loaf at home and complete the baking in their oven—you'll be able to present absolutely fresh bread or rolls for the dinner party.

**Baking instructions for parbaked bread:**

1. Follow preparation steps for any recipe in this book.

2. Begin baking at the recipe's usual temperature.

3. Remove the loaf from the oven when it just begins to darken in color; the idea is to just set the center of the loaf. For most loaves, that means nearly 90 percent of the baking time.

4. Allow the loaf to cool on a rack, and then place in a plastic bag. Freeze immediately if you plan to wait more than half a day to finish baking.

**To complete the baking:**

1. If frozen, completely defrost the loaf, still wrapped, at room temperature. Unwrap the defrosted loaf, place it on a preheated baking stone or directly on the oven rack, and bake at the recipe's recommended temperature. Bake until browned and appealing, usually about 5 to 10 minutes.

2. Cool on a rack as usual.

5

# THE MASTER RECIPE

We chose an artisan free-form loaf that the French call a *boule*—pronounced "bool," meaning "ball"—as the basic model for all the breads in this book (see color photo). You'll learn a truly revolutionary approach to bread baking: Take the needed amount of pre-mixed dough from the refrigerator, shape it, leave it to rest, then pop it in the oven and let it bake while you're preparing the rest of the meal.

The dough is made with nothing but all-purpose flour, yeast, salt, and water, and is the easiest to handle, shape, and bake. This white dough is used to make all of the recipes in Chapter 5; later chapters introduce other flours and flavors. You'll learn how wet the dough needs to be (wet, but not so wet that the finished loaf won't hold its shape), and how a "gluten cloak" substitutes for kneading. Wetter doughs encourage the development of sourdough character over two weeks of storage. And by omitting kneading, by mixing dough in bulk, and by storing and using it as it's needed over time, you'll truly be able to make this bread in five minutes a day (excluding resting and oven time).

**You should become familiar with the following recipe before going through the rest of the book.**

# The Master Recipe: Boule (Artisan Free-Form Loaf)

***Makes four loaves, slightly less than 1 pound each. The recipe is easily doubled or halved.***

| **Ingredient** | **Volume (U.S.)** | **Weight (U.S.)** | **Weight (Metric)** |
|---|---|---|---|
| Lukewarm water (100°F or below) | 3 cups | 1 pound, 8 ounces | 680 grams |
| Granulated yeast[1] | 1 tablespoon | 0.35 ounce | 10 grams |
| Kosher salt[1] | 1 to 1½ tablespoons | 0.6 to 0.9 ounce | 17 to 25 grams |
| All-purpose flour | 6½ cups (scoop-and-sweep) | 2 pounds | 910 grams |
| Cornmeal or parchment paper, for the pizza peel | | | |

[1]Can decrease (see pages 14 and 17)

## Mixing and Storing the Dough

1. **Warm the water slightly:** It should feel just a little warmer than body temperature, about 100°F. By using warm water, the dough will rise to the right point for storage in about 2 hours. You can use cold water and get the same final result, but the first rising will take longer (see "Tips and Techniques," page 14).

2. **Add yeast and salt to the water** in a 6-quart bowl or, preferably, in a lidded (not airtight) food container or food-grade plastic bucket. Don't worry about getting it all to dissolve.

3. **Mix in the flour—kneading is unnecessary:** Add all of the flour at once, measuring it in with dry-ingredient measuring cups, or by weighing the ingredients. If you measure with cups, use the scoop-and-sweep method, gently scooping up flour, then sweeping

**The scoop-and-sweep method:** It's easier to scoop and sweep if you store your flour in a bin rather than the bag it's sold in; it can be difficult to get the measuring cups into the bag without making a mess. **Don't use an extra-large, 2-cup-capacity measuring cup,** which allows the flour to overpack and measures too much flour.

the top level with a knife or spatula; don't press down into the flour as you scoop or you'll throw off the measurement by compressing. Mix with a wooden spoon or a heavy-duty stand mixer (with paddle) until the mixture is uniform. If you're hand-mixing and it becomes too difficult to incorporate all the flour with the spoon, you can reach into your mixing vessel with very wet hands and press the mixture together. Don't knead! It isn't necessary. You're finished when everything is uniformly moist, without dry patches. This step is done in a matter of minutes, and will yield a dough that is wet and loose enough to conform to the shape of its container.

**Other tools to use for the initial mixing:** If you're mixing by hand, a **Danish dough whisk** (page 27) is an effective alternative to a wooden spoon. It's much stouter than a flimsy egg-beating whisk, and it incorporates the wet and dry ingredients in no time flat. **Food processors** also work well—just replace the standard blade with the dough attachment that comes with most machines. Make sure the machine is rated to handle dough—the motor must be heavy duty. You'll also need the largest size made to mix a full batch—one with a 14-cup bowl. Make a half batch if your processor has a smaller bowl and stop the machine as soon as the ingredients are uniformly mixed (see Equipment, page 29).

4. **Allow to rise:** Cover with a lid that fits well to the container but can be cracked open so it's not completely airtight—most plastic lids fit the bill. If you're using a bowl, cover it loosely with plastic wrap. Towels don't work—they stick to wet dough. Lidded (or even vented) plastic buckets are readily available (see page 24). Allow the mixture to rise at

room temperature until it begins to collapse (or at least flattens on the top), about 2 hours, depending on the room's temperature and the initial water temperature—then refrigerate it and use over the next fourteen days. If your container isn't vented, allow gases to escape by leaving it open a crack for the first couple of days in the fridge—after that you can usually close it. If you forget about your rising dough on the counter, don't worry: longer rising times at room temperature, even overnight, will not harm the result (though egg-enriched dough should go into the fridge after 2 hours). You can use a portion of the dough any time after the 2-hour rise. Fully refrigerated wet dough is less sticky and is easier to work with than dough at room temperature, so the first time you try our method, it's best to refrigerate the dough overnight (or for at least 3 hours) before shaping a loaf. Once refrigerated, the dough will seem to have shrunk back upon itself and it will never rise again in the bucket—that's normal. Whatever you do, **do not punch down this dough.** With our method, you're trying to retain as much gas in the dough as possible, and punching it down knocks gas out and will make your loaves denser.

## On Baking Day

5. **The gluten cloak: *Don't* knead, just "cloak" and shape a loaf in 20 to 40 seconds.** (see sidebar page 58). Prepare a pizza peel with cornmeal or parchment paper to prevent your loaf from sticking to it when you slide it into the oven (the parchment paper slides right onto the stone along with the loaf).

   Dust the surface of your refrigerated dough with flour. Pull up and cut off a 1-pound (grapefruit-size) piece of dough, using a serrated knife or kitchen shears. Hold the dough and add more flour as needed so it won't stick to your hands. Gently stretch the surface of the dough around to the bottom on all four sides, rotating the ball a quarter-turn as you go. Most of the dusting flour will fall off; it's not intended to be incorporated into the dough. The bottom of the loaf may appear to be a collection of bunched ends, but it will flatten out and adhere during resting and baking. The correctly shaped loaf will be smooth and cohesive. The entire process should take no more than 20 to 40 seconds—don't work the dough longer or your loaves may be dense.

**Relax.** You don't need to monitor doubling or tripling of volume as in traditional recipes.

**What's a "gluten cloak"?** Just imagine a warm blanket being pulled around you on a cold night. Or, for the more technically inclined: What you are trying to do here is to add enough flour to the surface so it can be handled and the protein strands in the surface can be aligned, creating a resilient "cloak" around the mass of wet dough. Visualize a cloak being pulled around the dough, so that the entire ball is surrounded by a skin. ***Resist the temptation*** to get rid of all stickiness by incorporating flour. This could prevent the bread from developing a finished crumb with the typical artisanal "custard" (see page 35). See our YouTube channel for video of the gluten-cloak step (YouTube.com/BreadIn5).

**Adjusting the Resting Time:**

- **Lengthen the resting time** if your fridge or the room is particularly cold, if you're making larger loaves, or if you just want to get a more open and airy crumb structure. You can go as long as 90 minutes for a 1-pound loaf. When increasing the resting time (especially in dry environments), cover the loaf with plastic wrap or a roomy overturned bowl—plastic wrap won't stick if the surface is well dusted. Don't use a damp towel—that will stick.
- **Shorten the resting time by half** if you're using fresh, unrefrigerated dough.

6. **Rest the loaf and let it rise on a pizza peel:** Place the shaped ball on the prepared pizza peel, and allow it to rest for about 40 minutes. It doesn't need to be covered during the rest period unless you're extending the rest time to get a more "open" crumb (see sidebar, page 58, and "Tips and Techniques," page 35). You may not see much rise during this period; much more rising will occur during baking (oven spring).

**Don't have a pizza peel and baking stone?** You can rest the formed loaf on a baking sheet prepared with oil, butter, parchment paper, or a silicone mat. Then just place the baking sheet on an oven rack when ready to bake.

7. **Preheat a baking stone near the middle of the oven to 450°F**, which takes about 20 to 30 minutes. (You may consider a longer preheat; see page 43). Place an empty metal broiler tray for holding water on any shelf that won't interfere with rising bread. **Never use a glass pan to catch water for steam—it's likely to shatter.**

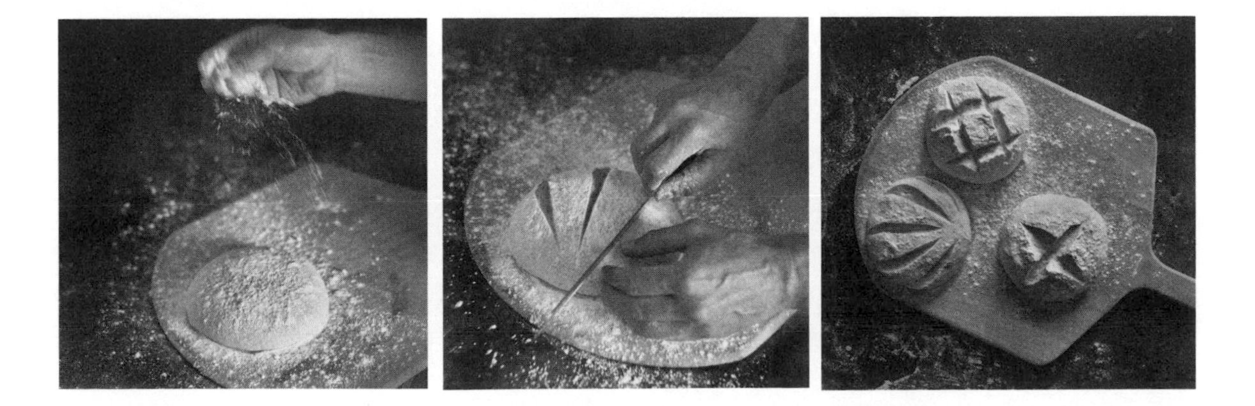

8. **Dust and slash:** Dust the top of the loaf liberally with flour, which will prevent the knife from sticking. Slash a ½-inch-deep cross, scallop, or tic-tac-toe pattern into the top, using a serrated bread knife held perpendicular to the bread (see photos). Leave the flour in place for baking; tap some of it off before eating.

9. **Baking with steam—slide the loaf onto the preheated stone:** Place the tip of the peel a few inches beyond where you want the bread to land. Give the peel a few quick forward-and-back jiggles, and pull it sharply

**Instant-read thermometers:** We're not in love with internal-temperature food thermometers, usually sold as "instant-read" thermometers (as opposed to oven thermometers, which we love, see page 23). They have a pointed probe that you stick into the bread to see if it's reached a target temperature. We find that the inexpensive ones (under $20) aren't all that "instant," which means that you're never sure how long to wait before the read-out stabilizes. The truly instant (and accurate) digital units are much more expensive (but can still give misleading results if its probe isn't well centered in the loaf). If you have confidence in your thermometer and your technique, here are some guidelines for fully baked bread:

- Lean dough (no eggs): 205°F to 210°F (96°C to 99°C)
- Egg-enriched dough, such as challah and brioche: 180°F to 185°F (82°C to 85°C)

out from under the loaf. Quickly but carefully pour about 1 cup of hot water from the tap into the broiler tray and close the oven door to trap the steam (see page 20 for steam alternatives). **If you used parchment paper instead of cornmeal, pull it out from under the loaf after about 20 minutes** for a crisper bottom crust. Bake for a total of about 30 to 35 minutes, or until the crust is richly browned and firm to the touch. Smaller or larger loaves will require adjustments in baking times (see page 36). Because the dough is wet, there is little risk of drying out the interior, despite the dark crust. When you remove the loaf from the oven, a perfectly baked loaf will audibly crackle, or "sing," when initially exposed to room-temperature air. Allow to cool completely (up to 2 hours), preferably on a wire cooling rack, for best flavor, texture, and slicing. The crust may initially soften, but will firm up again when cooled. If you're not getting the browning and crispness you want, test your oven temperature with an inexpensive oven thermometer (see page 23).

10. **Store the remaining dough in the refrigerator in your lidded or loosely plastic-wrapped container and use it over the next 14 days:** You'll find that even one day's storage improves the flavor and texture of your bread. This maturation continues over the 14-day storage period. If you store your dough in your mixing container, you'll avoid some cleanup. Cut off and shape more loaves as you need them. We often have several types of dough stored in our refrigerators at once. Lean doughs like this (those made without eggs, sweetener, or fat) can be

**Lazy sourdough shortcut:** When your dough bucket is finally empty, or nearly so, don't wash it. Immediately remix another batch in the same container. In addition to saving the cleanup step, the aged dough stuck to the sides of the container will give your new batch a head start on sourdough flavor. Just scrape it down and it will hydrate and incorporate into the new dough. Don't do this with egg- or dairy-enriched dough—with those, the container should be washed after each use.

You can take this even further by adding a more sizable amount of old dough from your last batch. You can use up to 2 cups; just mix it in with the water for your new batch and let it stand until it becomes soupy before you start mixing. An immersion blender is helpful for blending the old dough with water, but not required. Add the liquid to your dry ingredients as in the recipe. Professionals call this *pâte fermentée* (pot fair-mon-táy), which means nothing more than "fermented dough." **See safety note on immersion blenders** (Equipment, page 30).

**Amaze your friends with the "6-2-2-13" rule:** If you want to store enough for seven to eight 1-pound loaves, here's a simple mnemonic for the recipe: 6, 2, 2, and 13. Combine 6 cups water, 2 tablespoons salt*, and 2 tablespoons yeast; then mix in 13 cups of flour. Store in a 10- to 12-quart lidded container. That's it. It will amaze your friends when you do this in their homes without a recipe—but tell them to buy this book anyway!

*Adjust to your taste, see Ingredients, page 17.

frozen in 1-pound portions in an airtight container for up to 4 weeks and defrosted overnight in the refrigerator before use.

**VARIATION: HERB BREAD**

This simple recipe shows off the versatility of our approach. Herb-scented breads are great favorites for appetizers and snacks.

Follow the directions for mixing the Master Recipe and add 1 teaspoon dried thyme leaves (or 2 teaspoons fresh) and 1/2 teaspoon dried rosemary leaves (or 1 teaspoon fresh) to the water mixture. You can also use herbs with the other recipes in this chapter.

## Baguette

This is the quintessential thin and crusty loaf of France, served at every meal, and the symbol of an entire cuisine. Baguettes are defined as much by their crust as their crumb (interior); a crisp crust can make the loaf sensational (see color photo). Aside from the shaping, one important technique that differentiates the baguette from the boule in this chapter is that the baguette is *not* heavily dusted with flour, at least not traditionally. So, to keep the knife from sticking, brush water onto the surface of the loaf just before slashing. You'll also notice that for this loaf we use flour rather than cornmeal on the pizza peel, since cornmeal would impart too strong a flavor to classic baguettes.

Traditional recipes for baguettes are high maintenance, so if you've done this the old-fashioned way, our approach should be a relief. A 20-minute rest after shaping is all that is needed to create this light and airy loaf. So our baguette is delicious, and very, very fast. With your fresh baguette, create a sensational meal by making the Aubergine Tartine on page 68.

*"On my honeymoon in France we survived on twenty-five dollars a day, and this included accommodations. Every morning we would go to the café for a baguette and café au lait. For lunch it was a tartine (page 68), and dinner was often the same with the addition of a bottle of wine and pastry to follow. We didn't eat lavishly, but we ate well. The baguettes were essential. It's hard to match that experience, but we've found we can come very close with this recipe."*—Zoë

***Makes 1 baguette***

½ pound (orange-size portion) Master Recipe dough (page 53)
All-purpose flour, for dusting
Whole-wheat flour or parchment paper, for the pizza peel

1. **Preheat a baking stone near the middle of the oven to 450°F (20 to 30 minutes),** with an empty broiler tray on any shelf that won't interfere with rising bread.

2. Dust the surface of the refrigerated dough with flour and cut off a ½-pound (orange-size) piece. Dust with more flour and quickly shape it into a ball by stretching the surface of the dough around to the bottom on all four sides, rotating the ball a quarter-turn as you go. Once it's cohesive, begin to stretch and elongate the dough, dusting with additional flour as necessary. You may find it helpful to roll it back and forth with your hands on a flour-dusted surface. Form a cylinder approximately 1½ inches in diameter. Place the loaf on a pizza peel covered with whole wheat flour or parchment paper and allow to rest for 20 minutes (for professional shaping tips, see page 66).

3. After the dough has rested, paint the loaf with water, using a pastry brush. Slash the loaf with longitudinal cuts that move diagonally across the loaf, using a serrated bread knife (see photo, page 66).

4. Slide the loaf directly onto the hot stone. Pour 1 cup of hot water into the broiler tray and quickly close the oven door (see page 20 for steam alternatives). Bake for about 25 minutes, or until deeply browned and firm to the touch.

5. Allow to cool on a rack before cutting or eating.

**Fashion a perfect taper with the letter-fold technique:** Our simple stretch-and-roll method will give you a decent baguette, but you might not get the skinny taper of a professional baguette. Here's a more polished method—if you perfect this, yours will look just like the ones in the bakery window. In addition to using it for skinny baguettes, you can use the letter-fold to get professional tapered ends with your basic oval loaves, such as the Bâtard (page 70) or Deli-Style Rye Bread (page 111). Here's what you do:

1. Gently stretch the dough into a ½-inch-thick oval. Fold in one of the long sides and gently press it into the center, taking care not to compress the dough too much.

2. Bring up the other side to the center and pinch the seam closed. This letter-fold technique puts less dough on the ends—that's what gives you the nice taper.

3. Stretch very gently into a log, working the dough until you have a thin baguette. Again, try not to compress the air out of the dough. If the dough resists pulling, let it rest for 5 to 10 minutes to relax the gluten, then continue to stretch—don't fight the dough. You can continue to stretch lengthwise during the 20-minute rest, until you achieve the desired thin result, about 1½ inches wide.

# Aubergine Tartine (oh-ber-jean tar-teen)

This open-faced sandwich is a more sophisticated vegetarian cousin to our Croque Monsieur (page 80), with smoky grilled eggplant (*aubergine*) and roasted red pepper on a freshly baked baguette (page 64), topped with spicy greens and soft, ripe cheese.

***Makes 2 open-faced baguette sandwiches; serves 2 to 4***

Two ½-inch-thick slices of eggplant, cut lengthwise
Olive oil, for brushing the eggplant
Salt and freshly ground black pepper, to taste
½ red bell pepper, seeds and ribs removed
½ baguette (see page 64)
2 roasted garlic cloves (see sidebar)
1 dozen arugula leaves
3 ounces soft, ripened cheese, such as Brie or Camembert, sliced

1. Preheat a gas or charcoal grill, or a broiler. Brush the eggplant slices with olive oil. Sprinkle with salt and pepper and grill over a medium gas flame or charcoal, or under a broiler, until browned and soft but not overcooked, approximately 5 minutes on each side.

2. Flatten the half bell pepper, making additional cuts as needed to get it flat. Grill or broil the pepper under the broiler or on a

**To roast the garlic cloves:** Wrap, unpeeled, in aluminum foil and bake for 30 minutes at 400°F. Allow to cool and cut across the top of each clove. Squeeze out the soft roasted garlic pulp. You can even do this with an entire head of garlic.

gas or charcoal grill, keeping the skin side closest to the heat source. Check often and remove when the skin is blackened, 8 to 10 minutes. Drop the roasted pieces into an empty bowl and cover the bowl. As they steam, the skin will loosen over the next 10 minutes. Gently hand-peel the pepper and discard the blackened skin. Some dark bits will adhere to the pepper's flesh, which is not a problem. Cut the roasted pepper into thin strips.

3. Split the baguette lengthwise, spread it open, and tear out some of the inside. Smear roasted garlic over the cut surfaces. Top each half with the eggplant, red pepper strips, and arugula.

4. Top with the cheese and broil for 3 to 4 minutes until the cheese is melted, taking care not to burn the baguettes.

# Bâtard (báh-tar)

The *bâtard*, a short and wide French loaf with pointed ends, is more suitable to use for sandwiches than a baguette—it cuts into ample round slices that can accommodate sandwich fillings. You get more of the mellow-sweet crumb and less of the crispy caramelized crust. If you like, you can make the bâtard almost as wide as a sandwich loaf, but traditionally it is about 3 inches across at its widest point. Like a baguette, the bâtard is tapered to a point at each end. For a more perfectly shaped bâtard, you can use the letter-fold technique (see box, pages 66–67), just don't make it quite so skinny.

***Makes 1 bâtard***

1 pound (grapefruit-size portion) Master Recipe dough (page 53)
All-purpose flour, for dusting
Cornmeal or parchment paper, for the pizza peel

1. Follow steps 1 and 2 for the baguette on page 65, but shape the loaf to a diameter of about 3 inches.

2. When forming the loaf on the floured surface, concentrate pressure at the ends to form the bâtard's traditional taper.

3. Follow steps 3 through 5 for the baguette, but increase the resting time to 40 minutes, and the baking time to 30 minutes, or until deeply brown.

# Ciabatta (cha-báh-tah)

The word *ciabatta* is Italian for slipper, and refers to the shape of the bread, which is halfway between a flatbread and a loaf. It's made from very wet dough, and shaped as an elongated oval or rectangle—perhaps you have slippers shaped like this? (See color photo.) To achieve the very moist crumb, shape the loaf with wet hands rather than dusting with flour. The bread will be chewy and moist, with large and appealing air holes, especially if you used longer-aged dough. Ciabatta is baked without cornmeal on the bottom, so dust the pizza peel with an ample coating of white flour instead. And, since white flour is a less efficient "stick-preventer" than cornmeal, you may need to nudge the loaf off the peel with a steel dough scraper or spatula (or use parchment paper).

***Makes 1 ciabatta***

1 pound (grapefruit-size portion) Master Recipe dough (page 53)
All-purpose flour for dusting
White flour or parchment paper, for the pizza peel

1. Cut off a 1-pound (grapefruit-size) piece of refrigerated dough without dusting the surface with flour; wet hands will help prevent sticking. Using your wet hands, shape the dough into a ball by stretching the surface of the dough around to the bottom on all four sides, rotating the ball a quarter-turn as you go. With your wet fingers, flatten the ball into an elongated oval about ¾ inch thick. If you make it much thinner, it may puff like pita bread, which isn't desirable here.

2. **Preheat a baking stone near the middle of the oven to 450°F (20 to 30 minutes),** with an empty metal broiler tray on any shelf that won't interfere with rising bread.

3. Place the loaf on a flour-covered pizza peel and allow to rest for 20 minutes (increase to 40 minutes if you're not getting the large hole-structure you want). Dust the top with flour, but don't slash the loaf.

4. Slide the loaf directly onto the hot stone, using a steel dough scraper or spatula to nudge it off if it sticks (this won't be necessary if you're using parchment paper; just slide off onto the stone, paper and all). Pour 1 cup of hot water into the broiler tray and quickly close the oven door (see page 20 for steam alternatives). If you notice puffing through the oven door, poke the air bubbles with a long-handled fork. Bake for 20 to 25 minutes until deeply brown.

5. Allow to cool on a rack before cutting or eating.

## Couronne (cor-ówn)

This ring, or crown-shaped French loaf, is a specialty of Lyon. The *couronne* is quite simple to shape and is a beautiful, crustier alternative to the classic boule (see color photo).

***Makes 1 couronne***

1 pound (grapefruit-size portion) Master Recipe dough (page 53)
All-purpose flour, for dusting
Whole-wheat flour, cornmeal, or parchment paper, for the pizza peel

1. Dust the surface of the refrigerated dough with flour and cut off a 1-pound (grapefruit-size) piece. Dust the piece with more flour and quickly shape it into a ball by stretching the surface of the dough around to the bottom on all four sides, rotating the ball a quarter-turn as you go. When a cohesive ball has formed, poke your thumbs through the center of the ball and gradually stretch the hole so that it is about three times as wide as the wall of the ring; otherwise the hole will close up during baking.

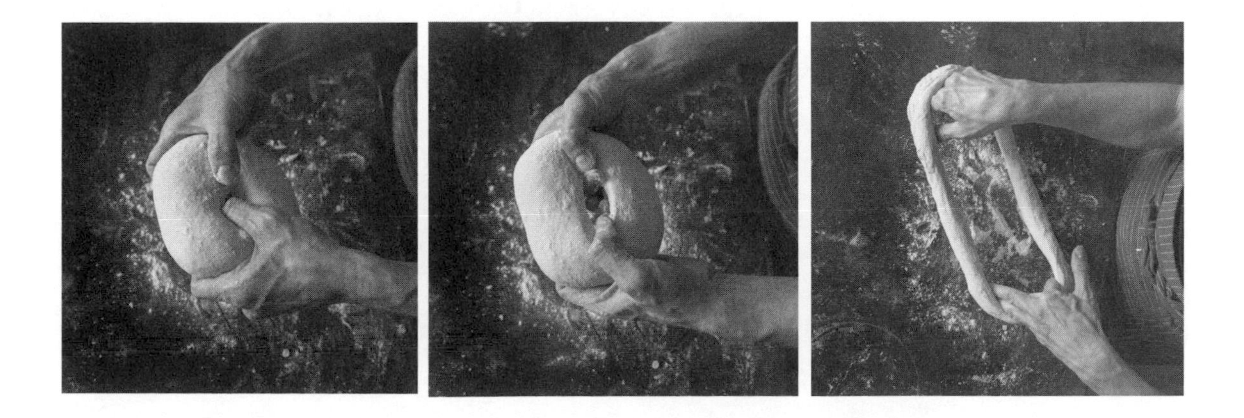

2. Place the loaf on a pizza peel covered with flour, cornmeal, or parchment paper and allow to rest for 20 minutes.

3. **Preheat a baking stone near the middle of the oven to 450°F (20 to 30 minutes),** with an empty metal broiler tray on any shelf that won't interfere with the rising bread.

4. Dust the couronne with flour and slash radially, like spokes in a wheel (see color photo).

5. Slide the loaf directly onto the hot stone. Pour 1 cup of hot water into the broiler tray and quickly close the oven door (see page 20 for steam alternatives). Bake for about 25 to 30 minutes, or until deeply browned and firm. Smaller or larger loaves will require adjustments in baking time.

6. Allow the bread to cool before cutting or eating.

# Pain d'Epí—Wheat Stalk Bread (pan deh-peé)

Fancifully shaped like a stalk of wheat with individual "grains," the *pain d'epí* is a simple yet impressive bread to present to guests (see color photo). To preserve the shape of those wheat grains, we call for bread flour, which makes a stiffer dough. If you don't have bread flour, you can use all-purpose, but increase it to 7 cups. You can make pain d'epí with many of our other doughs, but the illusion of the wheat grains won't be so well-defined.

*"I first ate pain d'epí when vacationing in the South of France. Maman, our adopted grandmother and host, had it delivered fresh every morning. I'd walk through a yard filled with fruit and herb trees to a special bread basket that hung next to the mailbox. I'd pick up this freshly baked wheat stalk and have to pinch myself to make sure it wasn't a dream. The bread was impossibly light, crisp, and absolutely perfect with coffee and jam in the morning, or with Maman's fish stew for dinner. It was heaven!"—Zoë*

***Makes seven ½-pound loaves. The recipe is easily doubled or halved.***

| Ingredient | Volume (U.S.) | Weight (U.S.) | Weight (Metric) |
|---|---|---|---|
| Lukewarm water (100°F or below) | 3 cups | 1 pound, 8 ounces | 680 grams |
| Granulated yeast[1] | 1 tablespoon | 0.35 ounce | 10 grams |
| Kosher salt[1] | 1 to 1½ tablespoons | 0.6 to 0.9 ounce | 17 to 25 grams |
| Bread flour | 6½ cups | 2 pounds, ½ ounce | 920 grams |
| Parchment paper, for the pizza peel | | | |

[1]Can decrease (see pages 14 and 17)

1. **Mixing and storing the dough:** Mix the yeast and salt with the water in a 6-quart bowl or a lidded (not airtight) food container.

2. Mix in the flour without kneading, using a spoon or a heavy-duty stand mixer (with paddle). If you're not using a machine, you may need to use wet hands to incorporate the last bit of flour.

3. Cover (not airtight) and allow to rest at room temperature until the dough rises and collapses (or flattens on top), approximately 2 hours.

4. The dough can be used immediately after initial rise, though it is easier to handle when cold. Refrigerate the container of dough and use over the next 14 days.

5. **Preheat a baking stone near the middle of the oven to 450°F (20 to 30 minutes),** with an empty metal broiler tray on any shelf that won't interfere with rising bread.

6. Dust the surface of the refrigerated dough with flour and cut off a ½-pound (orange-size) piece. Dust with more flour and quickly shape it into a ball by stretching the surface of the dough around to the bottom on all four sides, rotating the ball a quarter-turn as you go.

7. Using the letter-fold technique (see box, pages 66–67), form a slender baguette.

8. Lay the baguette on the edge of a prepared pizza peel. For this loaf, parchment paper is preferred because it will allow sliding it into the oven without distortion or sticking. Allow to rest for 20 minutes.

9. Dust the surface of the loaf with flour. Using kitchen shears and starting at one end of the loaf, cut into the dough at a very shallow

angle. If you cut too vertically, the "wheat grains" won't be as pointy. Cut with a single snip to within 1/4 inch of the work surface, but be careful not to cut all the way through the loaf or you'll have separate rolls (see photo).

10. As you cut, lay each piece over to one side. Continue to cut in this fashion until you've reached the end of the stalk (see photo).

11. Slide the loaf directly onto the hot stone. Pour 1 cup of hot water into the broiler tray and quickly close the oven door (see page 20 for steam alternatives). Bake for about 25 minutes or until richly browned and firm.

12. Allow to cool on a rack before eating.

# Crusty White Sandwich Loaf

This loaf is nothing like commercial white bread, that impossibly soft stuff best used for wadding up and tossing across lunchrooms. The crust is firm if not actually crackling. If you're looking for a flavorful, soft-crusted, and buttery loaf, try Soft American-Style White Bread (page 324) or Buttermilk Bread (page 327). The stored dough adds sourdough complexity to a traditionally plain recipe, and the steam adds crackle and caramelization to the crust. And loaf breads can be as artfully beautiful as free-form ones (see color photo).

This variation will give you some experience baking high-moisture dough in a loaf pan. Nonstick pans release more easily, but you can use a traditional loaf pan if it's heavy gauge and you grease it well; otherwise the loaf is likely to stick.

***Makes 1 loaf***

2 pounds (large cantaloupe-size portion) Master Recipe dough (page 53)
Oil, for greasing the pan

**You don't absolutely have to slash breads baked in a pan:** A loaf pan or a close-fitting cast-iron pot will prevent shape problems. The top crust may crack open randomly but it won't be misshapen.

1. Dust the surface of the refrigerated dough with flour and cut off a 2-pound (large cantaloupe-size) piece. Dust with more flour and quickly shape it into a ball by stretching the surface of the dough around to the bottom on all four sides, rotating the ball a quarter-turn as you go. Lightly grease an 8½ × 4½-inch nonstick loaf pan with oil (grease heavily if you're not using a nonstick pan).

2. Elongate the ball into an oval and drop it into the prepared pan.

3. **Cover with plastic wrap and allow to rest for 90 minutes** (page 58). Dust with flour and slash the top crust with a serrated bread knife.

4. **Preheat the oven to 450°F (20 to 30 minutes)**, with an empty metal broiler tray on any shelf that won't interfere with rising bread. A baking stone is not required, and omitting it shortens the preheat.

5. Place the loaf on a rack in the center of the oven. Pour 1 cup of hot water into the broiler tray and quickly close the oven door. Bake for about 45 minutes, or until brown and firm.

6. Remove the loaf from the pan and allow to cool completely on a rack before slicing; otherwise you won't get well-cut slices. If the loaf sticks, wait 10 minutes and it will steam itself out of the pan.

## Croque Monsieur and Panini

*Croque Monsieur*, the classic Parisian street snack, is a hearty and simple sandwich. Start with freshly baked sandwich bread, slather it with Dijon mayonnaise, add some Gruyère cheese and ham, and then grill it in butter. Serve it with a glass of light red wine and a salad for a little bit of heaven. See the *panini* variation below for the Italian version.

***Makes 1 sandwich***

1½ tablespoons mayonnaise
2 teaspoons whole-grain Dijon mustard
2 slices sandwich loaf bread (page 78)
1 teaspoon unsalted butter, plus more if needed
1½ ounces Gruyère cheese, grated
2 ounces ham, thinly sliced

1. Blend together the mayonnaise and mustard; set aside.

2. Butter one side of each slice of bread, and spread the other side with the mustard-mayonnaise mixture. Place one slice of bread, buttered side down, in a skillet.

3. Cover with half the cheese, then the ham. Finish with the remaining half of the cheese and second slice of bread, buttered side up.

4. Place the skillet over medium-low heat and grill the sandwich slowly for approximately 4 minutes per side, or until browned and crisp. Add additional butter to the pan if needed.

Boule, Master Recipe, page 53

Baguette, page 64

Ciabatta, page 71

*Couronne, page 73*

Pain d'Epi, page 75

Loaf breads

*Panini, page 80*

Crock Pot Bread, page 83

Rolls, clockwise from top: Pull-apart, Cloverleaf, Rosemary Crescent, Brötchen, page 88

From top left, Fougasse with Roasted Red Pepper, page 238, Olive Fougasse, page 235, and Olive Bread, page 103

*Pumpernickel, page 123, and Deli-Style Rye, page 111*

Caraway Swirl Rye, page 116

Italian Semolina Bread, page 143

Yeasted Thanksgiving Cornbread with Cranberries, page 151

Spicy Pork Buns, page 153

*Wurzelbrot, page 159*

**VARIATION: PANINI**

*Panini* (singular *panino*) are the Italian cousins to the French *croque monsieur.* Rather than flipping them in a buttered skillet, make them in a panini press prepared with olive oil. The press can be either automatic-electric or old-fashioned cast-iron (on the stovetop). Either way, you have two hot surfaces that grill the top and bottom of the sandwich simultaneously, compress it thin, and create mouthwatering caramelization in the form of beautiful sear marks (see color photo).

Health enthusiasts will appreciate the olive oil, but this is no dry toast—it's a decadent Italian treat. We've found that enriched breads (see page 295) tend to stick to the panini press, but otherwise, anything goes. A large pita (page 248) works nicely too; cut it into wedges after grilling to serve four. If you have an electric press, just follow the manufacturer's instructions for use, using olive oil rather than butter. If you love old-fashioned manual kitchen equipment, try the Lodge or Le Creuset cast-iron grill pans with matching panini press (see Sources, page 367).

1. Preheat the top and bottom surfaces of the panini press for 5 minutes over medium heat on the stovetop if you're using a manual press; otherwise follow the preheat instructions for your electric press.

2. During the preheat, slice your sandwich bread thinly (or slit a pita). Fill with slices of cheese and whatever meat, vegetable, or other fillings you are using. Place a slice of cheese next to the bread on both sides, and don't overstuff.

3. Stack the sandwich together and brush both sides with olive oil.

4. Once the press is hot, quickly rub both grill surfaces with olive oil, using a paper towel. Work quickly or the oil will smoke. Put the sandwich into the pan, cover with the panini press, and firmly press down.

**If you're finding it difficult to achieve prominent grill marks,** consider using very little oil, or (in a well-seasoned pan) none at all. The grill marks will be impressive, and if you want the richness of the usual panini, you can brush olive oil onto the sandwich after the grilling is complete.

5. Grill the sandwich over medium heat for 3 to 4 minutes, adjusting the heat as needed. If your manual press wasn't well preheated, you may need to flip the sandwich and grill for another 2 to 3 minutes (try to match up the grill marks).

6. Serve when appetizing grill marks have appeared and cheese is melted.

**VARIATIONS:**

**Meat filling ideas:** prosciutto, mortadella, soppressata, pancetta. Precook by searing, if raw.

**Vegetable filling ideas:** roasted red peppers, artichoke hearts, grilled asparagus

**Cheeses:** fresh mozzarella, provolone, Swiss, and ripened cheeses, such as Camembert and Brie

# Crock Pot Bread (Fast Bread in a Slow Cooker)

Everyone loves crock pots, bubbling away with Swedish meatballs, no-peek chicken, or chili. Over the years we've had requests for a method for baking our dough in one. **Bread in a crock pot? We had our doubts, lots of them.** We didn't think a slow cooker could get hot enough; thought it would take too long; didn't think it would bake through or have a nice crust. So we resisted trying it, convinced it would fail. **Oh, how wrong we were** (see color photo). The crock pot does indeed get hot enough, and it takes less time than using your oven because the rising time is included in the baking. Straight out of the pot, the crust is soft and quite pale, but just a few minutes under the broiler and you have a gorgeous loaf. In the summer there is no need to heat up the oven to get great bread, and at the holidays it is a perfect way to free up much needed oven space. You could even amaze your friends at work by baking a loaf under your desk.

***Makes 1 loaf***

1 pound (grapefruit-size portion) Master Recipe dough (page 53)
All-purpose flour, for dusting
Parchment paper, for baking

1. **On baking day,** dust the surface of the refrigerated dough with flour and cut off a 1-pound (grapefruit-size) piece. Dust with more flour and quickly shape it into a ball by stretching the surface of the dough around to the bottom on all four sides, rotating the ball a quarter-turn as you go. Place it on a sheet of parchment paper.

2. Lower the dough into a 4-quart crock pot or other slow cooker. Be sure to follow the manufacturer's instructions for proper use.

3. Turn the temperature to high and put on the cover. **(Not all crock pots behave the same, so you should keep an eye on the loaf after about 45 minutes to make sure it is not overbrowning on the bottom or not browning at all. You may need to adjust the time according to your appliance.)**

4. Bake for 1 hour (this will depend on your crock pot, you may need to increase or decrease the time). **To check for doneness**, it should feel firm when you gently poke the top of the loaf.

5. The bottom crust should be nice and crisp, but the top of the loaf will be quite soft. Some folks desire a softer crust, so they'll love this loaf. But if you want a darker or crisper crust . . .

**Check with your crock pot's manufacturer before trying this:** Some models' instructions specify that the crock pot has to be at least partially filled with a liquid to avoid safety or durability problems. And never bake bread in a crock pot unattended.

6. Remove the parchment paper and place the bread under the broiler for 5 minutes or until it is the color you like, with the rack positioned in the middle of the oven.

7. **Let the loaf cool completely before slicing.** Cutting into a hot loaf is tempting, but it won't slice well and may seem underbaked if you break into it before it's cooled.

# Pullman Sandwich Loaf

The beauty of a Pullman loaf is its perfectly square slices. The dough is baked in a pan with a lid, so it is forced into a neat and clean shape. This uniform style of loaf was developed by the Pullman company (of railroad car fame) to be baked in its compact kitchens and stacked in as little space as possible. It makes a great sandwich loaf or picture-perfect toast. Any of our bread doughs will work in this pan, but some rise more than others, so you may have to adjust the amounts.

***Makes 1 loaf***

2½ pounds (extra-large cantaloupe-size portion) Master Recipe dough (page 53)
Oil or unsalted butter, for greasing the pan

1. **On baking day,** grease a 9×4×4-inch nonstick Pullman loaf pan, including the lid, with butter or oil. Dust the surface of the refrigerated dough with flour and cut off a 2½-pound (large cantaloupe-size) piece. Dust with more flour and quickly shape it into a ball by stretching the surface of the dough around to the bottom on all four sides, rotating the ball a quarter-turn as you go.

2. Elongate the ball into an oval and drop it into the prepared pan. You want to fill the pan about three-quarters full, then cover the pan with the lid.

3. Allow the dough to rest for 1 hour and 45 minutes (see sidebar, page 58).

4. **Preheat the oven to 450°F.** A baking stone is not required, and omitting it shortens the preheat.

5. Place the loaf on a rack near the center of the oven. Bake for about 45 minutes, remove the lid, and bake for an additional 10 minutes.

6. Remove the loaf from the pan and allow to cool completely on a rack before slicing; otherwise you won't get well-cut sandwich slices. If the loaf sticks, wait 10 minutes and it will steam itself out of the pan.

# Soft Dinner Rolls, Brötchen, Baguette Buns, Cloverleaf Rolls, and Rosemary Crescents

Rolls are a delight to bake and adorable to look at (see color photo). They're small, so they need very little resting time before they go into the oven. And they don't have to cool completely like larger loaves do—it's okay to eat them slightly warm. You can make any of the following recipes with the Master Recipe, or try these easy shapes with other lean doughs, or even the enriched challah (page 296) or brioche (page 300) doughs, which yield softer rolls. **Be sure to decrease the oven temperature to 350°F when using egg-enriched dough, and increase baking time about 25 percent.**

***Makes five 3-ounce rolls***

1 pound (grapefruit-size portion) Master Recipe dough (page 53) or Egg-White–Enriched Brötchen dough (see sidebar, page 90)
All-purpose flour, for dusting
Egg white, for glazing brötchen
Melted unsalted butter or oil, for brushing dinner rolls
Unsalted butter, oil, or parchment paper, for the baking sheet

**Soft Dinner Rolls**

1. **Preheat a baking stone near the middle of the oven to 450°F (20 to 30 minutes).**

2. Cut off 3-ounce (small peach-size) pieces of Master Recipe dough and quickly shape into balls. Allow to rest, 2 inches apart, on a baking sheet lined with parchment paper or a silicone mat for 20 minutes.

3. Cut a cross into the top of each roll, using a serrated knife or kitchen shears and keeping the shears perpendicular to the work surface when you cut.

4. Brush the tops with melted butter or oil and place the baking sheet in the oven. Bake for about 25 minutes, or until richly browned.

5. For the softest result, brush with more butter or oil. Serve slightly warm.

**To make soft pull-apart rolls:** Cut off a 1-pound (grapefruit-size) piece of challah (page 296), brioche (page 300), or buttermilk bread dough (page 327), then divide the dough into 8 pieces and quickly shape them into balls. Place the dough balls in a greased 8 × 8-inch baking dish; they should be touching. Rest for 30 minutes. Preheat the oven to 350°F. Brush the tops of the rolls with melted butter before and after they go into the oven. Bake for about 30 minutes, or until golden brown. Serve slightly warm.

**Brötchen (bro-chin)**

On our website, people asked for German-style hard rolls, so we've included the most common: *brötchen* (German for "little bread"). They're traditionally made from dough enriched with egg whites, and then brushed with more egg white before baking at high temperature with steam. The egg white creates an incredible crust and crumb—see the sidebar (page 90) for an easy variation that turns the Master Recipe into brötchen dough for superb hard rolls.

1. Preheat the oven to 450°F, with an empty metal broiler tray on any shelf that won't interfere with the rising brötchen.

2. Cut off 3-ounce (small peach-size) pieces of **Egg White–Enriched Dough for Brötchen** (see page 90) and quickly shape into balls, then pinch to form

**Egg White–Enriched Dough for Brötchen:** Put 3 egg whites into the bottom of a measuring cup, then add water to bring the total volume to 3 cups of liquid in the Master Recipe (page 53). All other ingredient measurements are the same. Refrigerate for up to 5 days before freezing in 1-pound portions. This dough is great for brötchen but you can use it for other rolls or bread as well.

an oval shape. Allow to rest, 2 inches apart, on a baking sheet prepared with oil, butter, parchment paper, or a silicone mat for 20 minutes.

3. Brush the tops with egg white and cut a single lengthwise slash into the top of each roll, using a serrated knife.

4. Place baking sheet in the oven, pour 1 cup of hot water into the broiler tray, and quickly close the oven door. Bake the rolls for about 25 minutes, or until richly browned. Serve slightly warm.

**Baguette Buns**

1. **Preheat a baking stone near the middle of the oven to 450°F (20 to 30 minutes),** with an empty metal broiler tray on any other shelf.

2. Form a ½-pound baguette (see page 64) on a work surface; this will make about 6 buns. Using a dough scraper or a knife, make angled parallel cuts about 2 inches apart along the length of the baguette to form rolls. Allow them to rest, 2 inches apart, on a baking sheet prepared with butter, oil, parchment paper, or a silicone mat for 20 minutes.

3. Place baking sheet in the oven, pour 1 cup of hot water into the broiler tray, and quickly close the oven door. Bake the rolls for about 25 minutes, or until richly browned. Serve slightly warm.

### Cloverleaf Buns

1. **Preheat a baking stone near the middle of the oven to 450°F (20 to 30 minutes),** with an empty metal broiler tray on any other shelf. Grease a muffin pan.

2. Cut off 3-ounce (small peach-size) pieces of dough. Cut each of these pieces into 4 smaller pieces. Shape each one into a smooth ball. Put the 4 balls together to form the cloverleaf and place in a cup of the prepared muffin pan. Continue with the remaining dough. Allow to rest for 30 minutes.

3. Slide the muffin pan into the oven, pour 1 cup of hot water into the broiler tray, and quickly close the oven door. Bake for about 25 minutes, or until richly browned. Serve slightly warm.

### Rosemary Crescent Rolls

½ pound (orange-size portion) Master Recipe dough (page 53)
3 tablespoons olive oil
½ teaspoon kosher salt
2 tablespoons finely chopped fresh rosemary or other herbs

1. Prepare a baking sheet with parchment paper or a silicone mat.

2. Dust the surface of the refrigerated dough with flour and cut off a ½-pound (orange-size portion). Dust with more flour and quickly shape it into a ball by stretching the surface of the dough around to the bottom on all four sides, rotating the ball a quarter-turn as you go. With a rolling pin, roll out dough into a ⅛-inch-thick round. As you roll out the dough, use enough flour to prevent it from sticking to the work surface but not so much as to make the dough dry.

3. Spread 2 tablespoons of the olive oil over the dough and then sprinkle evenly with the salt and rosemary. Using a pizza cutter or a sharp knife, cut the dough into 8 equal-sized wedges, like a pizza.

4. Starting at the wider end, roll each wedge until the point is tucked securely under the bottom. Bend the ends in slightly to create the crescent shape. Brush the tops with the remaining olive oil and cover loosely with plastic wrap. Allow to rest about 40 minutes.

5. **Preheat the oven to 450°F.** A baking stone is not required, and omitting it shortens the preheat.

6. Bake about 25 minutes, until golden brown and well set in center.

6

# PEASANT LOAVES

The term "peasant bread" has come to mean the rougher, more rustic loaf that originated in the European countryside during the Middle Ages. These are breads made with whole-grain flours that, once upon a time, fell out of fashion with sophisticated European urbanites. How times have changed; since the 1980s, rustic breads have signaled sophistication just as surely as a perfect French baguette. Thank goodness we've come to realize the wonderful and complex flavors to be had by adding whole grains and rye to our bread.

Rye flour creates the tangy, slightly nutty fragrance and flavor that is basic to many of these breads, whether or not it's blended with whole wheat or other grains. Even if rye flour is not sold as "whole grain," it has more fiber (from rye bran) than white flours. The proteins and starches in rye flour, plus the extra boost of rye bran, mean that these breads have a substantial, chewy texture.

# European Peasant Bread

The round, whole-grain, country-style loaves of rural France (*pain de campagne*) and Italy (*pane rustica*) were once viewed as too rustic for stylish European tables—white flour was once an almost-unattainable luxury. Today people from all walks of life enjoy the crackling crust and moist chewy crumb that define this peasant bread.

We live in the upper Midwest, and in the wintertime we dream of Mediterranean vacations. The next best thing to being there is mixing up a batch of this bread and serving it with anchovies, a strong cheese, and a hearty fish soup with lots of garlic and fresh herbs (see page 149). On the next day, cut up the leftovers for Tuscan Bread Salad (page 97).

***Makes four loaves, slightly less than 1 pound each. The recipe is easily doubled or halved.***

| Ingredient | Volume (U.S.) | Weight (U.S.) | Weight (Metric) |
|---|---|---|---|
| Lukewarm water (100°F or below) | 3 cups | 1 pound, 8 ounces | 680 grams |
| Granulated yeast[1] | 1 tablespoon | 0.35 ounce | 10 grams |
| Kosher salt[1] | 1 to 1½ tablespoons | 0.6 to 0.9 ounce | 17 to 25 grams |
| Rye flour | ½ cup | 2⅛ ounces | 60 grams |
| Whole wheat flour[2] | ½ cup | 2¼ ounces | 65 grams |

[1]Can decrease (see pages 14 and 17)

[2]Can substitute white whole wheat (see page 11)

| Ingredient | Volume (U.S.) | Weight (U.S.) | Weight (Metric) |
| --- | --- | --- | --- |
| All-purpose flour | 5½ cups | 1 pound, 11½ ounces | 780 grams |
| Cornmeal or parchment paper, for the pizza peel | | | |

1. **Mixing and storing the dough:** Mix the yeast and salt with the water in a 6-quart bowl or a lidded (not airtight) food container.

2. Mix in the remaining ingredients without kneading, using a spoon or a heavy-duty stand mixer (with paddle). If you're not using a machine, you may need to use wet hands to incorporate the last bit of flour.

3. Cover (not airtight) and allow to rest at room temperature until the dough rises and collapses (or flattens on top), approximately 2 hours.

4. The dough can be used immediately after the initial rise, though it is easier to handle when cold. Refrigerate the container of dough and use over the next 14 days.

5. **On baking day,** dust the surface of the refrigerated dough with flour and cut off a 1-pound (grapefruit-size) piece. Dust with more flour and quickly shape it into a ball by stretching the surface of the dough around to the bottom on all four sides, rotating the ball a quarter-turn as you go. Allow to rest and rise on a pizza peel prepared with cornmeal or parchment paper for 40 minutes (see sidebar, page 58).

**Make a Bread Bowl:** Bake up a fresh loaf of bread, wait for it to cool, then scoop out the center, keeping the sides about an inch thick, to form a bowl (save the scraps for bread salad or pudding—see pages 97 and 99). Then you are ready to fill the hollowed bread with your favorite stew or dip. Make sure your filling is thick enough that it won't make the bread too soggy, but the bowl should absorb some of the chili or artichoke dip and become part of the meal—the soaked bread is the best part.

6. **Preheat a baking stone near the middle of the oven to 450°F (20 to 30 minutes),** with an empty metal broiler tray on any shelf that won't interfere with rising bread.

7. Sprinkle liberally with flour and slash the top, about 1/2 inch deep, using a serrated bread knife (see photos, page 59).

8. Slide the loaf directly onto the hot stone. Pour 1 cup of hot water into the broiler tray and quickly close the oven door (see page 20 for steam alternatives). Bake for about 35 minutes, or until richly browned and firm. Smaller or larger loaves will require adjustments in resting and baking time.

9. Allow to cool on a rack before slicing and eating.

# Tuscan Bread Salad (Panzanella)

Even great bread goes stale; here's a delicious way to use it. European Peasant Bread is our first choice for panzanella, but other unsweetened breads will also work well. This salad is a masterpiece when made with tomatoes at the peak of the summer season. If you grow your own, here's your chance to let them shine. If you want to turn this into a complete meal, add cannellini or Great Northern beans, or even sliced prosciutto ham.

***Makes 4 servings***

**The Salad**

10 slices stale bread (1 to 3 days old), cubed
3 medium tomatoes, cubed
1 medium cucumber, sliced
1 very small red onion, thinly sliced
1 teaspoon capers, drained
¼ cup pitted black olives, halved
2 anchovy fillets, chopped (optional)
15 fresh basil leaves, coarsely chopped
1 tablespoon coarsely grated Parmigiano-Reggiano cheese
¾ cup cooked or canned cannellini or Great Northern beans (optional)
3 ounces sliced prosciutto ham (optional)

**The Dressing**

⅓ cup olive oil
3 teaspoons red wine vinegar
1 garlic clove, finely minced
Salt and freshly ground black pepper (don't be stingy)

1. Prepare the salad ingredients and combine in a large bowl.

2. In a small bowl, whisk all the dressing ingredients until well blended.

3. Toss the dressing with the salad, and allow to stand for at least 10 minutes, or until the bread has softened.

# Savory Bread Pudding

This savory bread pudding reminds us of quiche, but is so much easier to make. Take your favorite loaf of bread, anything from a crusty boule to a soft brioche, soak it in a rich, savory custard, and layer it with caramelized onions, spinach, and cheese. It makes a simply elegant breakfast or side dish.

***Makes 8 servings***

1 pound day-old bread, cubed
5 large eggs
4 cups whole milk
2 cups half-and-half
Pinch of freshly grated nutmeg
½ teaspoon salt
Freshly ground black pepper
½ teaspoon dried thyme
½ cup chèvre and/or cream cheese, cut into small pieces
½ cup caramelized onions (see page 181)
¾ cup chopped spinach, fresh or frozen, thawed and well drained
1 cup shredded cheddar, Swiss, Gruyère, or other firm cheese

1. Preheat the oven to 325°F.

2. In a large mixing bowl, whisk together the eggs, milk, half-and-half, nutmeg, salt, pepper, and thyme until well combined.

3. Arrange the bread cubes in an 8 × 12 × 2-inch baking dish. Sprinkle the chèvre, cream cheese, onions, and spinach over the bread, then top with the shredded cheese. Pour the custard slowly over the bread;

let sit about 15 minutes. You may have to press the bread into the custard to make sure it's all soaked.

4. Tent loosely with aluminum foil, and poke a few holes in the top to allow steam to escape. Place on the center rack. Bake for 1 hour, or until the center is just firm.

5. Remove from the oven and allow to stand for 10 minutes. Serve warm.

# Pan Bagna (Provençal Tuna and Vegetable Sandwich)

This sandwich loaf is a specialty of Provence, where it's a time-honored way for families to use day-old country bread. *Pan bagna* (pan ban-ya) literally translated from the Provençal dialect means "bathed bread." The sandwich is similar to the New Orleans muffuletta, which is based on cold cuts rather than tuna steak (see variation below). In New Orleans, they use a concoction called "olive salad" rather than sliced olives, and you'll never find arugula on a traditional muffuletta.

You'll have an easier time making pan bagna if you shape a slightly flattened boule, rather than a high-domed one.

***Makes 4 sandwich wedges***

1-pound loaf European Peasant Bread (page 94), or Boule (page 53) dough
4 tablespoons olive oil
1 small garlic clove
1 tablespoon red wine vinegar
Salt and freshly ground black pepper
¼ pound soft goat cheese (chèvre)
6 Mediterranean-style olives, pitted and sliced
1 cup arugula leaves, rinsed and well dried
6 ounces cooked fresh tuna steak, thinly sliced, or substitute canned tuna in a pinch
3 small tomatoes, thinly sliced
10 large, fresh basil leaves, stacked, rolled, and cut crosswise into a chiffonade

1. Slice the bread in half horizontally and slightly hollow out the top and the bottom. Make fresh bread crumbs out of the discarded centers and

reserve for another use. Drizzle the cut surface of the halves with 1½ tablespoons of the oil.

2. In a blender, combine the remaining 2½ tablespoons oil with the garlic, vinegar, and salt to taste. Blend until smooth.

3. Spread the goat cheese on the bottom shell, top it with the olives and arugula, and season with salt and pepper to taste. Drizzle with one-third of the dressing, top with the tuna, season with salt and pepper to taste. Drizzle half of the remaining dressing over the tuna, top the tuna with the tomatoes and basil, and season with salt and pepper to taste. Drizzle with the remaining dressing, and cover with the top of the loaf.

4. Wrap the sandwich in plastic wrap, place it on a plate, and cover it with another plate with approximately 1 to 2 pounds of weight on top. Refrigerate for 1 hour, if possible (or eat right away if you can't wait). The sandwich may be made up to 6 hours in advance and kept covered and chilled.

5. Cut the pan bagna into 2-inch slices, and serve.

**VARIATION: MUFFULETTA**

Make a New Orleans muffuletta sandwich by substituting sliced ham, salami, and mortadella for the tuna steak; provolone for the goat cheese; and lettuce for the arugula and basil leaves. In New Orleans, locals use a regional product called "olive salad" in place of the sliced olives.

# Olive Bread

This bread is associated with the countries of the Mediterranean, especially Italy and France, where the olives are abundant and have incredible flavor (see color photo). Use the best-quality olives you can find; the wetter Kalamata variety work as well as the dry Niçoise type, so it's your choice. The rich salty flavors of the olives make this a perfect accompaniment to cheeses, pasta tossed with fresh tomatoes, or our Tuscan White Bean Dip (page 105).

This recipe is a great showcase for the versatility of our basic doughs—the recipe introduces a technique that shows how you can roll flavorful ingredients into a single loaf if you want to introduce some zest. But if you want a whole batch of olive dough, just mix a cup of halved olives into the initial mix of any of the doughs that we list.

***Makes 1 loaf***

1 pound (grapefruit-size portion) Master Recipe (page 53), European Peasant Bread (page 94), Olive Oil (page 214), Light Whole Wheat (page 131), or Italian Semolina (page 143) dough
¼ cup high-quality olives, pitted and halved

**Cornstarch Wash:** Using a fork, blend ½ teaspoon cornstarch with a small amount of water to form a paste. Add ½ cup water and whisk with a fork. Microwave or boil until the mixture appears glassy, about 30 to 60 seconds on high. It will keep in the refrigerator for 2 weeks.

Cornmeal or parchment paper, for the pizza peel
Cornstarch wash (see sidebar) or water, for brushing the loaf

1. Dust the surface of the refrigerated dough with flour and cut off a 1-pound (grapefruit-size) piece. Using your hands and a rolling pin, flatten the dough to a thickness of ½ inch. Cover with the olives and roll up to seal inside the dough. Crimp the ends shut and tuck them under to form an oval loaf. Cover with plastic wrap or an overturned bowl and allow to rest for 90 minutes on a pizza peel prepared with cornmeal or parchment paper (see sidebar, page 58).

2. **Preheat a baking stone near the middle of the oven to 450°F (20 to 30 minutes),** with an empty metal broiler tray on any shelf that won't interfere with rising bread.

3. Paint the surface of the loaf with cornstarch wash or water, and slash the top, about ½ inch deep, using a serrated bread knife (see photos, page 59).

4. Slide the loaf directly onto the hot stone. Pour 1 cup of hot water into the broiler tray and quickly close the oven door (see page 20 for steam alternatives). Bake for about 35 minutes, or until the top crust is richly browned and firm. Smaller or larger loaves will require adjustments in resting and baking time.

5. Allow to cool on a rack before slicing and eating.

# Tuscan White Bean Dip

We created this dip in the spirit of simplifying our lives and eating foods with rich, wonderful flavors. Simply puree beans with the aromatics and spread it over our Olive Bread (page 103) to make a delicious rustic hors d'oeuvre.

It's probably easier to find dried Great Northern white beans than the more authentic cannellini beans, so go with whatever you can find. And if you don't have time to roast the garlic, raw is fine, though it will have a stronger kick. Jarred roasted red peppers can be substituted, but the flavor is less intense.

***Makes about 2 cups dip***

1 cup dried Great Northern or cannellini beans (or one 16-ounce can, drained)
1 large roasted garlic clove (see sidebar, page 68)
2 tablespoons olive oil
1 teaspoon salt
Freshly ground black pepper
10 fresh basil leaves
1 small red bell pepper, roasted and peeled (see step 2, page 68)

1. Pick over the dried beans for stones, dirt, and debris. Rinse, drain, and then cover with water and soak overnight. Bring to a simmer and cook for 2 to 3 hours until soft, adding water as needed to keep the beans covered. Drain and reserve about 2 cups of the cooking liquid (though you probably won't need all of it). If using canned beans, discard the canning liquid and use plain water later in the recipe.

2. Peel the roasted garlic and place it in the food processor along with the cooked beans, olive oil, salt, and black pepper to taste. Process until

smooth, adding some of the reserved cooking liquid or water until you achieve a medium consistency.

3. Add the basil and roasted red pepper and pulse until coarsely chopped; taste and adjust seasonings as needed.

4. Refrigerate and serve with Olive Bread (page 103), European Peasant Bread (page 94), or a Baguette (page 64).

# Tapenade Bread

We enjoy tapenade, the delightful spread made from olives, anchovies, and capers. This recipe was originally developed with store-bought tapenade, but then we started making our own. It is easy and has a freshness that the commercial product can't match. But if you have a jar of great tapenade on hand, by all means use it. This bread is great with cheeses or grilled with tomato, basil, and garlic into mouthwatering Bruschetta (page 110).

***Makes four 1-pound loaves. The recipe is easily doubled or halved.***

| Ingredient | Volume (U.S.) | Weight (U.S.) | Weight (Metric) |
|---|---|---|---|
| Lukewarm water (100°F or below) | 3 cups | 1 pound, 8 ounces | 680 grams |
| Granulated yeast[1] | 1 tablespoon | 0.35 ounce | 10 grams |
| Kosher salt[1] | 1 to 1½ tablespoons | 0.6 to 0.9 ounce | 17 to 25 grams |
| Bread flour | 7 cups | 2 pounds, 3 ounces | 990 grams |
| Homemade (see sidebar) or store-bought tapenade | 1 cup | 8 ounces | 230 grams |

[1]Can decrease (see pages 14 and 17)

1. **Mixing and storing the dough:** Mix the yeast and salt with the water in a 6-quart bowl or a lidded (not airtight) food container.

**Making your own tapenade:** In a food processor, coarsely chop ½ pound pitted black olives, 4 teaspoons drained capers, 4 anchovy fillets, 1 garlic clove, pressed through or very finely chopped, ¼ teaspoon dried thyme, and ¼ cup olive oil.

2. Mix in the remaining ingredients without kneading, using a spoon or a heavy-duty stand mixer (with paddle). If you're not using a machine, you may need to use wet hands to incorporate the last bit of flour.

3. Cover (not airtight) and allow to rest at room temperature until the dough rises and collapses (or flattens on top), approximately 2 hours.

4. The dough can be used immediately after the initial rise, though it is easier to handle when cold. Refrigerate the container of dough and use over the next 7 days.

5. **On baking day,** dust the surface of the refrigerated dough with flour and cut off a 1-pound (grapefruit-size) piece. Dust the piece with more flour and quickly shape it into a ball by stretching the surface of the dough around to the bottom on all four sides, rotating the ball a quarter-turn as you go. Allow to rest and rise on a pizza peel prepared with cornmeal or parchment paper for 1 hour (see sidebar, page 58).

6. **Preheat a baking stone near the middle of the oven to 450°F (20 to 30 minutes),** with an empty metal broiler tray on any shelf that won't interfere with rising bread.

7. Sprinkle the loaf liberally with flour and slash the top, about ½-inch deep, using a serrated bread knife (see photos, page 59).

8. Slide the loaf directly onto the hot stone. Pour 1 cup of hot water into the broiler tray and quickly close the oven door (see page 20 for steam alternatives). Bake 35 to 40 minutes until deeply browned and firm. Smaller or larger loaves will require adjustments in baking time.

9. Allow to cool on a rack before slicing and eating.

# Bruschetta (bruss-kéh-ta)

Here's one more way to use stale bread, which, like Tuscan Bread Salad (page 97), comes from Italy. The Italians continually rearrange and reconstruct a limited number of delicious ingredients: bread, tomato, garlic, olive oil, and herbs. Every family seems to have its own take on the combo.

*"This was first made for me by my friend Marco, who was a visiting student from Livorno, Italy. He wanted to show off his family specialties, so he made a pasta dish with Parmigiano-Reggiano that he'd carried from Italy in his luggage, and to accompany it, this simple but memorable bruschetta."—Jeff*

***Makes 4 bruschetti***

4 thick slices of day-old Boule (page 53), European Peasant Bread (page 94), Tapenade Bread (page 107), or other non-enriched bread
1 garlic clove, halved
¼ cup seeded and chopped tomato, well drained
8 torn or chopped fresh basil leaves
Coarse salt
4 teaspoons olive oil

1. **Preheat the oven to 400°F.** Meanwhile, toast or grill the bread slices until crisp and browned.

2. Rub the crisped bread on both sides with the garlic, grating the garlic down into the toasted bread. Rub as much or as little as you like.

3. Place the bruschetti on a baking sheet and top with the tomato, basil, and a sprinkling of coarse salt. Finish with a liberal drizzling of olive oil; about a teaspoon per slice.

4. Bake for about 5 minutes, or until hot. Serve as an appetizer.

# Deli-Style Rye Bread

This loaf, our version of a classic sourdough rye, started Jeff's twenty-five-year obsession with bread baking (see color photo). The recipe produces a traditional rye comparable to those made with complicated starters—the kind that need to be "fed," incubated, and kept alive in your refrigerator. It's terrific on day one of the batch, but will be even better on day two or three. Along with the caraway seeds, which are part of the classic flavor, what sets this rye apart from other rustic breads is that there is no flour on the top crust; instead it's glazed with a cornstarch wash, which serves the triple function of anchoring the caraway seeds, allowing the slashing knife to pass easily without sticking, and adding flavor and color to the crust. If you're pressed for time, you can use plain water.

*"My grandmother truly did believe that this rye was better than cake. It turns out that elder immigrants from all over Europe felt the same way about 'a good piece of bread.' Friends of Dutch and Scandinavian heritage also recall older relatives shunning ordinary desserts in favor of extraordinary bread."*—Jeff

***Makes four loaves, slightly less than 1 pound each. The recipe is easily doubled or halved.***

| Ingredient | Volume (U.S.) | Weight (U.S.) | Weight (Metric) |
|---|---|---|---|
| Lukewarm water (100°F or below) | 3 cups | 1 pound, 8 ounces | 680 grams |
| Granulated yeast[1] | 1 tablespoon | 0.35 ounce | 10 grams |
| Caraway seeds | 1½ tablespoons, plus additional for sprinkling the top | 0.35 ounce | 10 grams |

[1]Can decrease (see pages 14 and 17)

(continued)

| Ingredient | Volume (U.S.) | Weight (U.S.) | Weight (Metric) |
|---|---|---|---|
| Kosher salt[1] | 1 to 1½ tablespoons | 0.6 to 0.9 ounce | 17 to 25 grams |
| Rye flour | 1 cup | 4¼ ounces | 120 grams |
| All-purpose flour | 5½ cups | 1 pound, 11½ ounces | 780 grams |
| Cornmeal or parchment paper, for the pizza peel | | | |
| Cornstarch wash (see sidebar page 104) or water, for brushing the top crust | | | |

1. **Mixing and storing the dough:** Mix the yeast, salt, and caraway seeds with the water in a 6-quart bowl or a lidded (not airtight) food container.

2. Mix in the flours without kneading, using a spoon or a heavy-duty stand mixer (with paddle). If you're not using a machine, you may need to use wet hands to incorporate the last bit of flour.

3. Cover (not airtight) and allow to rest at room temperature until the dough rises and collapses (or flattens on top), approximately 2 hours.

4. The dough can be used immediately after the initial rise, though it is easier to handle when cold. Refrigerate the container of dough and use over the next 14 days.

5. **On baking day,** dust the surface of the refrigerated dough with flour and cut off a 1-pound (grapefruit-size) piece. Dust the piece

with more flour and quickly shape it into a ball by stretching the surface of the dough around to the bottom on all four sides, rotating the ball a quarter-turn as you go. Elongate the ball to form an oval loaf—do it roughly or use the letter-fold technique (see sidebar, page 66). Allow to rest and rise on a pizza peel prepared with cornmeal or parchment paper for 40 minutes (see sidebar, page 58).

6. **Preheat a baking stone near the middle of the oven to 450°F (20 to 30 minutes),** with an empty metal broiler tray on any shelf that won't interfere with rising bread.

7. Using a pastry brush, paint the top crust with cornstarch wash or water and then sprinkle with additional caraway seeds. Slash with ½-inch-deep, parallel cuts across the loaf, using a serrated bread knife.

8. Slide the loaf directly onto the hot stone. Pour 1 cup of hot water into the broiler tray and quickly close the oven door (see page 20 for steam alternatives). Bake for about 30 to 35 minutes until deeply browned and firm. Smaller or larger loaves will require adjustments in baking time.

9. Allow to cool on a rack before slicing and eating.

**VARIATION: SAUERKRAUT RYE**

Add 1 cup (5 ounces/140 grams) well-drained sauerkraut to the initial mix, **decrease the water by 3 tablespoons**, and don't store the dough longer than 7 days. Decrease the salt if you're sensitive to it as sauerkraut is already salty. If you don't want to commit to a whole batch of sauerkraut dough, roll in 1/4 cup of well-drained sauerkraut to each loaf as it is being formed from plain rye dough (see page 116 for roll-in technique). If you use the roll-in technique, allow a 90-minute resting time after shaping, and cover with plastic wrap or an overturned bowl. Bake for about 35 minutes.

# Reuben Sandwich

This sandwich is the king of the American delicatessen: home-baked rye or pumpernickel bread (pages 111 and 123) grilled in butter, dripping with rich cheese and Russian dressing, and piled high with corned beef. It towers above the common sandwich. But Reuben's no snob—cold beer (or a Dr. Brown's cream soda) is the perfect accompaniment. The Reuben also works well when made as a panino (see page 80).

***Makes 1 sandwich***

1 teaspoon unsalted butter, plus more if needed
2 slices rye or pumpernickel bread
2 teaspoons Russian dressing
1 ounce thinly sliced Swiss or Emmenthaler cheese
2 ounces thinly sliced corned beef
2 tablespoons sauerkraut, well drained

1. Butter 1 side of each slice of bread. Place 1 slice of bread, buttered side down, in a skillet. Spread 1 teaspoon of Russian dressing on the face-up side of the bread.

2. Cover with half the cheese, the corned beef, and then the sauerkraut. Finish with the remaining half of the cheese.

3. Spread the remaining Russian dressing on the dry side of the second slice of bread to complete the sandwich.

4. Place the skillet over medium-low heat and grill slowly for about 4 minutes per side, or until browned and crisp. Add additional butter to the pan if needed.

# Caraway Swirl Rye

An extra jolt of caraway is swirled through this rye bread, producing a beautiful and flavorful crunch (see color photo).

***Makes 1 loaf***

1 pound (grapefruit-size portion) Deli-Style Rye dough (page 111)
2 tablespoons caraway seeds, plus more for sprinkling on the top
Cornmeal or parchment paper, for the pizza peel
Cornstarch wash (see sidebar, page 104) or water, for brushing the top crust

1. Dust the surface of the refrigerated dough with flour and cut off a 1-pound (grapefruit-size) piece. Dust the piece with more flour and quickly shape it into a ball by stretching the surface of the dough around to the bottom on all four sides, rotating the ball a quarter-turn as you go. Using your hands and a rolling pin, flatten the ball into a ½-inch-thick oval (avoid using too much flour here or you might get dry patches in the caraway swirl).

2. Sprinkle the dough with caraway seeds. The amount can vary according to your taste; reserve some for the top crust. Roll up the dough like a jelly roll, forming an oval loaf. Be sure that the end of the roll is at the bottom of the loaf, and allow to rest on a pizza peel prepared with cornmeal or parchment paper for 90 minutes.

3. **Preheat a baking stone near the middle of the oven to 450°F (20 to 30 minutes),** with an empty metal broiler tray on any shelf that won't interfere with rising bread.

4. Using a pastry brush, paint the top crust with the cornstarch wash or water and then sprinkle with the additional caraway seeds. Slash with ½-inch-deep, parallel cuts across the loaf, using a serrated bread knife.

5. Slide the loaf directly onto the hot stone. Pour 1 cup of hot water into the broiler tray and quickly close the oven door (see page 20 for steam alternatives). Bake for 30 to 35 minutes until deeply browned and firm. Smaller or larger loaves will require adjustments in baking time.

6. Allow to cool before slicing and eating.

# Onion Rye

The homey, comforting flavor of sautéed onion is one of life's simplest and most satisfying pleasures, especially when combined with hearty rye bread. Be sure to brown the onion to achieve the caramelization that makes this bread so savory. This recipe can be made with or without caraway seeds. Ordinary yellow or white onions work well and are readily available, but Vidalia or red varieties produce a milder onion flavor that some may prefer.

***Makes 1 loaf***

1 pound (grapefruit-size portion) Deli-Style Rye (page 111) or Pumpernickel (page 123) dough
1 medium onion, halved and thinly sliced
Vegetable oil, for sautéing the onions
Cornmeal or parchment paper, for the pizza peel
Cornstarch wash (see sidebar, page 104) or water, for brushing the top crust

1. Sauté the sliced onion in the oil over medium heat in a skillet for 10 minutes, or until brown and nicely caramelized.

2. Dust the surface of the refrigerated dough with flour and cut off a 1-pound (grapefruit-size) piece. Dust with more flour and quickly shape it into a ball by stretching the surface of the dough around to the bottom on all four sides, rotating the ball a quarter-turn as you go. Flatten the ball into a ½-inch-thick oval either with your hands or a rolling pin (avoid using much extra flour here or you might get dry patches).

3. Spread the surface of the flattened loaf with a thin layer of the browned onion. Then roll up the dough from the short end like a jelly

roll. Pinch the ends and tuck under to form an oval loaf. Cover with plastic wrap or an overturned bowl and allow to rest for 90 minutes on a pizza peel prepared with cornmeal or parchment paper (see sidebar, page 58).

4. **Preheat a baking stone near the middle of the oven to 450°F (20 to 30 minutes),** with an empty metal broiler tray on any shelf that won't interfere with rising bread.

5. Using a pastry brush, paint the top crust with cornstarch wash or water. Slash with ½-inch-deep, parallel cuts across the loaf, using a serrated bread knife.

6. Slide the loaf directly onto the hot stone. Pour 1 cup of hot water into the broiler tray and quickly close the oven door (see page 20 for steam alternatives). Bake for 30 to 35 minutes until richly browned and firm. Smaller or larger loaves will require adjustments in baking time.

7. Allow to cool on a rack before slicing and eating.

# Limpa

Here's a five-minute version of the traditional Swedish rye bread. Honey and orange zest mingle with the more exotic flavors of anise and cardamom to make a flavorful and fragrant treat. Make two loaves—the first loaf will go quickly, and you can use the second one for bread pudding (page 359).

***Makes four 1-pound loaves. The recipe is easily doubled or halved.***

| Ingredient | Volume (U.S.) | Weight (U.S.) | Weight (Metric) |
|---|---|---|---|
| Lukewarm water (100°F or below) | 3 cups | 1 pound, 8 ounces | 680 grams |
| Granulated yeast[1] | 1 tablespoon | 0.35 ounce | 10 grams |
| Kosher salt[1] | 1 to 1½ tablespoons | 0.6 to 0.9 ounce | 17 to 25 grams |
| Honey | ½ cup | 6 ounces | 170 grams |
| Anise seed, ground | ½ teaspoon | — | — |
| Cardamom, ground | 1 teaspoon | — | — |
| Orange zest (see Equipment, page 30) | 1½ teaspoons | — | — |
| Rye flour | 1 cup | 4¼ ounces | 120 grams |
| All-purpose flour | 5½ cups | 1 pound, 11½ ounces | 780 grams |

[1]Can decrease (see pages 14 and 17)

| Ingredient |
| --- |
| Whole wheat flour or parchment paper, for the pizza peel |
| Cornstarch wash (see sidebar, page 104) or water, for brushing the top crust |
| Spiced sugar for each loaf: mix together 1/4 teaspoon ground anise seed, 1/4 teaspoon ground cardamom, and 1 1/2 teaspoons sugar |

1. **Mixing and storing the dough:** Mix the yeast, salt, honey, spices, and orange zest with the water in a 6-quart bowl or a lidded (not airtight) food container.

2. Mix in the remaining dry ingredients without kneading, using a spoon or a heavy-duty stand mixer (with paddle). If you're not using a machine, you may need to use wet hands to incorporate the last bit of flour.

3. Cover (not airtight) and allow to rest at room temperature until the dough rises and collapses (or flattens on top), approximately 2 hours.

4. The dough can be used immediately after the initial rise, though it is easier to handle when cold. Refrigerate the container of dough and use over the next 7 days.

5. **On baking day**, dust the surface of the refrigerated dough with flour and cut off a 1-pound (grapefruit-size) piece. Dust the piece with more flour and quickly shape it into a ball by stretching the surface of the dough around to the bottom on all four sides, rotating the ball a quarter-turn as you go. Allow to rest and rise on a pizza peel prepared with whole wheat or parchment paper for 40 minutes (see sidebar, page 58).

6. **Preheat a baking stone near the middle of the oven to 375°F (20 to 30 minutes),** with an empty metal broiler tray on any shelf that won't interfere with rising bread.

7. Using a pastry brush, paint the top crust with cornstarch wash or water, then slash the top, about ½ inch deep, using a serrated bread knife. Sprinkle with the spiced-sugar mixture.

8. Slide the loaf directly onto the hot stone. Pour 1 cup of hot water into the broiler tray and quickly close the oven door (see page 20 for steam alternatives). Bake for about 40 to 45 minutes, or until golden brown and firm. Smaller or larger loaves will require adjustments in baking time. Due to the honey in the recipe, the crust on this bread will not be hard and crackling.

9. Allow to cool on a rack before slicing and eating.

# Pumpernickel Bread

Pumpernickel bread is really just a variety of rye bread (see color photo). What darkens the loaf and accounts for its mildly bitter but appealing flavor is powdered caramel coloring, cocoa, molasses, and coffee, not the flour. The caramel color is actually a natural ingredient made by overheating sugar until it is completely caramelized (available as a powder from King Arthur Flour, see Sources, page 367, or see the sidebar, page 125, to make your own liquid version). Traditional recipes use pumpernickel flour (a coarse rye with a lot of rye bran), but this grain doesn't do well in our recipes because it absorbs water unpredictably. Since it's really the caramel, coffee, and chocolate that give pumpernickel its unique flavor and color, we successfully created a pumpernickel bread *without* pumpernickel flour.

This bread is associated with Russia and caviar. Or just pile on the pastrami and corned beef.

***Makes four loaves, slightly less than 1 pound each. The recipe is easily doubled or halved.***

***Altus*, literally translated means "the old stuff":** Many traditional pumpernickel recipes call for the addition of altus, which is stale rye or pumpernickel bread crumbs, soaked in water and blended into the dough. If you want to find a use for some stale rye or pumpernickel bread, you can experiment with this approach, which some say adds moisture and flavor to many traditional rye breads. Add about a cup of altus to the liquid ingredients before the flours. Adjust the flour to end up with dough of your usual consistency.

| Ingredient | Volume (U.S.) | Weight (U.S.) | Weight (Metric) |
|---|---|---|---|
| Lukewarm water (100°F or below) | 3 cups | 1 pound, 8 ounces | 680 grams |
| Granulated yeast[1] | 1 tablespoon | 0.35 ounce | 10 grams |
| Kosher salt[1] | 1 to 1½ table-spoons | 0.6 to 0.9 ounce | 17 to 25 grams |
| Molasses | 2 tablespoons | 1¼ ounces | 35 grams |
| Cocoa powder, unsweetened | 1½ tablespoons | 0.4 ounce | 10 grams |
| Instant espresso or instant coffee powder[2] | 2 teaspoons | — | — |
| Caramel color | 1½ tablespoons | — | — |
| Rye flour | 1 cup | 4¼ ounces | 120 grams |
| All-purpose flour | 5½ cups | 1 pound, 11½ ounces | 780 grams |
| Cornmeal or parchment paper, for the pizza peel | | | |
| Cornstarch wash (see sidebar, page 104) or water, for brushing the top crust | | | |
| Whole caraway seeds for sprinkling on the top (optional) | | | |

[1]Can decrease (see pages 14 and 17)
[2]Can substitute brewed coffee for 2 cups of the water, keeping total volume at 3 cups

1. **Mixing and storing the dough:** Mix the yeast, salt, molasses, cocoa, espresso powder, and caramel color with the water in a 6-quart bowl or a lidded (not airtight) food container.

2. Mix in the flours without kneading, using a spoon or a heavy-duty stand mixer (with paddle). If you're not using a machine, you may need

to use wet hands to incorporate the last bit of flour.

3. Cover (not airtight) and allow to rest at room temperature until the dough rises and collapses (or flattens on top), approximately 2 hours.

4. The dough can be used immediately after the initial rise, though it is easier to handle when cold. Refrigerate the container of dough and use over the next 8 days.

5. **On baking day,** cut off a 1-pound (grapefruit-size) piece of dough. Using wet hands (don't use flour), quickly shape the dough into a ball by stretching the surface of the dough around to the bottom on all four sides, rotating the ball a quarter-turn as you go. Then form an oval-shaped loaf. Allow to rest and rise on a pizza peel prepared with cornmeal or parchment paper for 40 minutes (see sidebar, page 58).

**Make your own caramel color:** Caramel color can be made at home, but as a liquid rather than a powder. Put 3 tablespoons sugar and 1 tablespoon water into a saucepan. Over low heat, melt the sugar, then increase the heat to medium-high, cover, and bring to a boil for 2 minutes. Add a pinch of cream of tartar and continue to boil, uncovered, until the mixture becomes very dark. It will start to smoke at this point. Remove from heat and allow to cool partially. Very carefully, add ¼ cup of boiling water to the pan to dissolve the caramelized sugar (it may sputter and water may jump out of the pan, so wear gloves and be sure to shield your face). Cool to room temperature and use about ¼ cup of this mixture in place of the 1½ tablespoons of commercial caramel color powder in our Pumpernickel Bread (decrease the water in your initial mix by ¼ cup).

6. **Preheat a baking stone near the middle of the oven to 400°F (20 to 30 minutes),** with an empty metal broiler tray on any shelf that won't interfere with rising bread.

7. Using a pastry brush, paint the top crust with cornstarch wash or water and sprinkle with the caraway seeds, if using. Slash the loaf with ½-inch-deep, parallel cuts, using a serrated bread knife.

8. Slide the loaf directly onto the hot stone. Pour 1 cup of hot water into the broiler tray and quickly close the oven door (see page 20 for steam alternatives). Bake for 35 to 40 minutes until firm. Smaller or larger loaves will require adjustments in baking time.

9. Allow to cool on a rack before slicing and eating.

# Pumpernickel Date-and-Walnut Bread

The sweetness of the dried fruit and the richness of the nuts are wonderful with the aromatic pumpernickel dough. We finish the loaf with nothing but the traditional cornstarch wash, letting the fruit and nuts take center stage.

***Makes 1 loaf***

1 pound (grapefruit-size portion) Pumpernickel Bread dough (page 123)
¼ cup chopped walnuts
¼ cup chopped dates or raisins
Cornmeal or parchment paper, for the pizza peel
Cornstarch wash (see sidebar, page 104) or water, for brushing the top crust

1. **On baking day,** using wet hands instead of flour, cut off a 1-pound (grapefruit-size) piece of dough. Continuing with wet hands, quickly shape it into a ball by stretching the surface of the dough around to the bottom on all four sides, rotating the ball a quarter-turn as you go.

2. Flatten the dough with your wet hands to a thickness of ½ inch and sprinkle with the walnuts and dates. Roll up the dough like a jelly roll, to form a log. Crimp the ends shut and tuck them under to form an oval loaf.

3. Allow to rest and rise on a pizza peel prepared with cornmeal or parchment paper for 90 minutes (see sidebar, page 58).

4. **Preheat a baking stone near the middle of the oven to 400°F (20 to 30 minutes),** with an empty metal broiler tray on any shelf that won't interfere with rising bread.

5. Using a pastry brush, paint the top crust with cornstarch wash or water and then slash the loaf with ½-inch deep, parallel cuts, using a serrated bread knife.

6. Slide the loaf directly onto the hot stone. Pour 1 cup of hot water into the broiler tray and quickly close the oven door. Bake for 35 to 40 minutes until firm. Smaller or larger loaves will require adjustments in baking time.

7. Allow to cool on a rack before slicing and eating.

# Bran-Enriched White Bread

There's no point in belaboring the value of bran in the diet. Cup for cup, wheat bran is much higher in fiber than whole wheat flour, yet it doesn't affect the taste of bread as much. For those who don't care for the pleasantly bitter, nutty flavor of whole wheat, this loaf is a mild-tasting, high-fiber alternative.

***Makes three loaves, slightly more than 1 pound each. The recipe is easily doubled or halved.***

| Ingredient | Volume (U.S.) | Weight (U.S.) | Weight (Metric) |
|---|---|---|---|
| Lukewarm water (100°F or below) | 3 cups | 1 pound, 8 ounces | 680 grams |
| Granulated yeast[1] | 1 tablespoon | 0.35 ounce | 10 grams |
| Kosher salt[1] | 1 to 1½ tablespoons | 0.6 to 0.9 ounce | 17 to 25 grams |
| Wheat bran | ¾ cup | 2¼ ounces | 65 grams |
| All-purpose flour | 5¾ cups | 1 pound, 12¾ ounces | 815 grams |
| Cornmeal or parchment paper, for the pizza peel | | | |

[1]Can decrease (see pages 14 and 17)

1. **Mixing and storing the dough:** Mix the yeast and salt with the water in a 6-quart bowl or a lidded (not airtight) food container.

2. Mix in the remaining dry ingredients without kneading, using a spoon or a heavy-duty stand mixer (with paddle). If you're not using a

machine, you may need to use wet hands to incorporate the last bit of flour.

3. Allow to rest at room temperature until the dough rises and collapses (or flattens on top), approximately 2 hours.

4. The dough can be used immediately after the initial rise, though it is easier to handle when cold. Refrigerate the container of dough and use over the next 14 days.

5. **On baking day**, dust the surface of the refrigerated dough with flour and cut off a 1-pound (grapefruit-size) piece. Dust the piece with more flour and quickly shape it into a ball by stretching the surface of the dough around to the bottom on all four sides, rotating the ball a quarter-turn as you go. Then elongate to form an oval loaf. Allow to rest and rise on a pizza peel prepared with cornmeal or parchment paper for 40 minutes (see sidebar, page 58).

6. **Preheat a baking stone near the middle of the oven to 450°F (20 to 30 minutes),** with an empty metal broiler tray on any shelf that won't interfere with rising bread.

7. Sprinkle liberally with flour and slash the top, making ½-inch-deep, parallel cuts across the loaf, using a serrated bread knife.

8. Slide the loaf directly onto the hot stone. Pour 1 cup of hot water into the broiler tray and quickly close the oven door (see page 20 for steam alternatives). Bake for about 30 to 35 minutes until deeply browned and firm. Smaller or larger loaves will require adjustments in baking time.

9. Allow to cool on a rack before slicing and eating.

# Light Whole Wheat Bread

You'll find this recipe a basic workhorse when you want a versatile and healthy light wheat bread for sandwiches, appetizers, and snacks. The blend of all-purpose flour and whole wheat creates a bread that is lighter in texture, taste, and appearance than our other whole-grain breads.

***Makes four loaves, slightly less than 1 pound each. The recipe is easily doubled or halved.***

| Ingredient | Volume (U.S.) | Weight (U.S.) | Weight (Metric) |
|---|---|---|---|
| Lukewarm water (100°F or below) | 3 cups | 1 pound, 8 ounces | 680 grams |
| Granulated yeast[1] | 1 tablespoon | 0.35 ounce | 10 grams |
| Kosher salt[1] | 1 to 1½ tablespoons | 0.6 to 0.9 ounce | 17 to 25 grams |
| Whole wheat flour[2] | 1 cup | 4½ ounces | 130 grams |
| Unbleached all-purpose flour | 5½ cups | 1 pound, 11½ ounces | 780 grams |
| Whole wheat flour, cornmeal, or parchment paper, for the pizza peel | | | |

[1]Can decrease (see pages 14 and 17)
[2]Can substitute white whole wheat (see page 11)

1. **Mixing and storing the dough:** Mix the yeast and salt with the water in a 6-quart bowl or a lidded (not airtight) food container.

2. Mix in the remaining dry ingredients without kneading, using a spoon or a heavy-duty stand mixer (with paddle). If you're not using a

machine, you may need to use wet hands to incorporate the last bit of flour.

3. Cover (not airtight) and allow to rest at room temperature until the dough rises and collapses (or flattens on top), approximately 2 hours.

4. The dough can be used immediately after the initial rise, though it is easier to handle when cold. Refrigerate the container of dough and use over the next 14 days.

5. **On baking day**, dust the surface of the refrigerated dough with flour and cut off a 1-pound (grapefruit-size) piece. Dust with more flour and quickly shape it into a ball by stretching the surface of the dough around to the bottom on all four sides, rotating the ball a quarter-turn as you go. Allow to rest and rise on a pizza peel prepared with cornmeal, whole wheat flour, or parchment paper for 40 minutes (see sidebar, page 58).

6. **Preheat a baking stone near the middle of the oven to 450°F (20 to 30 minutes),** with an empty metal broiler tray on any shelf that won't interfere with rising bread.

7. Sprinkle liberally with flour and slash the top, about ½ inch deep, using a serrated bread knife (see photos, page 59).

8. Slide the loaf directly onto the hot stone. Pour 1 cup of hot water into the broiler tray and quickly close the oven door (see page 20 for steam alternatives). Bake for about 35 minutes, or until deeply browned and firm. Smaller or larger loaves will require adjustments in baking time.

9. Allow to cool on a rack before slicing and eating.

**VARIATION: SPELT BREAD**

Substitute spelt flour for the 1 cup of whole wheat—spelt, an ancient variety of wheat, has all the nutrition of whole grain but less of the bitter earthy flavor that some, particularly kids, don't like.

**VARIATION: MORE WHOLE WHEAT**

For a heartier loaf, increase the water by 1⁄8 cup (2 tablespoons). Then, increase the whole wheat to 3 cups and decrease the all-purpose flour to 3½ cups. Don't try to store this dough longer than 10 days. If you're using spelt flour, don't increase the water. For even more whole grains, see 100% Whole Wheat Sandwich Bread (page 134). And check out ***Healthy Bread in Five Minutes a Day*** (2009), where we use vital wheat gluten to get airier results with very high levels of whole grain.

## 100% Whole Wheat Sandwich Bread

Whole wheat flour has a nutty, slightly bitter flavor, and it caramelizes very easily, yielding a richly browned and flavorful loaf. We've used milk and honey as tenderizers, but the honey's sweetness also serves as a nice counterpoint to whole wheat's bitter notes. Although we've showcased a loaf-pan method here, this dough also makes lovely free-form loaves using the baking stone. If you want a lighter result in 100 percent whole-grain breads, see our ***Healthy Bread in Five Minutes a Day*** (2009), where we use vital wheat gluten to get airier results with very high levels of whole grain.

***Makes two 1½-pound loaves, with another pound left over for rolls (see page 88). The recipe is easily doubled or halved.***

| Ingredient | Volume (U.S.) | Weight (U.S.) | Weight (Metric) |
|---|---|---|---|
| Lukewarm water (100°F or below) | 1½ cups | 12 ounces | 340 grams |
| Lukewarm milk | 1½ cups | 12 ounces | 340 grams |
| Granulated yeast[1] | 1 tablespoon | 0.35 ounce | 10 grams |
| Kosher salt[1] | 1 to 1½ tablespoons | 0.6 to 0.9 ounce | 17 to 25 grams |
| Honey | ½ cup | 6 ounces | 170 grams |
| Oil, plus additional for greasing the pan | 5 tablespoons | 2¼ ounces | 65 grams |
| Whole wheat flour[2] | 6⅔ cups | 1 pound, 14 ounces | 850 grams |

[1]Can decrease (see pages 14 and 17)

[2]Can substitute white whole wheat (see page 11)

1. **Mixing and storing the dough:** Mix the yeast, salt, honey, and oil with the water and milk in a 6-quart bowl or a lidded (not airtight) food container.

2. Mix in the remaining dry ingredients without kneading, using a spoon or a heavy-duty stand mixer (with paddle). If you're not using a machine, you may need to use wet hands to incorporate the last bit of flour.

3. Cover (not airtight) and allow to rest at room temperature until the dough rises and collapses (or flattens on top), approximately 2 hours.

4. The dough can be used immediately after the initial rise, though it is easier to handle when cold. Refrigerate the container of dough and use over the next 5 days.

5. **On baking day**, grease an 8½ × 4½-inch nonstick loaf pan. Using wet hands, scoop out a 1½-pound (small cantaloupe-size) handful of dough. This dough is pretty sticky, and often it's easiest to handle with wet hands. Quickly shape it into a ball by stretching the surface of the dough around to the bottom on all four sides, rotating the ball a quarter-turn as you go. Elongate the ball to form an oval loaf.

6. Drop the loaf into the prepared pan.

7. Cover with plastic wrap and allow to rest for 90 minutes (see sidebar, page 58).

8. **Preheat the oven to 350°F,** with an empty metal broiler tray on any shelf that won't interfere with rising bread. A baking stone is not required and omitting it shortens the preheat.

9. Flour the top of the loaf and slash, using the tip of a serrated bread knife. Place the loaf on a rack in the middle of the oven. Pour 1 cup of hot water into the broiler tray and quickly close the oven door (see page 20 for steam alternatives). Bake for 50 to 60 minutes until deeply browned and firm.

10. Remove from the pan and allow to cool completely before slicing; otherwise you won't get well-cut sandwich slices. If the loaf sticks, wait 10 minutes and it will steam itself out of the pan.

# American-Style Whole Wheat Sandwich Bread

Here's a classic American-style whole-grain sandwich bread—a blend of grains, some sweetener, and butter that makes for a tender and flavorful loaf. Even though this bread is soft-crusted, we bake it with steam to improve the color and appearance. If you really want to dive into the world of whole-grain breads, see ***Healthy Bread in Five Minutes a Day*** (2009), where we use vital wheat gluten to get airier results with very high levels of whole grain.

***Makes two loaves, slightly less than 2 pounds each. The recipe is easily doubled or halved.***

| Ingredient | Volume (U.S.) | Weight (U.S.) | Weight (Metric) |
|---|---|---|---|
| Lukewarm water (100°F or below) | 3 cups | 1 pound, 8 ounces | 680 grams |
| Granulated yeast[1] | 1 tablespoon | 0.35 ounce | 10 grams |
| Kosher salt[1] | 1 to 1½ tablespoons | 0.6 to 0.9 ounce | 17 to 25 grams |
| Honey | ¼ cup | 3 ounces | 85 grams |
| Unsalted butter, melted, or neutral-flavored oil plus additional for greasing the pan | ¼ cup | 2 ounces | 55 grams |
| Rye flour | ¼ cup | 2 ounces | 55 grams |
| Whole wheat flour[2] | 2¾ cups | 13½ ounces | 380 grams |
| All-purpose flour | 3 cups | 15 ounces | 425 grams |

[1]Can decrease (see pages 14 and 17)
[2]Can substitute white whole wheat (see page 11)

1. **Mixing and storing the dough:** Mix the yeast, salt, honey, and butter or oil with the water in a 6-quart bowl or a lidded (not airtight) food container.

2. Mix in the remaining dry ingredients without kneading, using a spoon or a heavy-duty stand mixer (with paddle). If you're not using a machine, you may need to use wet hands to incorporate the last bit of flour.

3. Cover (not airtight) and allow to rest at room temperature until the dough rises and collapses (or flattens on top), approximately 2 hours.

4. The dough can be used immediately after the initial rise, though it is easier to handle when cold. Refrigerate the container of dough and use over the next 5 days.

5. **On baking day**, lightly grease an 8½ × 4½-inch nonstick loaf pan. Dust the surface of the refrigerated dough with flour and cut off a 1½-pound (small cantaloupe-size) piece. Dust with more flour and quickly shape it into a ball by stretching the surface of the dough around to the bottom on all four sides, rotating the ball a quarter-turn as you go. Elongate to form an oval loaf and place it into the prepared pan. Cover with plastic wrap and allow to rest for 90 minutes (see sidebar, page 58).

6. **Preheat the oven to 400°F**, with an empty metal broiler tray on any shelf that won't interfere with rising bread. A baking stone is not required and omitting it shortens the preheat.

7. Flour the top of the loaf and slash, using the tip of a serrated bread knife. Place the loaf on a rack in the center of the oven. Pour 1 cup of hot water into the broiler tray and quickly close the oven door

(see page 20 for steam alternatives). Bake for about 50 to 55 minutes until richly browned and firm. Smaller or larger loaves will require adjustments in resting and baking time.

8. Remove from the pan and allow to cool completely before slicing; otherwise you won't get well-cut sandwich slices.

# Cornell Bread: Healthy and Protein Packed

During World War II, food rationing had parents panicking about whether they would be able to provide nutritious food for their families. Back then, most Americans believed that you couldn't be healthy without eating meat, which was strictly rationed. The shortages prompted Cornell University nutrition professor Clive McKay to develop a homemade bread recipe that included nonfat dry milk, wheat germ, and soy flour—to provide protein and vitamins. Along with Victory Gardens, "Cornell Bread" was promoted to stretch budgets at a time of national emergency.

**What's so surprising about Cornell Bread is that it was made almost entirely from white flour—there was no whole grain in the original recipe at all.** Americans still hadn't embraced the nutritional value (and good taste) of whole grains, and McKay needed something that would appeal to everyone. So here's a whole-grain version of McKay's idea, and maybe the best news of all: **the ingredients for a 1-pound loaf cost less than 70 cents.**

***Makes four 1-pound loaves. The recipe is easily doubled or halved.***

| Ingredient | Volume (U.S.) | Weight (U.S.) | Weight (Metric) |
|---|---|---|---|
| Lukewarm water (100°F or below) | 3¼ cups | 1 pound, 10 ounces | 740 grams |
| Granulated yeast[1] | 1 tablespoon | 0.35 ounce | 10 grams |
| Kosher salt[1] | 1 to 1½ tablespoons | 0.6 to 0.9 ounce | 17 to 25 grams |
| Honey | 2 tablespoons | 1½ ounces | 45 grams |

[1]Can decrease (see pages 14 and 17)

| Ingredient | Volume (U.S.) | Weight (U.S.) | Weight (Metric) |
|---|---|---|---|
| Skim-milk powder | ½ cup | 1½ ounces | 40 grams |
| Wheat germ | ¼ cup | ¾ ounce | 20 grams |
| Soy flour | ½ cup | 1¾ ounces | 50 grams |
| Whole wheat flour[2] | 3½ cups | 15¾ ounces | 445 grams |
| All-purpose flour | 3 cups | 15 ounces | 425 grams |
| Cornmeal or parchment paper, for the pizza peel | | | |
| Cornstarch wash (see sidebar, page 104) or water, for brushing the top crust | | | |
| Seed mixture, for sprinkling the top: your choice of sesame, flax, caraway, raw sunflower, poppy, and/or anise—1 to 2 tablespoons per loaf | | | |

[2]Can substitute white whole wheat (see page 11)

1. **Mixing and storing the dough:** Mix the yeast, salt, honey, and skim-milk powder with the water in a 6-quart bowl or a lidded (not airtight) food container. The honey and skim-milk powder will not completely dissolve.

2. Mix in the wheat germ and the flours without kneading, using a spoon or a heavy-duty stand mixer (with paddle). If you're not using a machine, you may need to use wet hands to incorporate the last bit of flour.

3. Cover (not airtight) and allow to rest at room temperature until the dough rises and collapses (or flattens on top), approximately 2 hours.

4. The dough can be used immediately after the initial rise, though it is easier to handle when cold. Refrigerate the container of dough and use over the next 7 days.

5. **On baking day,** dust the surface of the refrigerated dough with flour and cut off a 1-pound (grapefruit-size) piece. Dust with more flour and quickly shape it into a ball by stretching the surface of the dough around to the bottom on all four sides, rotating the ball a quarter-turn as you go. Cover with plastic wrap or an overturned bowl and allow to rest for 40 minutes (see sidebar, page 58).

6. **Preheat a baking stone near the middle of the oven to 350°F (20 to 30 minutes),** with an empty metal broiler tray on any shelf that won't interfere with rising bread.

7. Paint the top crust with cornstarch wash or water. Sprinkle with seeds and slash the top, about ½ inch deep, using a serrated bread knife.

8. Slide the loaf directly onto the hot stone. Pour 1 cup of hot water into the broiler tray and quickly close the oven door (see page 20 for steam alternatives). Bake for about 40 minutes, or until richly browned and firm. Smaller or larger loaves will require adjustments in resting and baking time.

9. Allow to cool on a rack before slicing and eating.

# Italian Semolina Bread

This white free-form loaf, flavored with semolina and sesame seeds, is a fragrant masterpiece of southern Italian baking (see color photo). Semolina is a high-protein wheat flour that gives loaves a sweetness, and an almost winey aroma. In our minds, the flavor of the sesame seeds is inextricably linked to the semolina flavor (like caraway to rye). Try to use semolina flour that's labeled "durum"—other semolinas won't do as well in our method and can create a dry result because of their coarser grind. If you can't find durum, decrease the semolina to 1½ cups, and increase the all-purpose to 5 cups.

***Makes four loaves, slightly less than 1 pound each. The recipe is easily doubled or halved.***

| Ingredient | Volume (U.S.) | Weight (U.S.) | Weight (Metric) |
|---|---|---|---|
| Lukewarm water (100°F or below) | 3 cups | 1 pound, 8 ounces | 680 grams |
| Granulated yeast[1] | 1 tablespoon | 0.35 ounce | 10 grams |
| Kosher salt[1] | 1 to 1½ tablespoons | 0.6 to 0.9 ounce | 17 to 25 grams |
| Durum (semolina) flour | 3 cups | 15 ounces | 425 grams |
| All-purpose flour | 3¼ cups | 1 pound | 455 grams |
| Sesame seeds | 1 to 2 teaspoons | — | — |
| Cornmeal or parchment paper, for the pizza peel | | | |
| Cornstarch wash (see sidebar, page 104) or water, for brushing the top crust | | | |

[1]Can decrease (see pages 14 and 17)

1. **Mixing and storing the dough:** Mix the yeast and salt with the lukewarm water in a 6-quart bowl or a lidded (not airtight) food container.

2. Mix in the flours without kneading, using a spoon or a heavy-duty stand mixer (with paddle). If you're not using a machine, you may need to use wet hands to incorporate the last bit of flour.

3. Cover (not airtight) and allow to rest at room temperature until the dough rises and collapses (or flattens on top), approximately 2 hours.

4. The dough can be used immediately after the initial rise, though it is easier to handle when cold. Refrigerate the container of dough and use over the next 14 days.

5. **On baking day**, dust the surface of the refrigerated dough with flour and cut off a 1-pound (grapefruit-size) piece. Dust the piece with more flour and quickly shape it into a ball by stretching the surface of the dough around to the bottom on all four sides, rotating the ball a quarter-turn as you go. Elongate the ball to form an oval-shaped, free-form loaf. Allow to rest and rise on a cornmeal-covered pizza peel for 40 minutes (see sidebar, page 58).

6. **Preheat a baking stone near the middle of the oven to 450°F (20 to 30 minutes),** with an empty metal broiler tray on any shelf that won't interfere with rising bread.

7. Paint the surface with cornstarch wash or water, sprinkle with sesame seeds, and slash the surface with ½-inch-deep, parallel cuts, using a serrated bread knife.

8. Slide the loaf directly onto the hot stone. Pour 1 cup of hot water into the broiler tray and quickly close the oven door (see page 20 for steam alternatives). Bake for 30 to 35 minutes until deeply browned and firm. Smaller or larger loaves will require adjustments in resting and baking time.

9. Allow to cool on a rack before slicing and eating.

# Broa (Portuguese Cornbread)

Broa is a very rustic recipe from the Portuguese countryside. It's a dense, part-corn loaf that's perfect for sopping up hearty soups like our Portuguese Fish Stew (page 149). It bears little resemblance to American Southern cornbread, which is usually pretty sweet, and leavened with baking soda and powder.

Form the loaf as a relatively flattened ball, so that you'll get lots of crust. The flattened loaf is truer to the original and helps to prevent denseness from the corn.

***Makes four loaves, slightly less than 1 pound each. The recipe is easily doubled or halved.***

| Ingredient | Volume (U.S.) | Weight (U.S.) | Weight (Metric) |
|---|---|---|---|
| Lukewarm water (100°F or below) | 3 cups | 1 pound, 8 ounces | 680 grams |
| Granulated yeast[1] | 1 tablespoon | 0.35 ounce | 10 grams |
| Kosher salt[1] | 1 to 1½ tablespoons | 0.6 to 0.9 ounce | 17 to 25 grams |
| Cornmeal | 1½ cups | 8½ ounces | 240 grams |
| All-purpose flour | 5 cups | 1 pound, 9 ounces | 710 grams |
| Cornmeal or parchment paper, for the pizza peel, and extra cornmeal, for sprinkling on the loaf | | | |

[1]Can decrease (see pages 14 and 17)

1. **Mixing and storing the dough:** Mix the yeast and salt with the water in a 6-quart bowl or a lidded (not airtight) food container.

2. Mix in the remaining dry ingredients without kneading, using a spoon or a heavy-duty stand mixer (with paddle). If you're not using a machine, you may need to use wet hands to incorporate the last bit of flour.

3. Cover (not airtight) and allow to rest at room temperature until the dough rises and collapses (or flattens on top), approximately 2 hours.

4. The dough can be used immediately after the initial rise, though it is easier to handle when cold. Refrigerate the container of dough and use over the next 10 days.

5. **On baking day,** dust the surface of the refrigerated dough with flour and cut off a 1-pound (grapefruit-size) piece. Dust the piece with more flour and quickly shape it into a ball by stretching the surface of the dough around to the bottom on all four sides, rotating the ball a quarter-turn as you go. Flatten slightly and allow to rest and rise on a pizza peel prepared with cornmeal or parchment paper for 40 minutes (see sidebar, page 58).

6. **Preheat a baking stone near the middle of the oven to 450°F (20 to 30 minutes),** with an empty metal broiler tray on any shelf that won't interfere with rising bread.

7. Sprinkle liberally with cornmeal and slash the top, about ½ inch deep, using a serrated bread knife (see photos, page 59). Leave the cornmeal in place for baking; tap some of it off before eating.

8. Slide the loaf directly onto the hot stone. Pour 1 cup of hot water into the broiler tray and quickly close the oven door (see page 20

for steam alternatives). Bake for about 30 minutes, or until deeply browned and firm. Smaller or larger loaves will require adjustments in baking time.

9. Allow to cool on a rack before slicing and eating.

# Portuguese Fish Stew (Caldeirada de Peixe)

We include this simple and delicious recipe that was born to have Broa (page 146) dipped into it. The distinctive character of the soup comes from the orange zest and hot red pepper flakes, which make it quite different from French or Italian versions. Cod is a typical Portuguese choice, but the dish works well with any combination of boneless white-fleshed, non-oily fish and/or shellfish.

***Makes 6 to 8 servings***

¼ cup olive oil
1 large onion, chopped
2 leeks, well washed to remove interior soil and coarsely chopped
1 fennel bulb, white parts only, trimmed and coarsely chopped
5 garlic cloves, finely chopped
1 cup diced tomatoes, canned or fresh
1 red bell pepper, cored, seeded, and diced
1 bay leaf
Zest of 1 orange, grated with a microplane zester (page 30)
1 quart fish stock or water, or an 8-ounce bottle of clam juice plus 3 cups water
2 cups dry white wine
Scant ¼ teaspoon hot red pepper flakes
1 tablespoon salt
Freshly ground black pepper
3 pounds mixed white, non-oily boneless fish and shellfish, or just fish

1. Heat the olive oil in a large stockpot over medium heat, add the onions and leeks, and sauté until softened. Add the fennel and garlic and sauté until aromatic.

2. Add all of the remaining ingredients, except for the fish and shellfish, and bring to a boil. Cover, lower the heat, and simmer for 20 minutes.

3. While the stock is simmering, cut the fish into bite-size portions. Bring the stock back to a rapid boil, add the fish, and cook for 1 minute.

4. Add the shellfish, if using, and return to a simmer. Continue to simmer until the shells open, 1 to 2 minutes, shaking the pan occasionally to encourage clams and mussels to open. If using shrimp, turn off the heat as soon as all the shrimp lose their gray translucency; any longer and they quickly become tough and overcooked.

5. Serve hot with wedges of Broa.

# Yeasted Thanksgiving Cornbread with Cranberries

Traditional American cornbread is a butter or lard-enriched quick bread, risen with baking powder and baking soda. We make ours with yeasted Broa dough (page 146). For Thanksgiving, we stud the dough with sweetened cranberries. Playing on the American cornbread theme, we baked the loaf in a heated cast-iron pan, liberally greased with butter, lard, bacon grease, or oil, creating a rich and flavorful crust.

Like a baking stone, cast iron absorbs and retains heat well, and radiates it very evenly to the dough, promoting a nice brown crust (see color photo).

***Makes 1 loaf***

1½ pounds Broa dough (page 146), approximately 1 small cantaloupe-size piece, or enough to fill a 12-inch, cast-iron pan to a depth of about 1½ inches
½ cup fresh cranberries or ⅓ cup dried
¼ cup sugar
Zest of half an orange, grated with a microplane zester (page 30)
3 tablespoons softened unsalted butter, lard, bacon grease, or oil, for greasing the pan

1. Dust the surface of the refrigerated dough with flour and cut off a 1½-pound (small cantaloupe-size) piece. Dust the piece with more flour and quickly shape it into a ball by stretching the surface of the dough around to the bottom on all four sides, rotating the ball a quarter-turn as you go.

2. Flatten the ball with your hands and a rolling pin to a thickness of ½ inch. Sprinkle the dough with the cranberries, sugar, and orange zest. Roll up the dough, jelly-roll style, to incorporate the cranberries. Shape into a ball again, then flatten until it is about the size of your pan.

3. Grease a cast-iron pan with the butter, lard, bacon grease, or oil, being sure to coat the sides of the pan as well. Place the dough into the pan. Cover with plastic wrap or the pan's lid and allow the dough to rest for 90 minutes (see sidebar, page 58).

4. **Preheat the oven to 425°F,** with an empty metal broiler tray on any shelf that won't interfere with rising bread. A baking stone is not required, and omitting it shortens the preheat.

5. Just before baking, uncover and heat the pan over medium heat for 1 or 2 minutes to jump-start the baking process and promote caramelization of the bottom crust.

6. Place the pan on a rack near the center of the oven. Pour 1 cup of hot water into the broiler tray and quickly close the oven door (see page 20 for steam alternatives). Check for browning in about 20 minutes. The time required will depend on the size and weight of pan, but will probably be about 30 minutes. The loaf should be a rich yellow-brown when done.

7. Carefully turn the hot loaf out of the pan onto a serving plate, or just cut wedges directly from the pan.

# Spicy Pork Buns

We'd been searching for a simple way to re-create and reconstruct some of the flavor combinations in great tamales (see color photo). Here's a simple recipe combining the sweet flavor of corn from the Broa dough, meat, and two kinds of chili peppers. Children devour these, but if your kids won't eat spicy food, you may want to tone down the chipotles in adobo sauce (which are the really hot ones), or leave them out altogether. We serve this dish as a main course, with added sauce on the side. You can put more sauce inside the buns, but don't overdo it or the result may be soggy.

***Makes 4 large buns***

**The Meat Filling**

4 to 5 pounds pork roast (shoulder or butt), or beef brisket
One 28-ounce can crushed tomatoes
2 chipotle peppers from a can of chipotles in adobo sauce, finely chopped
2 dried chili peppers (New Mexico red, guajillo, or ancho variety), or substitute 1 tablespoon of your favorite chili powder
1 medium onion
1½ teaspoons cumin seeds
2 teaspoons salt
1 tablespoon cornstarch
2 tablespoons chopped fresh cilantro

**The Wrappers**

1 pound (grapefruit-size portion) Broa dough (page 146)

1. **Prepare the meat filling:** If you're grinding your own chili pepper, briefly toast the dried peppers in a 400-degree oven until fragrant but not burned, 1 to 2 minutes; they'll remain flexible. Break up the

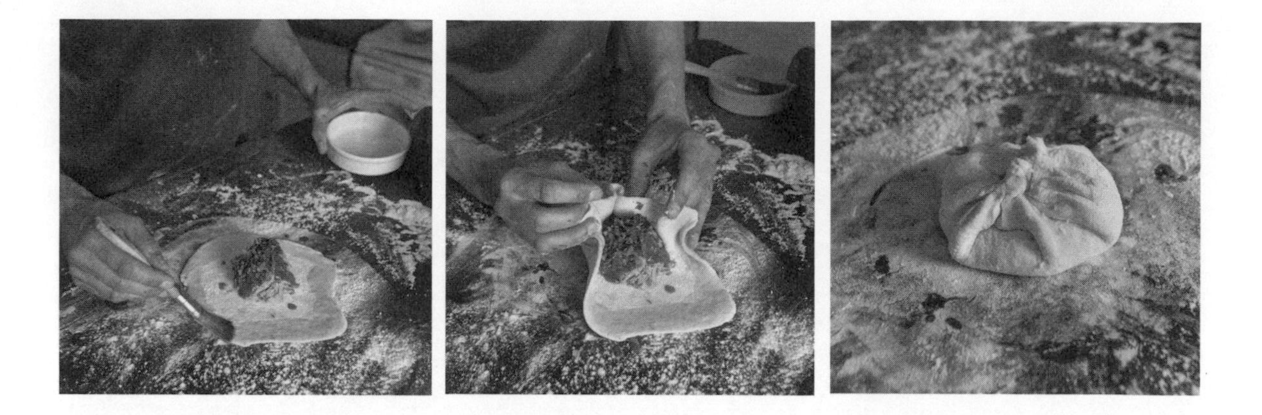

toasted peppers and discard the stems and seeds. Grind with the cumin seeds in a spice grinder (or coffee grinder used just for spices).

2. Place all of the ingredients for the meat filling, except for the cornstarch and cilantro, in a roomy pot on the stovetop. The pot should be large enough to hold the meat and still allow the cover to seal. The liquid should not come higher than about one-third of the way up the meat. Bring to a simmer and cook, covered, until very soft, approximately 3 hours, turning occasionally. Separate the meat and sauce and chill in the refrigerator.

3. Trim the meat of hardened fat; shred with knife, fork, and your fingers, pulling strips off the roast or brisket along the direction of the grain. You'll have plenty of meat left over for additional buns or other meals.

4. Skim the fat from the surface of the sauce. Anytime before assembling the buns, reheat the meat with the sauce. Mix the cornstarch with a small amount of sauce in a little cup to make a paste; then add to the pot. Simmer for 2 minutes, or until thickened.

5. **Preheat a baking stone near the middle of the oven to 450°F (20 to 30 minutes),** with an empty metal broiler tray on any shelf that won't interfere with the rising bread.

6. Dust the surface of the refrigerated dough with flour and cut off a 1-pound (grapefruit-size) piece. Divide the dough into four equal balls. Briefly shape, flattening out each ball with your fingers. Using a rolling pin, roll out 8- to 10-inch rounds, about ⅛ inch thick. Use minimal white flour on the work surface as you roll so that the dough sticks to it a bit.

7. **Assemble the buns:** Place approximately ½ cup of shredded meat in the center of each round of dough. Add about a tablespoon of sauce and ½ tablespoon of chopped cilantro. Wet the edges of the dough round with water. Gather the edges of the dough around the meat to form a pouch, pinching at the center to seal. Repeat with the remaining dough and filling.

8. Using a dough scraper, if necessary, transfer the finished buns to a cornmeal-covered pizza peel. No resting time is needed.

9. Slide the buns directly onto the hot stone. Pour 1 cup of hot water into the broiler tray and quickly close the oven door (see page 20 for steam alternatives). Check for browning in 15 minutes and continue baking, if needed, until the buns are medium brown.

10. Serve immediately, with the remaining sauce, and Mexican hot pepper sauce.

## English Granary-Style Bread

The English have created a great new cuisine based on super-fresh local ingredients, but when it comes to English bread, we're traditionalists. To accompany those new dishes, here is a staple of the old village bakery: a multi-grain loaf that includes malted wheat and barley malt powder (choose non-diastatic if you have a choice). The combination of grains creates a slightly sweet and old-fashioned flavor. Malted wheat flakes and barley malt powder can be ordered from King Arthur Flour (see Sources, page 367).

***Makes four loaves, slightly less than 1 pound each. The recipe is easily doubled or halved.***

| Ingredient | Volume (U.S.) | Weight (U.S.) | Weight (Metric) |
|---|---|---|---|
| Lukewarm water (100°F or below) | 3¼ cups | 1 pound, 10 ounces | 740 grams |
| Granulated yeast[1] | 1 tablespoon | 0.35 ounce | 10 grams |
| Kosher salt[1] | 1 to 1½ tablespoons | 0.6 to 0.9 ounce | 17 to 25 grams |
| Barley malt powder | ¼ cup | 1¼ ounces | 35 grams |
| Malted wheat flakes | 1 cup | 4¼ ounces | 120 grams |
| Whole wheat flour[2] | 1 cup | 4½ ounces | 130 grams |
| All-purpose flour | 5 cups | 1 pound, 9 ounces | 710 grams |
| Cornmeal or parchment paper, for the pizza peel | | | |

[1]Can decrease (see pages 14 and 17)

[2]Can substitute white whole wheat (see page 11)

| Ingredient |
|---|
| Cornstarch wash (see sidebar, page 104), or water, for brushing the top crust |
| Cracked wheat, for sprinkling on the top crust, 1 tablespoon |

1. **Mixing and storing the dough:** Mix the yeast, salt, and barley malt powder with the water in a 6-quart bowl or a lidded (not airtight) food container.

2. Mix in the wheat flakes and the flours without kneading, using a spoon or a heavy-duty stand mixer (with paddle). If you're not using a machine, you may need to use wet hands to incorporate the last bit of flour.

3. Cover (not airtight) and allow to rest at room temperature until the dough rises and collapses (or flattens on top), approximately 2 hours.

4. The dough can be used immediately after the initial rise, though it is easier to handle when cold. Refrigerate the container of dough and use over the next 10 days.

5. **On baking day,** dust the surface of the refrigerated dough with flour and cut off a 1-pound (grapefruit-size) piece. Dust the piece with more flour and quickly shape it into a ball by stretching the surface of the dough around to the bottom on all four sides, rotating the ball a quarter-turn as you go. Allow to rest and rise on a cornmeal-covered pizza peel for 40 minutes (see sidebar, page 58).

6. **Preheat a baking stone near the middle of the oven to 400°F (20 to 30 minutes),** with an empty metal broiler tray on any shelf that won't interfere with rising bread.

7. Brush the loaf with cornstarch wash or water and sprinkle with cracked wheat, then slash the top about ½ inch deep, using a serrated bread knife (see photos, page 59).

8. Slide the loaf directly onto the hot stone. Pour 1 cup of hot water into the broiler tray and quickly close the oven door (see page 20 for steam alternatives). Bake for about 35 minutes. Smaller or larger loaves will require adjustments in baking time.

9. Allow to cool on a rack before slicing and eating.

# Wurzelbrot (Swiss Twisted Bread)

"*Wurzel*" is German for "tree roots," and this particular "*brot*" from Switzerland, Germany, and Austria is distinctive for its rustic twisted look (see color photo). If you make a bunch of *wurzelbrot* (vóor-tsel-brot) they'll look like a pile of oak tree roots. It's supposed to look sloppy and rough-hewn, so forget about careful shaping. In Switzerland, wurzelbrot is a rustic white baguette, but in our version, molasses and just a little rye flour make for terrific deep browning and flavor.

*"The truth is, I almost never make a completely white baguette—even a little rye enhances the flavor of white bread—as little as 2 tablespoons changes the character of the batch."*—Jeff

***Makes four loaves, slightly less than 1 pound each. The recipe is easily doubled or halved.***

| Ingredient | Volume (U.S.) | Weight (U.S.) | Weight (Metric) |
|---|---|---|---|
| Lukewarm water (100°F or below) | 3 cups | 1 pound, 8 ounces | 680 grams |
| Granulated yeast[1] | 1 tablespoon | 0.35 ounce | 10 grams |
| Kosher salt[1] | 1 to 1½ tablespoons | 0.6 to 0.9 ounce | 17 to 25 grams |
| Molasses | 1 tablespoon | ¾ ounce | 15 grams |
| Rye flour | ½ cup | 2⅛ ounces | 60 grams |
| All-purpose flour | 6¼ cups | 1 pound, 15¼ ounces | 885 grams |
| Cornmeal or parchment paper, for the pizza peel | | | |

[1]Can decrease (see pages 14 and 17)

1. **Mixing and storing the dough:** Mix the yeast, salt, and molasses with the water in a 6-quart bowl or a lidded (not airtight) food container.

2. Mix in the flours without kneading, using a spoon or a heavy-duty stand mixer (with paddle). If you're not using a machine, you may need to use wet hands to incorporate the last bit of flour.

3. Cover (not airtight) and allow to rest at room temperature until the dough rises and collapses (or flattens on top), approximately 2 hours.

4. The dough can be used immediately after the initial rise, though it is easier to handle when cold. Refrigerate the container of dough and use over the next 14 days.

5. **On baking day,** dust the surface of the refrigerated dough with flour and cut off a 1-pound (grapefruit-size) piece. Dust the piece with more flour and quickly shape it into a ball by stretching the surface of the dough around to the bottom on all four sides, rotating the ball a quarter-turn as you go. Elongate the ball and continue to stretch until you have a long 1½-inch-wide rope. Cut the rope into thirds.

6. Hold one end in your hand and twist the other end to create an irregular twisted shape—it usually takes about 6 twists to create the effect (see photo). Sprinkle with more dusting flour after you finish the twist, and repeat with the other ropes.

7. **Preheat a baking stone near the middle of the oven to 450°F (20 to 30 minutes),** with an empty metal broiler tray on any shelf that won't interfere with rising bread.

8. Allow to rest and rise on a pizza peel prepared with cornmeal or parchment paper for 40 minutes (see sidebar, page 58). Or, for a more rustic dense crumb and to preserve the twisted shape, bake immediately with no rest.

9. Slide the loaf directly onto the hot stone (no need for slashing). Pour 1 cup of hot water into the broiler tray and quickly close the oven door (see page 20 for steam alternatives). Bake for about 30 minutes, or until deeply browned and firm. Smaller or larger loaves will require adjustments in baking time.

10. Allow to cool on a rack before slicing and eating.

## Oatmeal Maple Bread

This high-fiber loaf is lightly sweetened with maple syrup and tastes great cut into thick slices and then slathered with butter and Laura's Three-Citrus Marmalade (page 165). It also makes a great sandwich with smoked turkey and cheese.

***Makes two loaves, slightly less than 2 pounds each. The recipe is easily doubled or halved.***

| Ingredient | Volume (U.S.) | Weight (U.S.) | Weight (Metric) |
|---|---|---|---|
| Lukewarm water (100°F or below) | 2¾ cups | 1 pound, 6 ounces | 625 grams |
| Granulated yeast[1] | 1 tablespoon | 0.35 ounce | 10 grams |
| Kosher salt[1] | 1 to 1½ tablespoons | 0.6 to 0.9 ounce | 17 to 25 grams |
| Pure maple syrup | ¾ cup, plus 1 tablespoon for brushing the top | 6 ounces | 170 grams |
| Oil, plus more for greasing the pan | ¼ cup | 2 ounces | 55 grams |
| Wheat bran | ¾ cup | 2 ounces | 55 grams |
| Old-fashioned rolled oats | 1½ cups | 5 ounces | 140 grams |
| Whole wheat flour[2] | 1 cup | 4½ ounces | 130 grams |
| All-purpose flour | 4 cups | 1 pound, 4 ounces | 570 grams |

[1]Can decrease (see pages 14 and 17)

[2]Can substitute white whole wheat (see page 11)

1. **Mixing and storing the dough:** Mix the yeast and salt with the water, the ¾ cup maple syrup, and the oil in a 6-quart bowl or a lidded (not airtight) food container.

2. Mix in the remaining dry ingredients without kneading, using a spoon or a heavy-duty stand mixer (with paddle). If you're not using a machine, you may need to use wet hands to incorporate the last bit of flour.

3. Cover (not airtight) and allow to rest at room temperature until the dough rises and collapses (or flattens on top), approximately 2 hours.

4. The dough can be used immediately after the initial rise, though it is easier to handle when cold. Refrigerate the container of dough and use over the next 7 days.

5. **On baking day,** grease an 8½ × 4½-inch nonstick loaf pan. Dust the surface of the refrigerated dough with flour and cut off a 2-pound (large cantaloupe-size) piece. Dust the piece with more flour and quickly shape it into a ball by stretching the surface of the dough around to the bottom on all four sides, rotating the ball a quarter-turn as you go.

6. Elongate the ball to form an oval loaf and place it into the prepared pan. Cover with plastic wrap and allow to rest for 90 minutes (see sidebar, page 58).

7. **Preheat the oven to 350°F.** A baking stone is not required, and omitting it shortens the preheat.

8. Using a pastry brush, paint the top crust with the remaining 1 tablespoon maple syrup.

9. Place the loaf on a rack near the center of the oven. Bake for 50 to 60 minutes or until browned and firm. Smaller or larger loaves will require adjustments in resting and baking time.

10. Remove from the pan and allow to cool on a rack before slicing and eating.

# Laura's Three-Citrus Marmalade

Here's a traditional English preserve—something sweet yet startlingly tart to put on your English Granary-Style Bread (page 156), Oatmeal Maple Bread (page 162), or just about anything else. Citrus is available year-round but, if you wait until the height of the season, the selection increases. Try substituting blood oranges or tangerines for the navel oranges when in season.

*"My wife, Laura, does the canning at our house, and she makes a marmalade that everyone loves. I wish I could say that the recipe was whispered to her in an Italian citrus grove, but Laura enjoys telling foodies that it's adapted from the instruction sheet inside the Sure-Jell box. But she is too modest. Laura made it her own by adding pink grapefruit, which brings a touch of extra tartness."* —Jeff

If you don't want to bother canning, you can just refrigerate or freeze (see step 8).

***Makes 7 cups marmalade***

4 navel oranges
1 lemon
½ pink grapefruit
2½ cups water
⅛ teaspoon baking soda
5½ cups sugar
One 1.75-ounce box Sure-Jell fruit pectin

1. Using a vegetable peeler, remove the colored zest from the fruits and discard the white pith. Chop the zest coarsely.

2. Chop the fruit, discarding any seeds and reserving the juice.

3. Put the zests, water, and baking soda in a saucepan and bring to a boil. Reduce the heat; cover, and simmer for 20 minutes, stirring occasionally. Add the fruit and juice and simmer another 10 minutes.

4. Measure the sugar and set aside. Do not reduce the amount of sugar, or the marmalade may not set properly.

5. Stir the fruit pectin into the fruit mixture and bring to a full, rolling boil.

6. Stir in the sugar quickly, return to a full rolling boil, and cook for 1 minute. Remove from the heat and skim off any foam.

7. Pour the hot marmalade into sterilized canning jars. Process according to the canner's and U.S. Department of Agriculture (USDA) recommendations.

8. If you're intimidated by canning, simply skip the sterilization procedure in the final step and refrigerate the marmalade for up to 2 months or freeze for up to 1 year.

## Raisin-Walnut Oatmeal Bread

Full of the flavors we associate with oatmeal—raisins, walnuts, and a touch of maple syrup—this will remind you of the breakfast your mother made you when you were a kid. If not, it will be the breakfast your kids beg you to make.

***Makes 1 loaf***

Oil, for greasing the pan
1½ pounds (small cantaloupe-size portion) Oatmeal Maple Bread dough (page 162)
1 cup raisins
¾ cup walnuts
Egg wash (1 egg beaten with 1 tablespoon of water)

1. **On baking day,** grease an 8½ × 4½-inch nonstick loaf pan. Dust the surface of the refrigerated dough with flour and cut off a 1½-pound (small cantaloupe-size) piece. Dust the piece with more flour and quickly shape it into a ball by stretching the surface of the dough around to the bottom on all four sides, rotating the ball a quarter-turn as you go.

2. Flatten the dough with your hands and roll out into a ½-inch-thick rectangle. As you roll out the dough, use enough flour to prevent it from sticking to the work surface but not so much as to make the dough dry.

3. Sprinkle the raisins and walnuts over the dough and roll it up, jelly-roll style, to incorporate them. Shape into a ball.

4. Place the loaf in the prepared pan, and allow to rest for approximately 90 minutes (see sidebar, page 58).

5. **Preheat the oven to 350°F.** A baking stone is not required, and omitting it shortens the preheat.

6. Using a pastry brush, paint the loaf with the egg wash.

7. Place the loaf on a rack near the center of the oven. Bake for approximately 45 minutes, or until golden brown. Smaller or larger loaves will require adjustments in baking time.

8. Remove from the pan and allow to cool on a rack before slicing and eating.

# Oatmeal Pumpkin Bread

Here's a great use for leftover pumpkin puree. Roasting the pumpkin caramelizes the sugars and intensifies the flavors, so it's worth the effort to make your own rather than substituting with canned pumpkin puree. If you do roast your own, be sure to use the smaller "pie" pumpkin and not the watery and flavorless decorative pumpkin.

*"In the fall at my house, there is almost always a pumpkin roasting for pie and a batch of oatmeal cooking for breakfast. This is Minnesota and these are the things that keep us warm and happy. One day I had both going, and decided to try combining them into a bread. Well, it worked beautifully and is now one of my family's favorites. For obvious reasons I tend to make a lot of it right around Thanksgiving. It's perfect with leftover turkey."*—Zoë

***Makes two loaves slightly less than 2 pounds each. The recipe is easily doubled or halved.***

| Ingredient | Volume (U.S.) | Weight (U.S.) | Weight (Metric) |
|---|---|---|---|
| Fresh or canned 100% pure pumpkin puree | 1 cup | 8½ ounces | 240 grams |
| Lukewarm water | 2 cups | 1 pound | 455 grams |
| Granulated yeast[1] | 1 tablespoon | 0.35 ounce | 10 grams |
| Kosher salt[1] | 1 to 1½ tablespoons | 0.6 to 0.9 ounce | 17 to 25 grams |
| Unsalted butter, melted | 5 tablespoons | 2½ ounces | 70 grams |
| Honey | ⅓ cup | 4 ounces | 115 grams |

[1]Can decrease (see pages 14 and 17)

*(continued)*

| Ingredient | Volume (U.S.) | Weight (U.S.) | Weight (Metric) |
|---|---|---|---|
| Old-fashioned rolled oats | ½ cup | 2 ounces | 55 grams |
| Whole wheat flour[2] | ¾ cup | 3½ ounces | 100 grams |
| Rye flour | ¾ cup | 3⅛ ounces | 90 grams |
| All-purpose flour | 4 cups | 1 pound, 4 ounces | 565 grams |
| Unsalted butter or oil, for greasing the pan | | | |

[2]Can substitute white whole wheat (see page 11)

1. **To roast the pumpkin:** Preheat the oven to 350°F. Split the pumpkin in half starting at the stem and place cut side down on a silicone mat–lined or a lightly greased baking sheet. Bake for 45 minutes. The pumpkin should be very soft all the way through when poked with a knife. Cool slightly before scooping out the seeds.

2. Scoop out the roasted flesh of the pumpkin and mash it with a fork, or puree it in the food processor. Set aside 1 cup for the dough and use the rest in your favorite pie recipe.

3. **Mixing and storing the dough:** Mix the yeast and salt with the water, melted butter, and honey in a 6-quart bowl or a lidded (not airtight) food container.

4. Mix in the rolled oats, pumpkin puree, and flours without kneading, using a spoon or a heavy-duty stand mixer (with paddle). If you're not using a machine, you may need to use wet hands to incorporate the last bit of flour.

5. Cover (not airtight) and allow to rest at room temperature until the dough rises and collapses (or flattens on top), approximately 2 hours.

6. The dough can be used immediately after the initial rise, though it is easier to handle when cold. Refrigerate the container of dough and use over the next 7 days.

7. **On baking day,** grease an 8½ × 4½-inch nonstick loaf pan. Dust the surface of the refrigerated dough with flour and cut off a 2-pound (large cantaloupe-size) piece. Dust the piece with more flour and quickly shape it into a ball by stretching the surface of the dough around to the bottom on all four sides, rotating the ball a quarter-turn as you go.

8. Elongate the ball to form an oval loaf and place into the prepared pan. Allow to rest and rise for 90 minutes.

9. **Preheat the oven to 350°F.** A baking stone is not required, and omitting it shortens the preheat.

10. Place the loaf on a rack in the center of the oven. Bake for 50 to 60 minutes until browned and firm. Smaller or larger loaves will require adjustments in resting and baking time.

11. Remove from the pan and allow to cool on a rack before slicing and eating.

# Oatmeal–Pumpkin Seed Bread

To jazz up the Oatmeal Pumpkin Bread (page 169), roll in pumpkin seeds and dried cranberries. They add both a sweet and a tart element that is wonderful with the other flavors, and nothing could be more appropriate for Thanksgiving. You can buy shelled, toasted pumpkin seeds in most groceries, usually in the Mexican food aisle, where they might be labeled *pepitas*.

***Makes 1 loaf***

Oil, for greasing the pan
2 pounds (large cantaloupe-size portion) Oatmeal Pumpkin dough (page 169)
⅓ cup hulled, toasted pumpkin seeds
⅓ cup dried cranberries
Egg wash (1 egg beaten with 1 tablespoon of water)

1. **On baking day,** grease an 8½ × 4½-inch nonstick loaf pan. Dust the surface of the refrigerated dough with flour and cut off a 2-pound (large cantaloupe-size) piece. Dust the piece with more flour and quickly shape it into a ball by stretching the surface of the dough around to the bottom on all four sides, rotating the ball a quarter-turn as you go.

2. Flatten the dough with your hands and roll out into a ½-inch-thick rectangle. As you roll out the dough, use enough flour to prevent it from sticking to the work surface but not so much as to make the dough dry.

3. Sprinkle the seeds and cranberries over the dough and roll it up, jelly-roll style, to encase them. Fold the dough over again and gently knead for 20 seconds to work in the seeds. Then form into a ball.

4. Using a small amount of flour, elongate the ball to form an oval loaf and place into the prepared pan. Allow to rest and rise for 90 minutes, covered with plastic wrap.

5. **Preheat the oven to 350°F.** A baking stone is not required, and omitting it shortens the preheat.

6. Using a pastry brush, paint the top crust with egg wash.

7. Place the loaf on a rack in the center of the oven. Bake for 50 to 60 minutes until browned and firm. Smaller or larger loaves will require adjustments in resting and baking time.

8. Remove from the pan and allow to cool on a rack before slicing and eating.

# Oat Flour Bread

If you're looking for a delicious way to get kids to eat more fiber, here's a simple recipe with a milder flavor than most whole-grain breads. Oat flour has more soluble fiber than whole wheat flour.

***Makes two loaves, slightly less than 2 pounds each. The recipe is easily doubled or halved.***

| Ingredient | Volume (U.S.) | Weight (U.S.) | Weight (Metric) |
|---|---|---|---|
| Lukewarm water (100°F or below) | 3¼ cups | 1 pound, 10 ounces | 740 grams |
| Granulated yeast[1] | 1 tablespoon | 0.35 ounce | 10 grams |
| Kosher salt[1] | 1 to 1½ tablespoons | 0.6 to 0.9 ounce | 17 to 25 grams |
| Oat flour | 1 cup | 3¾ ounces | 105 grams |
| All-purpose flour | 5½ cups | 1 pound, 11½ ounces | 780 grams |
| Oil, for greasing the pan | | | |

[1]Can decrease (see pages 14 and 17)

1. **Mixing and storing the dough:** Mix the yeast and salt with the water in a 6-quart bowl or a lidded (not airtight) food container.

2. Mix in the flours without kneading, using a spoon or a heavy-duty stand mixer (with paddle). If you're not using a machine, you may need to use wet hands to incorporate the last bit of flour.

3. Cover (not airtight) and allow to rest at room temperature until the dough rises and collapses (or flattens on top), approximately 2 hours.

4. The dough can be used immediately after the initial rise, though it is easier to handle when cold. Refrigerate the container of dough and use over the next 10 days.

5. **On baking day,** lightly grease an 8½ × 4½-inch nonstick loaf pan. Dust the surface of the refrigerated dough with flour and cut off a 2-pound (cantaloupe-size) piece. Dust the piece with more flour and quickly shape it into a ball by stretching the surface of the dough around to the bottom on all four sides, rotating the ball a quarter-turn as you go. Elongate to form an oval loaf and drop into the prepared pan. Cover with plastic wrap or an overturned bowl and allow to rest for 90 minutes (see sidebar, page 58).

6. **Preheat the oven to 400°F,** with an empty metal broiler tray on any shelf that won't interfere with rising bread. A baking stone is not required, and omitting it shortens the preheat.

7. Place the loaf on a rack near the center of the oven. Pour 1 cup of hot water into the broiler tray and quickly close the oven door (see page 20 for steam alternatives). Bake for about 45 minutes, or until richly browned and firm. Smaller or larger loaves will require adjustments in baking time.

8. Allow to cool on a rack before slicing and eating.

# Vermont Cheddar Bread

Great cheese bread is a wonderful American specialty, and a complete meal in a slice. The success of this loaf will depend on the cheese you use, so go with a great one.

*"I grew up in Vermont, where eating sharp, aged cheddar is a birthright. Every Vermont bakery offers its own version of cheddar bread, using cheese from local dairies. We lived near Shelburne Farms, and I'm still loyal to their cheddar even since moving to the Midwest. It can be found at Whole Foods and other grocers with a good cheese counter. Feel free to substitute your favorite cheddar or other sharp-flavored hard cheese."*—Zoë

***Makes four loaves, slightly less than 1 pound each. The recipe is easily doubled or halved.***

| Ingredient | Volume (U.S.) | Weight (U.S.) | Weight (Metric) |
|---|---|---|---|
| Lukewarm water (100°F or below) | 3 cups | 1 pound, 8 ounces | 680 grams |
| Granulated yeast[1] | 1 tablespoon | 0.35 ounce | 10 grams |
| Kosher salt[1] | 1 to 1½ tablespoons | 0.6 to 0.9 ounce | 17 to 25 grams |
| Sugar | 1½ tablespoons | ¾ ounce | 20 grams |
| All-purpose flour | 6½ cups | 2 pounds | 910 grams |
| Grated cheddar cheese | 1 cup | 4 ounces | 115 grams |
| Cornmeal or parchment paper, for the pizza peel | | | |

[1]Can decrease (see pages 14 and 17)

[2]Can substitute white whole wheat (see page 11)

*Crisp Cheesy Bread Sticks, page 178*

Pizza Margherita, page 219

Spinach Feta Bread, page 183

Bagels and Bialys, page 198

Soft Pretzels, page 204

Pita, page 248

Fattoush, page 252

Lavash, page 254

Naan, page 260

*Gluten-free breads, page 267*

Braided Challah, page 296, and Turban-Shaped Challah with Raisins, page 303

Sticky Pecan Caramel Rolls (this page and opposite), page 307

*John Barrymore Onion Pletzel, page 305*

Almond Brioche (Bostock), page 312, and Apple and Pear Coffee Cake, page 345

*Chocolate-Filled Beignets,* page 318

1. **Mixing and storing the dough:** Mix the yeast, salt, and sugar with the water in a 6-quart bowl or a lidded (not airtight) food container.

2. Mix in the dry ingredients and the cheese without kneading, using a spoon or a heavy-duty stand mixer (with paddle). If you're not using a machine, you may need to use wet hands to incorporate the last bit of flour.

3. Cover (not airtight) and allow to rest at room temperature until the dough rises and collapses (or flattens on top), approximately 2 hours.

4. The dough can be used immediately after the initial rise, though it is easier to handle when cold. Refrigerate the container of dough and use over the next 7 days.

5. **On baking day,** dust the surface of the refrigerated dough with flour and cut off a 1-pound (grapefruit-size) piece. Dust the piece with more flour and quickly shape it into a ball by stretching the surface of the dough around to the bottom on all four sides, rotating the ball a quarter-turn as you go. Allow to rest and rise on a cornmeal or parchment paper–covered pizza peel for 1 hour (see sidebar, page 58).

6. **Preheat a baking stone near the middle of the oven to 450°F (20 to 30 minutes),** with an empty metal broiler tray on any shelf that won't interfere with rising bread.

7. Sprinkle liberally with flour and slash the top, about ½-inch deep, using a serrated bread knife (see photos, page 59).

8. Slide the loaf directly onto the hot stone. Pour 1 cup of hot water into the broiler tray and quickly close the oven door (see page 20 for steam

alternatives). Bake for about 30 minutes or until richly browned and firm. Smaller or larger loaves will require adjustments in resting and baking time.

9. Allow to cool on a rack before slicing and eating.

**VARIATION: CRISP CHEESY BREAD STICKS**

To make thin crispy bread sticks (see color photo), follow the directions below with Vermont Cheddar Bread dough or any lean dough in the book:

1. Preheat the oven to 400°F. Grease a baking sheet with oil or butter, or line with parchment paper. Roll out the dough into an 8 × 13-inch rectangle, about 1⁄8 inch thick, then cut along the long side into 1⁄8-inch-wide strips, using a pizza cutter or sharp knife.

2. Lay the strips on the prepared baking sheet, spacing them about 1⁄2 inch apart. Using a pastry brush, daub olive oil over each strip and sprinkle with coarse salt.

3. Bake the bread sticks in the center of the oven for 10 to 16 minutes. The bread sticks are done when nicely browned and beginning to crisp; they will firm up when cool.

# Wisconsin Beer-Cheese Bread

Anyone who has been to Wisconsin knows beer and cheese were meant to be paired. Cross the border into the "Cheese State" and you'll find this combo on every menu. Be sure to use a strong-tasting beer and a sharp cheese, so you can savor both. We find the flavor of the bread gets even better when the dough has had a couple of days to brew.

***Makes four 1-pound loaves. The recipe is easily doubled or halved.***

| Ingredient | Volume (U.S.) | Weight (U.S.) | Weight (metric) |
|---|---|---|---|
| Lukewarm water | 1¾ cups | 14 ounces | 400 grams |
| Beer | 1½ cups | 12 ounces | 340 grams |
| Granulated yeast[1] | 1 tablespoon | 0.35 ounce | 10 grams |
| Kosher salt[1] | 1 to 1½ tablespoons | 0.6 to 0.9 ounce | 17 to 25 grams |
| Sugar | 1½ tablespoons | ¾ ounce | 20 grams |
| All-purpose flour | 6 cups | 1 pound, 14 ounces | 850 grams |
| Whole wheat flour[2] | 1 cup | 4½ ounces | 130 grams |
| Grated sharp cheddar cheese | 1 cup | 4 ounces | 115 grams |

[1]Can decrease (see pages 14 and 17)
[2]Can substitute white whole wheat (see page 11)

1. **Mixing and storing the dough:** Mix the yeast, salt, and sugar with the water and beer in a 6-quart bowl or a lidded (not airtight) food container.

2. Mix in the flours and the cheese without kneading, using a spoon or a heavy-duty stand mixer (with paddle). If you're not using a machine, you may need to use wet hands to incorporate the last bit of flour.

3. Cover (not airtight) and allow to rest at room temperature until the dough rises and collapses (or flattens on top), approximately 2 hours.

4. The dough can be used immediately after the initial rise, though it is easier to handle when cold. Refrigerate the container of dough and use over the next 7 days.

5. **On baking day,** dust the surface of the refrigerated dough with flour and cut off a 1-pound (grapefruit-size) piece. Dust the piece with more flour and quickly shape it into a ball by stretching the surface of the dough around to the bottom on all four sides, rotating the ball a quarter-turn as you go. Allow to rest and rise on a pizza peel prepared with cornmeal or parchment paper for 1 hour (see sidebar, page 58).

6. **Preheat a baking stone near the middle of the oven to 450°F (20 to 30 minutes),** with an empty metal broiler tray on any shelf that won't interfere with rising bread.

7. Sprinkle liberally with flour and slash the top, about ½ inch deep, using a serrated bread knife (see photos, page 59).

8. Slide the loaf directly onto the hot stone. Pour 1 cup of hot water into the broiler tray and quickly close the oven door (see page 20 for steam alternatives). Bake for about 30 minutes, or until richly browned and firm. Smaller or larger loaves will require adjustments in resting and baking time.

9. Allow to cool on a rack before slicing and eating.

# Caramelized Onion and Herb Dinner Rolls

*"My friend Rey once told me she times her cooking so that the onions are caramelizing as her guests arrive, claiming there is nothing more aromatic and inviting. I can't help but agree with her."—Zoë*

Caramelizing onions is easy and rewarding, and they can be used to dress up any of our savory doughs. Another favorite is to add Manchego cheese to the onion mixture, which also makes a great pizza topping (page 219). Because it takes some time to achieve perfectly caramelized onions you may want to double the recipe to have some on hand; they freeze for months.

***Makes 6 dinner rolls***

1 pound (grapefruit-size portion) Master Recipe (page 53), Vermont Cheddar (page 176), or European Peasant (page 94) dough
3 tablespoons olive oil
2 large onions, chopped
1 teaspoon salt
1 tablespoon vermouth or white wine
1 teaspoon white wine vinegar
2 tablespoons brown sugar
1 teaspoon dried thyme or oregano (or 2 teaspoons chopped fresh thyme or oregano leaves)
4 tablespoons water
Freshly ground black pepper
Cornmeal or parchment paper, for the pizza peel.

1. **To prepare the onions:** Heat the olive oil in a large skillet on medium-low heat. Add the onions, salt, vermouth, vinegar, brown sugar, herbs, and water and cook for about 25 minutes, stirring occasionally, until

the onions are nicely caramelized. Add more water, as needed, to prevent burning. Season with pepper to taste.

2. **On baking day,** dust the surface of the refrigerated dough with flour and cut off a 1-pound (grapefruit-size) piece. Dust with more flour and quickly shape it into a ball by stretching the surface of the dough around to the bottom on all four sides, rotating the ball a quarter-turn as you go.

3. To form the dinner rolls, divide the ball into 6 roughly equal portions (each about the size of a plum). Shape each one into a smooth ball. Arrange on the prepared baking sheet so that the rolls have plenty of space to rise without touching. Allow to rest for 20 minutes.

4. **Preheat the oven to 450°F**, with an empty metal broiler tray on any shelf that won't interfere with rising rolls. A baking stone is not required, and omitting it shortens the preheat.

5. Cut a ½-inch-deep cross into the top of each roll, using a serrated bread knife or sharp kitchen shears. Fill the resulting space with about 1 tablespoon of the caramelized onion mixture.

6. Slide the baking sheet into the oven. Pour 1 cup of hot water into the broiler tray and quickly close the oven door (see page 20 for steam alternatives). Bake for 25 minutes, or until deeply browned and firm.

7. Allow to cool slightly before eating.

# Spinach Feta Bread

Spinach and feta cheese are usually seen wrapped in flaky phyllo pastry dough as savory Greek spinach pies. Our bread version is hearty, satisfying, and much easier to make (see color photo). Serve with tapenade (page 108) for a fantastic and easy appetizer.

***Makes four loaves, slightly less than 1 pound each. The recipe is easily doubled or halved.***

| Ingredient | Volume (U.S.) | Weight (U.S.) | Weight (Metric) |
|---|---|---|---|
| Cooked chopped spinach, squeezed dry | 1 cup | 6 ounces | 170 grams |
| Lukewarm water (100°F or below) | 3 cups | 1 pound, 8 ounces | 680 grams |
| Granulated yeast[1] | 1 tablespoon | 0.35 ounce | 10 grams |
| Kosher salt[1] | 1 to 1½ tablespoons | 0.6 to 0.9 ounce | 17 to 25 grams |
| Crumbled feta cheese | ¾ cup | 4 ounces | 115 grams |
| Sugar | 1½ tablespoons | ¾ ounce | 20 grams |
| All-purpose flour | 6½ cups | 2 pounds | 910 grams |
| Cornmeal or parchment paper, for the pizza peel | | | |

[1]Can decrease (see pages 14 and 17)

1. Mixing and storing the dough: Mix the yeast, salt, spinach, cheese, and sugar with the water in a 6-quart bowl or a lidded (not airtight) food container.

2. Mix in the flour without kneading, using a spoon or a heavy-duty stand mixer (with paddle). If you're not using a machine, you may need to use wet hands to incorporate the last bit of flour.

3. Cover (not airtight) and allow to rest at room temperature until the dough rises and collapses (or flattens on top), approximately 2 hours.

4. The dough can be used immediately after the initial rise, though it is easier to handle when cold. Refrigerate the container of dough and use over the next 7 days.

5. **On baking day,** dust the surface of the refrigerated dough with flour and cut off a 1-pound (grapefruit-size) piece. Dust the piece with more flour and quickly shape it into a ball by stretching the surface of the dough around to the bottom on all four sides, rotating the ball a quarter-turn as you go. Allow to rest and rise on a pizza peel prepared with cornmeal or parchment paper for 1 hour (see sidebar, page 58).

6. **Preheat a baking stone near the middle of the oven to 450°F (20 to 30 minutes),** with an empty metal broiler tray on any shelf that won't interfere with rising bread.

7. Brush the top of the loaf with water and slash the top, about ½ inch deep, using a serrated bread knife (see photos, page 59).

8. Slide the loaf directly onto the hot stone. Pour 1 cup of hot water

into the broiler tray and quickly close the oven door (see page 20 for steam alternatives). Bake for about 35 minutes, or until richly browned and firm. Smaller or larger loaves will require adjustments in resting and baking time.

9. Allow to cool on a rack before slicing and eating.

# Sun-Dried Tomato and Parmesan Bread

Bright and intense tomato flavors harmonize with the richness of aged Italian cheese. That's a combination we love in pasta dishes, so we created a bread with those flavors. If you can get authentic Parmigiano-Reggiano cheese, use it here; if not, use whatever hard Italian-style grating cheese you use on your pasta.

***Makes 1 loaf***

1 pound (grapefruit-size portion) Master Recipe (page 53), European Peasant (page 94), Olive Oil (page 214), Light Whole Wheat (page 131), or Italian Semolina (page 143) dough

Olive oil, for brushing the loaf

½ cup oil-packed, sun-dried tomatoes, roughly chopped

½ cup grated Parmigiano-Reggiano cheese (or other Italian-style grating cheese)

Cornmeal or parchment paper, for the pizza peel

1. **On baking day,** dust the surface of the refrigerated dough with flour and cut off a 1-pound (grapefruit-size) piece. Dust the piece with more flour and quickly shape it into a ball by stretching the surface of the dough around to the bottom on all four sides, rotating the ball a quarter-turn as you go.

2. Roll out the ball into a ¼-inch-thick rectangle. As you roll out the dough, use enough flour to prevent it from sticking to the work surface but not so much as to make the dough dry.

3. Brush the dough with olive oil. Scatter the sun-dried tomatoes evenly over the dough and sprinkle the cheese over the tomatoes. Starting

from the short end, roll the dough into a log and gently tuck the ends under to form an oval loaf. Allow to rest and rise on a cornmeal or parchment paper–covered pizza peel for 90 minutes (see sidebar, page 58).

4. **Preheat a baking stone near the middle of the oven to 450°F (20 to 30 minutes),** with an empty metal broiler tray on any shelf that won't interfere with rising bread.

5. Brush the top of the dough lightly with olive oil and slash ½-inch-deep, parallel cuts across the loaf, using a serrated bread knife.

6. Slide the loaf directly onto the hot stone. Pour 1 cup of hot water into the broiler tray and quickly close the oven door (see page 20 for steam alternatives). Bake for 30 to 35 minutes until deeply browned and firm.

7. Allow to cool on a rack before slicing and eating.

# Aunt Melissa's Granola Bread

The key to great granola bread is—surprise—great homemade granola (recipe follows). You can use packaged granola for this bread, but it won't have quite the same flavor. Make lots of your own granola and there'll be plenty left over for breakfast.

*"As a small child, I lived on a commune in the Northeast Kingdom of Vermont with my dad and my aunt Melissa, where they made granola and bread to sell at the local co-op. My main contribution was to eat great quantities of the granola. I still remember the sweet earthy smell of the house when Melissa would bake. Aunt Melissa has since passed away, and with her went the original recipe, but this is a very close approximation."*—Zoë

***Makes about two 1½-pound loaves. The recipe is easily doubled or halved.***

| Ingredient | Volume (U.S.) | Weight (U.S.) | Weight (Metric) |
|---|---|---|---|
| Lukewarm water (100°F or below) | 2 cups | 1 pound | 455 grams |
| Granulated yeast[1] | 1 tablespoon | 0.35 ounce | 10 grams |
| Honey | ½ cup | 6 ounces | 170 grams |
| Vegetable oil | 1 tablespoon | ½ ounce | 15 grams |
| Ground cinnamon | 1 teaspoon | — | — |
| Kosher salt[1] | 1 to 1½ tablespoons | 0.6 to 0.9 ounce | 17 to 25 grams |
| Whole wheat flour[2] | 1½ cups | 6¾ ounces | 190 grams |

[1]Can decrease (see pages 14 and 17)

[2]Can substitute white whole wheat (see page 11)

| Ingredient | Volume (U.S.) | Weight (U.S.) | Weight (Metric) |
|---|---|---|---|
| All-purpose flour | 2½ cups | 12½ ounces | 355 grams |
| Granola, plus a few tablespoons for sprinkling the top (see page 191 for Homemade Granola) | 1½ cups | 6½ ounces | 185 grams |
| Unsalted butter, melted, or oil, for greasing the pan | | | |
| Egg wash (1 egg beaten with 1 tablespoon of water) | | | |

1. **Mixing and storing the dough:** Mix the yeast, honey, vegetable oil, cinnamon, and salt with the water in a 6-quart bowl or a lidded (not airtight) food container.

2. Mix in the flours and granola without kneading, using a spoon or a heavy-duty stand mixer (with paddle). If you're not using a machine, you may need to use wet hands to incorporate the last bit of flour.

3. Cover (not airtight) and allow to rest at room temperature until the dough rises and collapses (or flattens on top), approximately 2 hours.

4. The dough can be used immediately after the initial rise, though it is easier to handle when cold. Refrigerate the container of dough and use over the next 5 days.

5. **On baking day,** grease an 8½ × 4½-inch nonstick loaf pan. Dust the surface of the refrigerated dough with flour and cut off a 1½-pound (small cantaloupe-size) piece. Dust the piece with more flour and

quickly shape it into a ball by stretching the surface of the dough around to the bottom on all four sides, rotating the ball a quarter-turn as you go.

6. Elongate the ball into an oval and place into the prepared pan. Cover with plastic wrap or an overturned bowl and allow to rest for 90 minutes (see sidebar, page 58).

7. **Preheat the oven to 350°F.** A baking stone is not required, and omitting it shortens the preheat.

8. Brush the loaf lightly with egg wash, sprinkle with granola, and place in the center of the oven, and bake for about 45 minutes, or until richly browned and firm. Smaller or larger loaves will require adjustments in resting and baking time.

9. Allow to cool on a rack before slicing and eating.

# Homemade Granola for Granola Bread

Use this granola in Aunt Melissa's Granola Bread, or enjoy it with milk for breakfast.

***Makes about 6 cups granola***

⅓ cup honey
⅓ cup maple syrup
⅓ cup vegetable oil
2 tablespoons water
½ teaspoon pure vanilla extract
¼ teaspoon ground cinnamon
¼ teaspoon salt
4 cups rolled oats
¼ cup sesame seeds
¾ cup chopped pecans, or the nut of your choice
¾ cup shredded sweetened or unsweetened coconut
½ cup raisins
½ cup dried cherries, chopped dried apricots, or dried cranberries (or a combination)

1. **Preheat the oven to 350°F.** Prepare a high-sided, rimmed baking sheet or a lasagna pan with parchment paper, oil, butter, or a large silicone mat.

2. Mix together the honey, maple syrup, oil, water, and vanilla extract in a large measuring cup.

3. In a large bowl, combine the liquid mixture with the dry ingredients, except for the dried fruit, and mix until everything is coated. Spread out the mixture evenly in the prepared baking sheet. Bake for about

30 minutes, stirring every 10 minutes, until the granola is golden brown. The baking time will vary, depending on the depth of granola in the baking sheet or pan.

4. After the baking is complete, add the dried fruit.

5. Allow to cool, store in jars, and use in Aunt Melissa's Granola Bread (page 188).

# Roasted Garlic Potato Bread

Skin on and roughly mashed is the way we prefer our potatoes, but if you want yours peeled and perfectly pureed that will work as well. The roasted garlic is sweet and pungent; this bread explodes with aroma when you break into it.

***Makes four 1-pound loaves. The recipe is easily doubled or halved.***

| Ingredient | Volume (U.S.) | Weight (U.S.) | Weight (Metric) |
|---|---|---|---|
| 1 head roasted garlic, squeezed out of its skin (see sidebar, page 68) | | | |
| Lukewarm water (100°F or below) | 3 cups | 1 pound, 8 ounces | 680 grams |
| Granulated yeast[1] | 1 tablespoon | 0.35 ounce | 10 grams |
| Kosher salt[1] | 1 to 1½ tablespoons | 0.6 to 0.9 ounce | 17 to 25 grams |
| Sugar | 1½ tablespoons | ¾ ounce | 20 grams |
| Mashed potato | 1 cup | 7¾ ounces | 220 grams |
| All-purpose flour | 6½ cups | 2 pounds, ½ ounce | 920 grams |
| Cornmeal or parchment paper, for the pizza peel | | | |

[1]Can decrease (see pages 14 and 17)

1. Mix the yeast, salt, sugar, mashed potato, and roasted garlic with the water in a 6-quart bowl or a lidded (not airtight) food container.

2. Mix in the flour without kneading, using a spoon or a heavy-duty stand mixer (with paddle). If you're not using a machine, you may need to use wet hands to incorporate the last bit of flour.

3. Cover (not airtight) and allow to rest at room temperature until the dough rises and collapses (or flattens on top), approximately 2 hours.

4. The dough can be used immediately after the initial rise, though it is easier to handle when cold. Refrigerate the container of dough and use over the next 7 days.

5. **On baking day,** dust the surface of the refrigerated dough with flour and cut off a 1-pound (grapefruit-size) piece. Dust the piece with more flour and quickly shape it into a ball by stretching the surface of the dough around to the bottom on all four sides, rotating the ball a quarter-turn as you go. Allow to rest and rise on a pizza peel prepared with cornmeal or parchment paper for 60 minutes (see sidebar, page 58).

6. **Preheat a baking stone near the middle of the oven to 450°F (20 to 30 minutes),** with an empty metal broiler tray on any shelf that won't interfere with rising bread.

7. Sprinkle liberally with flour and slash the top, about ½ inch deep, using a serrated bread knife (see photos, page 59).

8. Slide the loaf directly onto the hot stone. Pour 1 cup of hot water into the broiler tray and quickly close the oven door (see page 20 for steam alternatives). Bake for 30 to 35 minutes until deeply browned and firm. Smaller or larger loaves will require adjustments in baking time.

9. Allow to cool on a rack before slicing and eating.

# Eastern European Potato-Rye Bread

Here's another potato bread, but one with an Eastern European accent—hold the roasted garlic and bring on the caraway seeds. This rustic beauty will still be fresh the day after baking, thanks to the moisture-holding potato and rye.

***Makes four 1-pound loaves. The recipe is easily doubled or halved.***

| Ingredient | Volume (U.S.) | Weight (U.S.) | Weight (Metric) |
|---|---|---|---|
| Lukewarm water (100°F or below) | 3 cups | 1 pound, 8 ounces | 680 grams |
| Granulated yeast[1] | 1 tablespoon | 0.35 ounce | 10 grams |
| Kosher salt[1] | 1 to 1½ tablespoons | 0.6 to 0.9 ounce | 17 to 25 grams |
| Mashed potato | 1 cup | 7¾ ounces | 220 grams |
| Caraway seeds, plus additional for sprinkling the top | 1½ tablespoons | 0.35 ounce | 10 grams |
| Rye flour | 1 cup | 4¼ ounces | 120 grams |
| All-purpose flour | 5½ cups | 1 pound, 11½ ounces | 780 grams |
| Cornmeal or parchment paper, for the pizza peel | | | |
| Cornstarch wash (see sidebar, page 104) or water, for brushing the top crust | | | |

[1]Can decrease (see pages 14 and 17)

1. **Mixing and storing the dough:** Mix the yeast, salt, mashed potato, and caraway seeds with the water in a 6-quart bowl or a lidded (not airtight) food container.

2. Mix in the flours without kneading, using a spoon or a heavy-duty stand mixer (with paddle). If you're not using a machine, you may need to use wet hands to incorporate the last bit of flour.

3. Cover (not airtight) and allow to rest at room temperature until the dough rises and collapses (or flattens on top), approximately 2 hours.

4. The dough can be used immediately after the initial rise, though it is easier to handle when cold. Refrigerate the container of dough and use over the next 9 days.

5. **On baking day,** dust the surface of the refrigerated dough with flour and cut off a 1-pound (grapefruit-size) piece. Dust the piece with more flour and quickly shape it into a ball by stretching the surface of the dough around to the bottom on all four sides, rotating the ball a quarter-turn as you go. Allow to rest and rise on a pizza peel prepared with cornmeal or parchment paper for 60 minutes (see sidebar, page 58).

6. **Preheat a baking stone near the middle of the oven to 450°F (20 to 30 minutes),** with an empty metal broiler tray on any shelf that won't interfere with rising bread.

7. Using a pastry brush, paint the top crust with cornstarch wash or water and then sprinkle with the additional caraway seeds. Slash ½-inch-deep, parallel cuts across the loaf, using a serrated bread knife.

8. Slide the loaf directly onto the hot stone. Pour 1 cup of hot water into the broiler tray and quickly close the oven door (see page 20 for steam alternatives). Bake for 30 to 35 minutes, until deeply browned and firm. Smaller or larger loaves will require adjustments in baking time.

9. Allow to cool on a rack before slicing.

# Bagels

Bagels get their traditional texture and flavor from a brief trip into a malty boiling pot before baking (see color photo). You can substitute sugar for the malt in both the dough and the boiling water, but the flavor won't be quite as authentic. Bagels are meant to be chewy, so we use bread flour. This dough stores as well as any of our other recipes and can be used for soft pretzels (page 204), bialys (page 202), or even free-form loaves.

***Makes about 20 bagels. The recipe is easily doubled or halved.***

## The Dough

| Ingredient | Volume (U.S.) | Weight (U.S.) | Weight (Metric) |
| --- | --- | --- | --- |
| Lukewarm water (100°F or below) | 3 cups | 1 pound, 8 ounces | 680 grams |
| Granulated yeast[1] | 1 tablespoon | 0.35 ounce | 10 grams |
| Kosher salt[1] | 1 to 1½ tablespoons | 0.6 to 0.9 ounce | 17 to 25 grams |
| Malt powder (non-diastatic) or sugar | 2 tablespoons | 1 ounce | 30 grams |
| Bread flour | 6½ cups | 2 pounds | 910 grams |
| Whole wheat flour, for the pizza peel | | | |

[1]Can decrease (see pages 14 and 17)

**The Boiling Pot**

| Ingredient | Volume (U.S.) | Weight (U.S.) | Weight (Metric) |
|---|---|---|---|
| Boiling water | 8 quarts | 16 pounds | 7.3 kilograms |
| Malt powder (non-diastatic) or sugar | ¼ cup | 2 ounces | 55 grams |
| Baking soda | 1 teaspoon | — | — |
| Poppy or sesame seeds, for sprinkling | | | |
| Extra flour, for dusting the towel | | | |

1. **Mixing and storing the bagel dough:** Mix the yeast, salt, and malt powder or sugar with the water in a 6-quart bowl or a lidded (not airtight) food container.

2. Mix in the flour without kneading, using a spoon or a heavy-duty stand mixer (with paddle). If you're not using a machine, you may need to use wet hands to incorporate the last bit of flour.

3. Cover (not airtight) and allow to rest at room temperature until the dough rises and collapses (or flattens on top), approximately 2 hours.

4. The dough can be used immediately after the initial rise, though it is easier to handle when cold. Refrigerate the container of dough and use over the next 14 days.

5. **Preheat a baking stone near the middle of the oven to 500°F (20 to 30 minutes),** with an empty metal broiler tray on any shelf that won't interfere with the bagels.

6. Dust the surface of the refrigerated dough with flour and cut off a 1-pound (grapefruit-size) piece. Divide the dough into 5 equal pieces. Dust each piece with more flour and quickly shape it into a ball by stretching the surface of the dough around to the bottom on all four sides, rotating the ball a quarter-turn as you go.

7. Repeat to form the rest of the bagels. Cover the balls loosely with plastic wrap and allow to rest at room temperature for 20 minutes.

8. **Prepare the boiling-pot:** Bring a large saucepan or stockpot full of water to a boil. Reduce to a simmer and add the malt powder or sugar and baking soda.

9. Punch your thumb through each dough-ball to form a hole. Ease the hole open with your fingers and stretch until the diameter is about triple the width of the bagel wall.

10. Drop the bagels into the simmering water one at a time, raising the flame as necessary to continue at a slow simmer. They need enough room to float without crowding or they will be misshapen (though they may touch a little). Let them simmer for 1 minute and then flip them over with a slotted spoon to cook the other side for another 30 seconds.

11. Remove them from the water using the slotted spoon, and place on a clean kitchen towel that has been dusted with flour. This will absorb some of the excess water. After they've drained a bit, place them on a peel covered with whole wheat flour. Sprinkle the bagels with poppy seeds or sesame seeds.

12. Slide the bagels directly onto the hot stone. Pour 1 cup of hot water into the broiler tray and quickly close the oven door (see page 20 for steam alternatives). Bake for 15 to 20 minutes until deeply browned and firm.

13. Break the usual rule for cooling, and serve these a bit warm.

# Bialys

*"Bialys have always been something of an obsession for my mother. When I was a little girl, we'd visit my great aunts in Brighton Beach, Brooklyn, and my mother would always stop to pick up bialys and knishes, two things that couldn't be found anywhere in Vermont, where we lived. Mom's obsession was in full bloom during a recent trip to New York City with her best friend, Barbara. As they left the ballet at Lincoln Center, my mother decided that late-night bialys would make the evening truly perfect. They jumped onto a bus and headed for Kossar's Bakery in lower Manhattan, one of the world's last great bastions of "bialydom." One can only imagine the sight of two women dressed for the ballet getting out of a bus at midnight in front of Kossar's. Only someone obsessed with fresh bialys would understand. Now my mother can make bialys at home."*—Zoë

***Makes about 5 bialys***

1 pound Bagel dough (page 198)
1 tablespoon vegetable oil
½ onion, finely chopped
¾ teaspoon poppy seeds
Salt and freshly ground black pepper
Whole wheat flour, for the pizza peel

1. **On baking day,** dust the surface of the refrigerated dough with flour and cut off a 1-pound (grapefruit-size) piece. Divide the dough into 5 equal pieces. Dust each piece with more flour and quickly shape it into a ball by stretching the surface of the dough around to the bottom on all four sides, rotating the ball a quarter-turn as you go. Press the balls into 3-inch disks and let rest on a floured surface for 30 minutes.

2. **Preheat a baking stone near the middle of the oven to 450°F (20 to 30 minutes),** with an empty metal broiler tray on any shelf that won't interfere with the rising bialys.

3. While the dough is resting and the oven is preheating, in a skillet over medium heat, sauté the onions in the vegetable oil until they are translucent and slightly golden. Don't overbrown at this stage, or they will burn in the oven. Remove from heat and add the poppy seeds, and salt and pepper to taste.

4. Press the center of each bialy to flatten it, working your way out until there is a ½-inch rim of dough that is not pressed flat, and the bialy is about 4 inches wide. Fill the center of each bialy with 1 tablespoon of the onion mixture and press it firmly into the bialy dough.

5. Transfer the bialys to a pizza peel dusted with whole wheat flour, and slide them directly onto the hot stone, making sure they are spaced about 1 inch apart so they have room to expand. Pour 1 cup of hot water into the broiler tray and quickly close the oven door (see page 20 for steam alternatives). Bake for about 12 minutes, until golden brown. Do not overbake the bialys or they will lose their chewy, soft texture.

6. Allow to cool slightly before eating.

# Soft Pretzels

Pretzels are closely related to bagels, and you can make fantastic ones using our standard Bagel dough, and twisting it into the pretzel shape—an ancient symbol of earth and sun (see color photo). A brief bath in a boiling alkaline solution (we use baking soda) transforms ordinary bread crust into the essence of pretzels. We love them warm, with mustard.

*"Food writer Mimi Sheraton wrote a newspaper article on homemade pretzels about thirty-five years ago, and it stuck in my teenage mind—I was taken by her description of the crusty pretzels baked by her Stuttgart hosts. I still have the original clipping from 1978, so we've adapted her recipe here."*—Jeff

***Makes about 5 pretzels***

**The Pretzels**

1 pound (grapefruit-size portion) Bagel dough (page 198)
Extra flour, for dusting the kitchen towel
Coarse salt or "pretzel" salt
Whole wheat flour, for the pizza peel

**The Boiling Pot**

8 quarts boiling water
1/4 cup baking soda
2 tablespoons sugar

1. **On baking day,** dust the surface of the refrigerated dough with flour and cut off a 1-pound (grapefruit-size) piece. Divide the dough into 5 equal pieces. Dust each piece with more flour and quickly shape it

into a ball by stretching the surface of the dough around to the bottom on all four sides, rotating the ball a quarter-turn as you go. Elongate the ball, dusting with additional flour as necessary. Roll it back and forth with your hands on a flour-dusted surface to form a long rope about 20 inches long, approximately ½ inch in diameter at the center, and tapered on the ends.

2. Twist the dough rope into a pretzel shape by first forming a horseshoe with the ends facing away from you. Fold the tapered ends

**We didn't use lye in the boiling pot:** When we published our pretzel recipe in the first edition, a few people wrote to express their dismay that we didn't use lye in the boiling pot—that's right, the same chemical used in drain cleaner. They claimed that it's the crucial ingredient to get the absolutely authentic German-style pretzel crust they craved. They may have a point, but we doubted we'd be able to convince home bakers to try this particularly wacky ingredient. For this edition, we actually went so far as to purchase food-grade lye, but then we read the label: "*. . . wear chemical-resistant gloves. Wear protective clothing. Wear goggles . . .*" And our favorite, advising users to watch out for "*digestive tract burns*" (though the manufacturer helpfully advises against swallowing the lye). We found that baking soda makes a terrific substitute—it's alkaline enough. We must admit, we never opened that container of lye.

down to the thick part of the rope, crossing them, one over the other. Extend the ends an inch beyond the bottom loop and gently press them together.

3. **Preheat a baking stone near the middle of the oven to 450°F (20 to 30 minutes),** with an empty metal broiler tray on any shelf that won't interfere with rising pretzels.

4. Keep the pretzels covered loosely with plastic wrap as you repeat the process to shape the remaining dough. Let the pretzels rest at room temperature for 20 minutes.

5. **Prepare the boiling pot:** Bring a large saucepan or stockpot full of water to a boil. Reduce to a simmer and add the baking soda and sugar. Drop the pretzels into the simmering water one at a time, making sure they are not crowding one another. They need enough room to float without touching or they will be misshapen. Let them simmer for 1 minute and then flip them over with a slotted spoon to cook the other side for another 30 seconds.

6. Remove them from the water using the slotted spoon, and place on a clean kitchen towel that has been dusted with flour. This will absorb some of the excess water from the pretzels. Then place them on a peel covered with whole wheat flour. Sprinkle with coarse salt.

7. Slide the pretzels directly onto the hot stone. Pour 1 cup of hot water into the broiler tray and quickly close the oven door (see page 20 for steam alternatives). Bake for about 15 minutes, until deeply browned and firm. If you want crisp pretzels, bake 5 to 10 minutes longer.

8. Serve these a bit warm, with a hefty stein of beer.

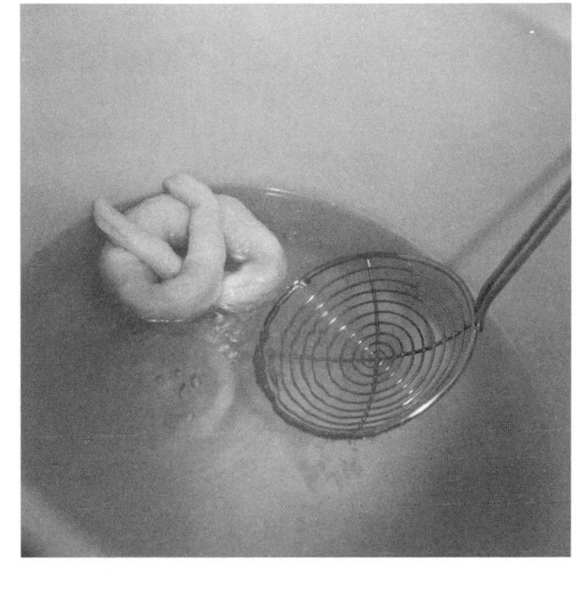

**VARIATION: PRETZEL BUNS**

Divide a 1-pound ball of Bagel dough (page 198) into 8 smooth balls, then allow to rest for 20 minutes. Boil as above but **shorten the boil to 20 seconds on each side,** drain as above, and space 2 inches apart on a baking sheet prepared with oil, butter, parchment paper, or a silicone mat. Sprinkle with coarse salt and bake with steam for 20 minutes at 450°F.

# Montreal Bagels

These differ from American bagels—they're sweeter, and they have toppings on both sides (poppy seed and sesame are the classics). In Montreal, bagels are traditionally baked in a wood-fired oven, which imparts a wonderful smokiness, but the ones made on the baking stone at home are excellent as well. This recipe calls for bread flour to ensure that the bagels are nice and chewy.

*"One of the first dates with my husband was to visit his hometown, Montreal. As soon as we arrived, we drove to Fairmont Bagels and got a dozen fresh from the oven—I was in love. Several years later, after a New Year's Eve party in Montreal, Graham proposed to me while we were eating Fairmont bagels. Now we live in the Midwest with no easy way to get our favorite bagels, so I create my own. They may not be baked in a wood-fired oven but they are close, really close, to what I remember."*—Zoë

***Makes about 1 dozen bagels. The recipe is easily doubled or halved.***

### The Bagels

| Ingredient | Volume (U.S.) | Weight (U.S.) | Weight (Metric) |
|---|---|---|---|
| Lukewarm water (100°F or below) | 1½ cups | 12 ounces | 340 grams |
| Granulated yeast[1] | 1 tablespoon | 0.35 ounce | 10 grams |
| Kosher salt[1] | 1 to 1½ tablespoons | 0.6 to 0.9 ounce | 17 to 25 grams |
| Sugar | 5 tablespoons | 2½ ounces | 70 grams |
| Honey | 2 tablespoons | 1½ ounces | 45 grams |

[1]Can decrease (see pages 14 and 17)

| Ingredient | Volume (U.S.) | Weight (U.S.) | Weight (Metric) |
|---|---|---|---|
| Large egg | 1 | 2 ounces | 55 grams |
| Vegetable oil | 3 tablespoons | 1½ ounces | 45 grams |
| Malt powder (non-diastatic) | 3 tablespoons | 1½ ounces | 45 grams |
| Bread flour | 4¼ cups | 1 pound, 5¼ ounces | 600 grams |
| Poppy seeds or sesame seeds, for sprinkling | | | |
| Whole wheat flour, for the pizza peel | | | |
| Extra flour, for dusting the towel | | | |

### The Boiling Pot

| Ingredient | Volume (U.S.) | Weight (U.S.) | Weight (Metric) |
|---|---|---|---|
| Water | 4 quarts | 8 pounds | 4 kilos |
| Honey | 2 tablespoons | 1½ ounces | 45 grams |
| Malt powder (non-diastatic) | 2 tablespoons | 1 ounce | 25 grams |

1. **Mixing and storing the bagel dough:** Mix the yeast, salt, sugar, honey, egg, oil, and malt powder with the water in a 6-quart bowl or a lidded (not airtight) food container.

2. Mix in the flour without kneading, using a spoon or a heavy-duty stand mixer (with paddle). If you're not using a machine, you may need to use wet hands to incorporate the last bit of flour.

3. Cover (not airtight) and allow to rest at room temperature until the dough rises and collapses (or flattens on top), approximately 2 hours.

4. The dough can be used immediately after the initial rise, though it is easier to handle when cold. Refrigerate the container of dough and use over the next 7 days.

5. **Preheat a baking stone near the middle of the oven to 500°F (20 to 30 minutes),** with an empty metal broiler tray on any shelf that won't interfere with the bagels.

6. **On baking day,** dust the surface of the refrigerated dough with flour and cut off a 1-pound (grapefruit-size) piece. Divide the dough into 5 equal pieces. Dust each piece with more flour and quickly shape it into a ball by stretching the surface of the dough around to the bottom on all four sides, rotating the ball a quarter-turn as you go.

7. Cover the balls loosely with plastic wrap and allow to rest at room temperature for 20 minutes.

8. **Prepare the boiling pot:** Bring a large saucepan or stockpot full of water to a boil. Reduce to a simmer, and add the honey and malt.

9. Punch your thumb through each dough ball to form a hole. Ease the hole open with your fingers and stretch until the diameter is about triple the width of the bagel wall.

10. Drop the bagels into the simmering water, one at a time, raising the flame as necessary to continue at a slow simmer. They need enough room to float without crowding or they will be misshapen (though they may touch a little). Let them simmer for 30 seconds and then flip

them over with a slotted spoon to cook the other side for another 30 seconds.

11. Remove them from the water, using the slotted spoon, and place on a clean kitchen towel that has been dusted with flour. This will absorb some of the excess water.

12. Dredge both sides of each bagel in poppy seeds or sesame seeds and place on a pizza peel. (If making plain bagels, cover the peel with whole wheat flour.) Slide the bagels directly onto the hot stone. Pour 1 cup of hot water into the broiler tray and quickly close the oven door (see page 20 for steam alternatives). Bake for about 15 to 20 minutes until richly browned and firm.

13. Break the usual rule for cooling and serve these a bit warm.

# 7

# FLATBREADS AND PIZZAS

Flatbreads from southern Europe, like Italian *focaccia* and French Provençal *fougasse,* have been popular in the United States for years (though not as long as pizza). When they first arrived on the scene, they seemed rich and exotic, with their strong flavors and their dependence on luxurious, savory olive oil. But their originators would have laughed—this was simple peasant fare, without pretension. These fragrant rounds were born in regions where dairy and butter were greater luxuries than olive oil.

And the Middle East has been producing leavened-but-flat breads of all kinds for thousands of years. Most Americans are familiar with puffed pita flatbread, but the aromatic spice-topped Arab *za'atar* flatbread is uncommon outside the Middle East.

Flatbread is marvelously suited to very fast preparation. Because flatbreads are so thin, the dough will warm to room temperature quickly, which means a very short resting time is needed after shaping. Pizza, lavash, and pita, among others, need none. And thicker flatbreads like focaccia do very well with just fifteen to twenty minutes, so preheat the oven while you're shaping them.

Once they've had their brief rest, flatbreads also bake faster, as quickly as five minutes for lavash and pita (pages 254 and 248). So if you've stored some dough, you can have fresh flatbread on the table in about twenty-five minutes.

## Olive Oil Dough

This versatile, rich dough is terrific in pizza, focaccia, and olive bread. The fruitier the olive oil, the better the flavor.

***Makes four loaves, slightly less than 1 pound each. The recipe is easily doubled or halved.***

| Ingredient | Volume (U.S.) | Weight (U.S.) | Weight (Metric) |
|---|---|---|---|
| Lukewarm water (100°F or below) | 2¾ cups | 1 pound, 6 ounces | 625 grams |
| Granulated yeast[1] | 1 tablespoon | 0.35 ounce | 10 grams |
| Kosher salt[1] | 1 to 1½ tablespoons | 0.6 to 0.9 ounce | 17 to 25 grams |
| Sugar | 1 tablespoon | ½ ounce | 15 grams |
| Olive oil | ¼ cup | 2 ounces | 55 grams |
| All-purpose flour | 6½ cups | 2 pounds, ½ ounce | 920 grams |

[1]Can decrease (see pages 14 and 17)

1. Mix the yeast, salt, sugar, and olive oil with the water in a 6-quart bowl or a lidded (not airtight) food container.

2. Mix in the flour without kneading, using a spoon or a heavy-duty stand mixer (with paddle). If you're not using a machine, you may need to use wet hands to incorporate the last bit of flour.

3. Cover (not airtight) and allow to rest at room temperature until the dough rises and collapses (or flattens on top), approximately 2 hours.

4. Dough can be used immediately after the initial rise, though it is easier to handle when cold. Refrigerate the container of dough and use over the next 12 days.

# Neapolitan-Style Pizza with Eggplant and Anchovy

We like crisp, thin-crusted, Neapolitan- (Naples) style pizza, baked at a high temperature directly on the stone. In home ovens, the maximum temperature is 500°F or 550°F—not 905°F as in Naples, but baking right on a stone helps achieve crisp crust even at the lower temperature. Pizza made this way at home, especially if you can get fresh mozzarella, is unlike anything most of us are used to eating. The secret to Neapolitan pizza is to keep the crust thin, don't overload it with toppings, and bake it very quickly at a high temperature so it doesn't all cook down to a soup—you should be able to appreciate the individual ingredients in the topping. And of course, you can put any toppings you like on this pizza—as in our variations below, including the classic Pizza Margherita (see color photo).

***Makes one 12-inch pizza; serves 2 to 4***

½ pound (orange-size portion) Master Recipe (page 53), European Peasant (page 94), Olive Oil (page 214), Light Whole Wheat (page 131), or Italian Semolina (page 143) dough
⅓ cup canned Italian-style chopped tomatoes, strained and pressed to drain liquid (or substitute prepared tomato sauce)
3 ounces mozzarella cheese, cut into ½-inch chunks
½ small eggplant, sliced into ⅛-inch-thick rounds, brushed with olive oil, and cut into bite-size pieces
4 canned or jarred anchovy fillets, chopped
1 tablespoon grated Parmigiano-Reggiano cheese
Flour, for the pizza peel

1. **Preheat a baking stone to your oven's highest temperature (550°F or 500°F)**, placing the stone near the bottom of the oven to help crisp the

bottom crust without burning the cheese. Most stones will be hot enough in 20 to 30 minutes (see page 43 for longer preheat options). You won't be using steam, so omit the broiler tray.

2. Prepare and measure all the toppings in advance. The key to a pizza that slides right off the peel is to work quickly—don't let the dough sit on the peel any longer than necessary.

3. Dust the surface of the refrigerated dough with flour and cut off a ½-pound (orange-size) piece. Dust the piece with more flour and quickly shape it into a ball by stretching the surface of the dough around to the bottom on all four sides, rotating the ball a quarter-turn as you go.

4. Flatten the dough with your hands and a rolling pin on the work surface to produce a ⅛-inch-thick round, and dust with flour to keep the dough from sticking. A little sticking can be helpful in overcoming the dough's resistance to stretch, so don't overuse flour, and consider using a dough scraper to "unstick" the dough. You may also need to let the partially rolled dough sit for a few minutes to "relax" to allow further rolling. At this point, stretching by hand may help, followed by additional rolling. Place the rolled-out dough onto a pizza peel dusted liberally with flour (as you get better at sliding your pies off the peel, you can use less flour).

**Smoother pizza sauces:** If you prefer a perfectly smooth tomato sauce, food-process the tomatoes, then reduce them in a saucepan over medium-low heat until thickened. Or make a thicker, slightly sweet sauce by food-processing tomato paste (one 6-ounce can) with canned tomatoes (one 14½-ounce can). This makes enough sauce for several pizzas and doesn't require draining or reduction of liquid to produce a thick, pizza-ready sauce.

**For thicker-crusted American-style pizza** that can support more toppings, use up to twice as much dough and only stretch the crust to a thickness of ¼ inch. Then pile on the extra cheese (within reason).

**Don't Get Smoked Out of House and Home:** This recipe calls for an exhaust fan because there may be some smoke with such a hot stone. Make sure the stone is scraped clean before preheating. If you don't have an exhaust fan and smoke is a problem, choose a lower oven temperature (450°F), and bake about 15 to 20 percent longer. Another option is to bake the pizza on an outdoor gas grill (see ***Artisan Pizza and Flatbread in Five Minutes a Day,*** 2011).

5. Spread the tomato over the surface of the dough with a spoon (smooth sauces apply well with a pastry brush). Do not cover the dough thickly or your pizza will not crisp.

6. Scatter the mozzarella over the surface of the dough, then the eggplant, anchovies, and Parmigiano-Reggiano. If you skipped the anchovies, consider a light sprinkling of kosher salt. No further resting is needed prior to baking.

7. If you have an exhaust fan, turn it on now, because some of the flour on the pizza peel will smoke at this temperature (see sidebar at left). Place the tip of the peel near the back of the stone, close to where you want the far edge of the pizza to land. Give the peel a few quick forward-and-back jiggles and pull it sharply out from under the pizza. Check for doneness in 8 to 10 minutes; at this time, turn the pizza around in the oven if one side is browning faster than the other. It may need 5 or more

minutes in the oven, depending on your pizza's thickness and your oven's temperature.

8. Allow to cool slightly on a cooling rack before serving to allow the cheese to set.

VARIATIONS

**Pizza Margherita:** This is the classic Italian pizza, with nothing but mozzarella, tomato, and fresh basil (substitute a sprinkling of dried oregano for the basil in a pinch, or fresh oregano if you have it). Drizzle with a little olive oil just before baking for authenticity and flavor. A light sprinkle of salt will boost tomato flavor. Try this with in-season fresh tomatoes, drained of seeds and liquid and thinly sliced.

**Sausage or Pepperoni Pizza:** Layer sliced cooked sausage or pepperoni on top of the cheese in a basic tomato and cheese pizza. Rendering the sausage of some if its fat beforehand can make for a crisper crust. No need for extra salt when using sausage or cured meats.

**Caramelized Onion and Manchego Cheese Pizza:** This is a sophisticated combination of flavors, both sweet and savory. Use ¾ cup of caramelized onions (page 181) covered with ½ cup of grated Manchego cheese.

# Rustic Wild Mushroom and Potato Pizza Provençal

*Herbes de Provence* give this rustic creation a luscious flavor that will transport you to the lavender-and-thyme-scented hillsides of the South of France.

***Makes one 12-inch pizza; serves 2 to 4***

½-pound (orange-size portion) Master Recipe (page 53), European Peasant (page 94), Olive Oil (page 214), Light Whole Wheat (page 131), or Italian Semolina (page 143) dough
2 small, unpeeled, red new potatoes, thinly sliced
6 large wild mushrooms such as chanterelles, shiitakes, porcini, portobellos, or oyster mushrooms, or white mushrooms if wild are not available, thinly sliced
2 tablespoons olive oil
1 teaspoon herbes de Provence
Salt and freshly ground black pepper
5 oil-packed sun-dried tomatoes, thinly sliced
2 ounces finely grated Parmigiano-Reggiano cheese
Flour or cornmeal, for the pizza peel

1. **Preheat a baking stone to your oven's highest temperature (550°F or 500°F),** placing the stone near the bottom of the oven to help crisp the bottom crust without burning the toppings. Most stones will be hot enough in 20 to 30 minutes. You won't be using steam, so omit the broiler tray.

2. Prepare and measure all of the toppings in advance. The key to a pizza that slides right off the peel is to work quickly—don't let the dough sit on the peel any longer than necessary.

3. In a skillet over medium heat, sauté the potatoes and mushrooms in the olive oil until the potatoes are soft. Season with the herbes de Provence and salt and pepper to taste.

4. Dust the surface of the refrigerated dough with flour and cut off a ½-pound (orange-size) piece. Dust the piece with more flour and quickly shape it into a ball by stretching the surface of the dough around to the bottom on all four sides, rotating the ball a quarter-turn as you go.

5. Flatten the dough with your hands and a rolling pin on the work surface to produce a ⅛-inch-thick round. Dust with flour to keep the dough from sticking. A little sticking can be helpful in overcoming the dough's resistance to stretch, so don't overuse flour, and consider using a dough scraper to "unstick" the dough. You may also need to let the partially rolled dough sit for a few minutes to "relax" and allow further rolling. At this point, stretching by hand may help, followed by additional rolling. Place the rolled-out dough onto a pizza peel covered with flour or cornmeal (as you get better at sliding your pies off the peel, you can use less flour).

6. Distribute the potatoes, mushrooms, and sun-dried tomatoes over the surface of the dough. Do not cover the dough thickly; the quantity specified will leave some of the dough surface exposed. Finish by sprinkling the cheese over the surface of the dough.

7. If you have an exhaust fan, turn it on now, because some of the flour or cornmeal on the pizza peel will smoke at this temperature (see sidebar, page 218). Place the tip of the peel near the back of the stone, close to where you want the far edge of the pizza to land. Give the peel a few quick forward-and-back jiggles and pull it sharply out from under the pizza. Check for doneness in 8 to 10 minutes; at this time, turn the

pizza around in the oven if one side is browning faster than the other. It may need 5 or more minutes in the oven, depending on your pizza's thickness and the oven's temperature.

8. Allow to cool slightly on a cooling rack before serving to allow the cheese to set.

# Spinach and Cheese Calzone

Traditional pizzerias turn out these folded cheese pies using some of the basic ingredients that appear in pizza (usually without the tomato). Whole-milk ricotta makes for a richer and creamier filling, but part-skim versions also work well. The doubled dough thickness means that you need to bake at a lower oven temperature than used for the flat Neapolitan pizza.

***Makes 1 medium-size calzone; serves 2 to 4***

½ pound (orange-size portion) Master Recipe (page 53), European Peasant (page 94), Olive Oil (page 214), Light Whole Wheat (page 131), or Italian Semolina (page 143) dough
1 large garlic clove, minced
1 to 2 tablespoons olive oil
½ cup fresh or thawed and drained frozen spinach leaves
1 large egg
1 cup whole-milk ricotta cheese
¼ teaspoon salt
Freshly ground black pepper
¼ cup grated mozzarella cheese
Whole wheat flour, for the pizza peel

1. **Preheat a baking stone near the middle of the oven to 450°F (20 to 30 minutes),** with an empty metal broiler tray on any shelf that won't interfere with rising calzone.

2. In a skillet over medium-low heat, briefly sauté the garlic in the olive oil until fragrant. Add the spinach and sauté for 2 minutes, until wilted. Drain and squeeze the spinach, discarding any liquid that may have accumulated.

3. In a bowl, beat the egg and then blend with the ricotta cheese, spinach, salt, and pepper to taste.

4. Dust the surface of the refrigerated dough with flour and cut off a ½-pound (orange-size) piece. Dust the piece with more flour and quickly shape it into a ball by stretching the surface of the dough around to the bottom on all four sides, rotating the ball a quarter-turn as you go.

5. Flatten the dough with your hands and a rolling pin on the work surface to produce a ⅛-inch-thick round, dusting lightly with flour, as needed, to keep the dough from sticking. A little sticking can be helpful in overcoming the dough's resistance to stretch, so don't overuse flour, and consider using a dough scraper to "unstick" the dough. You may also need to let the partially rolled dough sit for a few minutes to "relax" and allow for further rolling. At this point, hand-stretching may also help, followed by additional rolling. Place the rolled-out dough onto a pizza peel liberally covered with whole wheat flour (as you get better at sliding your pies off the peel, you can use less flour).

6. Cover half the dough round with the cheese-spinach mixture, leaving a 1-inch border at the edge, then top the mixture with grated mozzarella. Using a pastry brush, wet the border with water. Fold the bare side of the dough over the cheese mixture and seal the border by pinching it closed with your fingers. Cut three slits in the top crust, using a serrated knife. No resting time is needed.

7. Slide the calzone directly onto the hot stone. Pour 1 cup of hot water into the broiler tray and quickly close the oven door (see page 20 for steam alternatives). Bake for about 25 minutes, or until golden brown.

8. Allow to cool for 10 minutes before serving to allow the cheese to set a bit.

# Philadelphia Stromboli with Sausage

Both of us lived briefly in Philadelphia and fondly remember this local specialty. It's really just a folded pizza made with tomatoes, sausage, and mozzarella. It was brought to the table still puffed from the oven and glistening with olive oil. Unlike calzone (page 223) or red pepper fougasse (page 238), this is a flatbread that is meant to puff exuberantly, like pita bread, so don't slit the top crust prior to baking.

***Makes 1 medium-size stromboli; serves 2 to 4***

½ pound (orange-size portion) Master Recipe (page 53), European Peasant (page 94), Olive Oil (page 214), Light Whole Wheat (page 131), or Italian Semolina (page 143) dough
½ cup canned Italian-style chopped tomatoes, well drained
1 sweet or hot Italian sausage, grilled and cut into ⅛-inch-thick slices
10 fresh basil leaves, torn or cut into thin ribbons (chiffonade)
½ pound sliced mozzarella cheese
Olive oil, for brushing the top
Whole wheat flour, for the pizza peel

1. **Preheat a baking stone near the middle of the oven to 450°F (20 to 30 minutes),** with an empty metal broiler tray on any shelf that won't interfere with rising stromboli.

2. Dust the surface of the refrigerated dough with flour and cut off a ½-pound (orange-size) piece. Dust the piece with more flour and quickly shape it into a ball by stretching the surface of the dough around to the bottom on all four sides, rotating the ball a quarter-turn as you go.

3. Flatten the dough with your hands and a rolling pin on the work surface to produce a ⅛-inch-thick round, dusting lightly with flour, as needed, to keep the dough from sticking. A little sticking can be helpful in overcoming the dough's resistance to stretch, so don't overuse flour, and consider using a dough scraper to "unstick" the dough. You may also need to let the partially rolled dough sit for a few minutes to "relax" and allow for further rolling. At this point, hand-stretching may also help, followed by additional rolling. Place the rolled-out dough onto a pizza peel, liberally covered with whole wheat flour (as you get better at sliding your pies off the peel, you can use less flour).

4. Cover half the dough round with the tomato, sausage, basil, and then the cheese, leaving a 1-inch border at the edge.

5. Using a pastry brush, wet the border with water. Fold the bare side of the dough over the cheese and seal the border by pinching closed with your fingers. Do not slit or slash the dough; stromboli is meant to puff. Brush the top crust with olive oil. No resting or rising time is needed.

6. Slide the stromboli directly onto the hot stone. Pour 1 cup of hot water into the broiler tray and quickly close the oven door (see page 20 for steam alternatives). Bake for about 25 minutes, or until golden brown.

7. Allow to cool for 10 minutes before serving.

# Prosciutto and Olive Oil Flatbread

*"My friend Ralph's mother comes from Naples, and she remembers a bread from her childhood that was studded with pieces of pork fatback. The lard from the pork melted into the bread and created a fantastic rich crumb—it was called* pane di lardo. *Since your local supermarket isn't likely to carry Italian-style pork fatback, we decided to try a more universally loved Italian meat. Prosciutto is an aged Italian ham, but there are tasty domestic versions available as well. Spanish serrano ham is close to prosciutto in style, and can also be used. Rosemary complements the sweet and savory flavors of the meat for a fantastic flavor that goes beautifully with chilled Prosecco, an Italian sparkling wine—it's a sublime appetizer."*—Jeff

***Makes 6 appetizer portions***

1 pound (grapefruit-size portion) Olive Oil dough (page 214)
¼ teaspoon dried rosemary, crumbled, or ½ teaspoon fresh
2 ounces (⅛ pound) sliced prosciutto or serrano ham, cut into 1-inch squares
Olive oil, for brushing the top
Cornmeal, for the pizza peel

1. Dust the surface of the refrigerated dough with flour and cut off a 1-pound (grapefruit-size) piece. Dust the piece with more flour and quickly shape it into a ball by stretching the surface of the dough around to the bottom on all four sides, rotating the ball a quarter-turn as you go. Using your hands and a rolling pin, flatten it to a thickness of about ½ inch.

2. Layer the meat onto the dough round and sprinkle it with the rosemary. Roll up the dough and shape into a ball. Flatten the ball to a

thickness of approximately 1 inch and allow to rest and rise on a cornmeal-covered pizza peel for 40 minutes (see sidebar, page 58).

3. **Preheat a baking stone near the middle of the oven to 450°F (20 to 30 minutes),** with an empty metal broiler tray on any shelf that won't interfere with rising bread.

4. Brush with olive oil (page 104) and slash the top, about ½ inch deep, using a serrated bread knife (see photos, page 59).

5. Slide the loaf directly onto the hot stone. Pour 1 cup of hot water into the broiler tray and quickly close the oven door (see page 20 for steam alternatives). Bake for about 25 minutes, or until richly browned and firm. Smaller or larger loaves will require adjustments in resting and baking time.

6. Allow to cool before cutting into wedges and eating.

# Pissaladière

When Julia Child showed us that much of the French repertoire could be mastered by casual home chefs in *Mastering the Art of French Cooking* (1961), she included a delightful recipe for Pissaladière Niçoise, an onion tart with anchovies and black olives in a rich pastry shell. As served in the South of France, *pissaladière* is often based on a rustic flatbread or pizza base rather than a pastry shell, so we adapted Julia's recipe for our approach. The original called for dry black Niçoise-style olives but we've found we like it just as well with black olives done in the wetter, Greek Kalamata style. We like fresh, bulk-sold olives, but use whatever you like. Pre-pitted olives have a bit less flavor but they're a timesaver. This makes a great summertime hors d'oeuvre, served with dry white wine.

***Makes 6 appetizer portions***

½ pound (orange-size portion) Master Recipe (page 53), European Peasant (page 94), Olive Oil (page 214), Light Whole Wheat (page 131), or Italian Semolina (page 143) dough
3 medium onions, minced
4 tablespoons olive oil
4 parsley sprigs, chopped
¼ teaspoon dried thyme, or ½ teaspoon fresh
½ bay leaf
2 large garlic cloves, chopped
½ teaspoon salt
Freshly ground black pepper
8 canned or jarred anchovy fillets, chopped
16 Niçoise or Kalamata olives, pitted and halved
Flour or cornmeal, for the pizza peel

1. **Preheat a baking stone to your oven's highest temperature (550°F or 500°F),** placing the stone near the bottom of the oven to help crisp the bottom crust without burning the onions. You won't be using steam, so omit the broiler tray.

2. In a skillet over medium-low heat, sauté the onions in olive oil with the herbs, garlic, salt, and pepper to taste until barely browned, about 30 minutes. Do not overbrown, or they will burn while baking.

3. Dust the surface of the refrigerated dough with flour and cut off a ½-pound (orange-size) piece. Dust the piece with more flour and quickly shape it into a ball by stretching the surface of the dough around to the bottom on all four sides, rotating the ball a quarter-turn as you go.

4. Flatten the dough with your hands and a rolling pin on the work surface to produce a ⅛-inch-thick round, dusting lightly with flour, as needed, to keep the dough from sticking. A little sticking can be helpful in overcoming the dough's resistance to stretch, so don't overuse flour and consider using a dough scraper to "unstick" the dough. You may also need to let the partially rolled dough sit for a few minutes to "relax" and allow for further rolling. At this point, hand-stretching may also help, followed by additional rolling. Place the rolled-out dough onto a pizza peel liberally covered with flour or cornmeal (as you get better at sliding your pies off the peel, you can use less flour).

5. Remove the bay leaf and spread the onion mixture and its oil over the dough. Scatter the anchovies and olives on top. If you have an exhaust fan, turn it on now, because some of the flour or cornmeal will burn at this temperature (see sidebar, page 218).

6. Place the tip of the peel near the back of the stone, close to where you want the far edge to land. Give the peel a few quick forward-and-back

jiggles and pull it sharply out from under the pissaladière. Check for browning in 8 to 10 minutes. At this time you may have to turn the pissaladière around to achieve even doneness. It may need up to 5 more minutes in the oven.

7. Cool slightly, cut into wedges or squares, and serve.

# Focaccia with Onion and Rosemary

Here's the ultimate Tuscan hors d'oeuvre, with onion and rosemary topping an olive oil–dough flatbread. Try it with something simple, like rustic antipasto, or as an accompaniment to soups or pastas.

We bake onion focaccia at a slightly lower temperature than usual to avoid burning the onions, and we bake it on a rimmed baking sheet rather than directly on a stone since the oil would leak onto the stone and create an annoying problem with kitchen smoke that would continue into the next several baking sessions.

The key to success with this recipe is to go light on the onion. If you completely cover the dough surface with onions, the focaccia won't brown and the result, though delicious, will be pale.

***Makes 6 appetizer portions***

Olive oil, for greasing a rimmed baking sheet

1 pound (grapefruit-size portion) Olive Oil dough (our first choice, page 214). You can also use the Master Recipe (page 53), European Peasant (page 94), Light Whole Wheat (page 131), or Italian Semolina (page 143) dough

¼ medium white or yellow onion, thinly sliced

2 tablespoons olive oil, preferably extra virgin, plus 1 teaspoon for drizzling

¾ teaspoon dried rosemary leaves (or 1½ teaspoons fresh)

Coarse salt and freshly ground pepper, for sprinkling the top

1. **Preheat a baking stone near the middle of the oven to 425°F (20 to 30 minutes),** with an empty metal broiler tray on any shelf that won't interfere with rising focaccia. The baking stone is not essential when using a baking sheet; if you omit the stone the preheat can be as short as 5 minutes.

2. Grease a baking sheet with olive oil or line with parchment paper or a silicone mat. Set aside. Dust the surface of the refrigerated dough with flour and cut off a 1-pound (grapefruit-size) piece. Dust the piece with more flour and quickly shape it into a ball by stretching the surface of the dough around to the bottom on all four sides, rotating the ball a quarter-turn as you go.

3. Flatten it into a ½- to ¾-inch-thick round, using your hands and/or a rolling pin and a minimal amount of flour. Place the round on the prepared baking sheet.

4. In a skillet, sauté the onion slices over medium heat in the 2 tablespoons of the olive oil until softened but not browned; if you brown them they'll burn in the oven. Strew the onion over the surface of the dough, leaving a 1-inch border at the edge. Allow some of the dough surface to show through the onion, you may have some leftover onion at the end. If you can't see much dough surface, you're using too much onion and your focaccia won't brown attractively.

5. Sprinkle with the rosemary and coarse salt, and freshly ground black pepper to taste. Finish with a light drizzle of the remaining olive oil, about 1 teaspoon, but not so much that it starts dripping off the sides.

6. Allow the focaccia to rest and rise for 20 minutes.

7. After the focaccia has rested, place the baking sheet on a rack in the center of the oven. Pour 1 cup of hot water into the broiler tray and quickly close the oven door (see page 20 for steam alternatives). Bake for about 25 minutes, or until the crust is medium brown. Be careful not to

burn the onions. The baking time will vary according to the focaccia's thickness. Focaccia will not develop a crackling crust, because of the olive oil.

8. Cut into wedges and serve warm.

# Olive Fougasse

Provençal *fougasse* and Italian focaccia share a linguistic and culinary background. It's said that both may have Ancient Greek or Etruscan roots. Fougasse distinguishes itself with artful cutouts that resemble a leaf or ladder; this delivers a crustier flatbread, with lots more surface exposed to the oven heat. As with focaccia, it's best to bake it on a baking sheet to prevent oil from being absorbed into your baking stone (see color photo).

***Makes 6 appetizer portions***

1 pound (grapefruit-size portion) Olive Oil (page 214), Master Recipe (page 53), European Peasant (page 94), Light Whole Wheat (page 131), or Italian Semolina (page 143) dough
½ cup high-quality black olives, preferably Niçoise or Kalamata, pitted and halved or quartered if large
Olive oil, for greasing the baking sheet and brushing the fougasse
Flour, for dusting the board

1. **Preheat a baking stone near the middle of the oven to 400°F (20 to 30 minutes),** with an empty metal broiler tray on any shelf that won't interfere with rising bread. Grease a baking sheet with a bit of olive oil. Set aside. The baking stone is not essential for breads made on a baking sheet; if you omit it the preheat can be as short as 5 minutes.

2. Dust the surface of the refrigerated dough with flour and cut off a 1-pound (grapefruit-size) piece. Dust the piece with more flour and quickly shape it into a ball by stretching the surface of the dough around to the bottom on all four sides, rotating the ball a quarter-turn as you go.

3. Flatten the mass of dough to a thickness of about ½ inch on a work surface dusted with flour and sprinkle it with olives. Roll up the dough, jelly-roll style, then shape it into a ball. Form a flat round approximately ½ inch thick. Because you will need to be able to cut slits into the dough that do not immediately close up and re-adhere to each other, this dough needs to be drier than most; so use flour accordingly. Place the round on a pizza peel liberally dusted with flour.

4. Cut angled slits into the circle of dough (see above photo). You may need to add more flour to be able to cut the slits and keep them spread adequately during baking so they don't close up. Gently pull the holes to open them.

5. Gently lift the slitted dough round onto the prepared baking sheet and brush with additional olive oil. Allow it to rest for 20 minutes.

6. Place the baking sheet with the fougasse near the middle of the oven. Pour 1 cup of hot water into the broiler tray and quickly close the oven door (see page 20 for steam alternatives). Check for doneness at about 20 minutes and continue baking, as needed, until golden brown, which may be 5 minutes longer. Fougasse will not develop a crackling crust because of the olive oil.

7. Serve warm.

# Fougasse Stuffed with Roasted Red Pepper

This is a very festive folded flatbread with a roasted red pepper filling (see color photo). It uses some of the same techniques used in making the olive fougasse, but the dough is folded after slitting, on one side only, to reveal the roasted red pepper layered inside. The rich and smoky red pepper perfumes the whole loaf. It's a fantastic and impressive hors d'oeuvre, sliced or just broken into pieces.

***Makes 6 appetizer portions***

½ pound (orange-size portion) Olive Oil (page 214), Master Recipe (page 53), European Peasant (page 94), Light Whole Wheat (page 131), or Italian Semolina (page 143) dough
1 red bell pepper, roasted and cut into strips (see step 2, page 68, or substitute equivalent amount of jarred roasted red pepper, drained and patted dry)
Coarse salt, for sprinkling
¼ teaspoon dried thyme
Olive oil, preferably extra virgin, for brushing the loaf
Whole wheat flour, for the pizza peel

1. **Preheat a baking stone near the middle of the oven to 450°F (20 to 30 minutes),** with an empty metal broiler tray on any shelf that won't interfere with rising bread.

2. Dust the surface of the refrigerated dough with flour and cut off a ½-pound (orange-size) piece. Dust the piece with more flour and quickly shape it into a ball by stretching the surface of the dough around to the bottom on all four sides, rotating the ball a quarter-turn as you go.

3. Using a rolling pin, form a large flat oval or rectangle approximately ⅛ inch thick. Add a little more flour than usual when cloaking, shaping, and rolling the dough, because you will need to be able to cut slits into

the dough that do not close and immediately re-adhere to one another. Place the dough on a flour-covered pizza peel.

4. Cut angled slits into the dough on only one half of the oval (see above photo). You may need to add more flour to decrease stickiness so the slits stay open during handling. Gently spread the holes open with your fingers.

5. Place the roasted red pepper strips in a single layer on the unslit side of the fougasse, leaving a 1-inch border at the edge. Sprinkle with coarse salt and thyme. Dampen the dough edge, fold the slitted side over to cover the peppers, and pinch to seal. The peppers should peek brightly through the slitted windows. Brush the loaf with olive oil.

6. Slide the fougasse directly onto the hot stone. Pour 1 cup of hot water into the broiler tray and quickly close the oven door (see page 20 for steam alternatives). Bake for about 25 minutes, or until golden brown.

7. Allow to cool, then slice or break into pieces and serve.

## Sweet Provençal Flatbread with Anise Seeds

Provençal bakers are justly famous for their savory flatbreads such as Pissaladière (page 229), but their lesser-known, gently sweetened breads are just as delicious. The anise, which has a distinctive licorice flavor, is a perfect complement to the orange zest.

***Makes four loaves, slightly less than 1 pound each. The recipe is easily doubled or halved.***

| Ingredient | Volume (U.S.) | Weight (U.S.) | Weight (Metric) |
|---|---|---|---|
| Lukewarm water (100°F or below) | 2¼ cups | 1 pound, 2 ounces | 510 grams |
| Orange juice | ½ cup | 4 ounces | 115 grams |
| Olive oil, preferably extra virgin | ¼ cup | 2 ounces | 55 grams |
| Granulated yeast[1] | 1 tablespoon | 0.35 ounce | 10 grams |
| Kosher salt[1] | 1 to 1½ tablespoons | 0.6 to 0.9 ounce | 17 to 25 grams |
| Anise seeds | 1 tablespoon for dough, plus more for topping | — | — |
| Sugar | ⅓ cup | 2¼ ounces | 65 grams |
| Zest of ½ orange | — | — | — |
| All-purpose flour | 6½ cups | 2 pounds | 910 grams |

[1]Can decrease (see pages 14 and 17)

| Ingredient |
| --- |
| Cornmeal or parchment paper, for the pizza peel |
| Cornstarch wash (see sidebar, page 104) or water, for brushing the top crust |

1. **Mixing and storing the dough:** Mix together the yeast, salt, anise seeds, sugar, and orange zest with all the liquid ingredients in a 6-quart bowl or a lidded (not airtight) food container.

2. Mix in the flour without kneading, using a spoon or a heavy-duty stand mixer (with paddle). If you're not using a machine, you may need to use wet hands to incorporate the last bit of flour.

3. Cover (not airtight) and allow to rest at room temperature until the dough rises and collapses (or flattens on top), approximately 2 hours.

4. The dough can be used immediately after the initial rise, though it is easier to handle when cold. Refrigerate the container of dough and use over the next 14 days.

5. **On baking day,** dust the surface of the refrigerated dough with flour and cut off a 1-pound (grapefruit-size) piece. Dust the piece with more flour and quickly shape it into a ball by stretching the surface of the dough around to the bottom on all four sides, rotating the ball a quarter-turn as you go.

6. Flatten the ball with your hands and then, using a rolling pin and minimal dusting flour, roll out into a ½-inch-thick round. Cut the

round into several triangles for an authentic Provençal look, or just form into a single round flatbread, about ½ inch thick.

7. **Preheat a baking stone near the middle of the oven to 450°F (20 to 30 minutes),** with an empty metal broiler tray on any shelf that won't interfere with rising bread.

8. Allow the bread to rest and rise on a cornmeal-covered pizza peel for 20 minutes. Using a pastry brush, paint the surface with cornstarch wash or water and sprinkle with additional anise seeds. If you have shaped a single large loaf, slash it, using a serrated knife.

9. Slide the loaf/loaves directly onto the hot stone. Pour 1 cup of hot water into the broiler tray and quickly close the oven door (see page 20 for steam alternatives). Bake for 15 to 20 minutes, or until richly browned and firm. Smaller or larger loaves will require adjustments in resting and baking time.

10. Allow to cool before eating.

# Pine Nut–Studded Polenta Flatbread

Here's another recipe that plays with some classic Italian flavors: pine nuts, polenta, and olive oil. Polenta, coarse-ground northern Italian–style cornmeal, creates a marvelous texture and crunch, the pine nuts add richness and flavor, and olive oil pulls it all together. You can make this with Broa dough (page 146), but the flavor will be more subtle and the texture less crunchy. The bread is a natural for dipping into hearty soups, or for dips and hors d'oeuvres.

***Makes four loaves, slightly less than 1 pound each. The recipe is easily doubled or halved.***

| Ingredient | Volume (U.S.) | Weight (U.S.) | Weight (Metric) |
|---|---|---|---|
| Lukewarm water (100°F or below) | 3 cups | 1 pound, 8 ounces | 680 grams |
| Granulated yeast[1] | 1 tablespoon | 0.35 ounce | 10 grams |
| Kosher salt[1] | 1 to 1½ tablespoons | 0.6 to 0.9 ounce | 17 to 25 grams |
| Pine nuts | ½ cup | 2.5 ounces | 70 grams |
| Ground polenta meal | ¾ cup | 4½ ounces | 130 grams |
| All-purpose flour | 5¾ cups | 1 pound, 12¾ ounces | 815 grams |
| Olive oil, for brushing the top | | | |

[1]Can decrease (see pages 14 and 17)

1. **Mixing and storing the dough:** Mix the yeast, salt, and pine nuts with the water in a 6-quart bowl or a lidded (not airtight) food container.

2. Mix in the remaining dry ingredients without kneading, using a spoon or a heavy-duty stand mixer (with paddle). If you're not using a machine, you may need to use wet hands to incorporate the last bit of flour.

3. Cover (not airtight) and allow to rest at room temperature until the dough rises and collapses (or flattens on top), approximately 2 hours.

4. The dough can be used immediately after the initial rise, though it is easier to handle when cold. Refrigerate the container of dough and use over the next 7 days.

5. **On baking day**, dust the surface of the refrigerated dough with flour and cut off a 1-pound (grapefruit-size) piece. Dust the piece with more flour and quickly shape it into a ball by stretching the surface of the dough around to the bottom on all four sides, rotating the ball a quarter-turn as you go.

6. Flatten the ball and shape a 1-inch-thick, free-form loaf. Place on a cornmeal- or polenta-covered pizza peel. Press the pine nuts back into the dough if they're peeking out (they will burn if directly exposed to oven heat). Brush with olive oil. Allow to rest and rise for 40 minutes.

7. **Preheat a baking stone near the middle of the oven to 400°F (20 to 30 minutes),** with an empty metal broiler tray on any shelf that won't interfere with rising bread.

8. Slide the loaf directly onto the hot stone. Pour 1 cup of hot water into the broiler tray and quickly close the oven door (see page 20 for

steam alternatives). Bake for about 20 to 25 minutes, or until richly browned and firm. Smaller or larger loaves will require adjustments in resting and baking time.

9. Allow to cool before eating.

# Za'atar Flatbread

*Za'atar* spice has a lemony tang that is a bracing departure from everyday Western flavors. The distinctive taste comes from the ground sumac berries mixed with dried thyme and sesame seeds. You can blend your own or buy it at a Middle Eastern market. If you can't find it locally, try Penzey's Spices by mail order or online, where it is spelled "zatar." To make your own, mix together 1 part ground sumac berries, 2 parts dried thyme, and 1 part sesame seeds.

Don't worry if you end up with a large supply of za'atar spice blend—we have more recipes in the book where you can use it up: Jim's Spicy Kebabs (page 251) and Fattoush, the beautiful Middle Eastern bread salad (page 252).

*"I first had za'atar bread in Minneapolis at an Iraqi grocery. The flavor of the spice mixture was so memorable that years later I returned to find the stuff and bake my own. The shopkeeper smiled at my pronunciation, but I was now the proud owner of a very reasonably priced three-year supply of za'atar."*—Jeff

***Makes 1 flatbread***

1 pound (grapefruit-size portion) Master Recipe (page 53), European Peasant (page 94), Light Whole Wheat (page 131), Olive Oil (page 214), or Italian Semolina (page 143) dough
3 tablespoons olive oil, plus more for greasing the pan
1 tablespoon za'atar spice mix (see headnote above)
Coarse salt, for sprinkling

1. Grease a baking sheet with a bit of olive oil and set aside. Dust the surface of the refrigerated dough with flour and cut off a 1-pound (grapefruit-size) piece. Dust the piece with more flour and quickly shape it into a ball by stretching the surface of the dough around to the bottom on all four sides, rotating the ball a quarter-turn as you go.

2. Flatten the ball into a round, approximately ½ to ¾ inch thick. Place the round on an olive oil–greased baking sheet.

3. Sprinkle the za'atar spice mix over the dough round. Using your fingertips, poke holes into the surface of the dough at approximately 1-inch intervals. It's okay if the holes partially "re-fill" with dough as soon as fingers are removed.

4. Drizzle the oil over the surface of the dough, taking care to fill indentations that remain from your finger-poking (do this even if you've started with Olive Oil Dough). Some of the oil will run off the surface and find its way under the bread. Finish with a sprinkling of coarse salt, which strikingly accentuates the sourness of the za'atar. Use salt sparingly if your za'atar spice blend already contains salt.

5. **Preheat a baking stone near the middle of the oven to 450°F (20 to 30 minutes),** with an empty metal broiler tray on any shelf that won't interfere with rising flatbread. The baking stone is not essential with the baking sheet; if you omit it the preheat may be as short as 5 minutes.

6. After the za'atar bread has rested 20 minutes, place the baking sheet on a rack in the center of the oven. Pour 1 cup of hot water into the broiler tray and quickly close the oven door (see page 20 for steam alternatives).

7. Check for doneness at 15 minutes, and continue baking until medium brown. The baking time will vary according to the thickness of the za'atar bread. Za'atar bread does not develop a crackling crust because of the oil.

8. Cut into wedges and serve warm.

# Pita

Pita bread is the puffy, flour-dusted flatbread of the Middle East (see color photo). It is a simple and elemental bread, and for reasons we can't explain, it's just about our most fragrant one. Aside from being delicious, this bread is among the fastest in the book to make. It's easy to produce beautiful puffed loaves. The secret to the puffing is to roll the dough thinly and use a hot oven. Because pita isn't slashed, steam is trapped inside. As soon as the top and bottom crusts set, steam in the interior pushes them apart. It can't miss! Pita is delicious warm from the oven—unlike loaf breads, it doesn't need to cool completely.

*"My friend Jim became an expert on great pita because his job often took him to the Middle East. He once asked me to prepare pita to accompany a kebab dish he was making—a recipe he'd loved overseas. Perfect: hot and spicy food from the desert, served with pita, in Minnesota in January. We made the za'atar flatbread as an appetizer (page 246), and puffed pita for kebabs. The flavors and smells of the Mediterranean transported us to a different, warmer place."*—Jeff

***Makes one 12-inch pita, or 2 small individual pitas***

½ pound (orange-size portion) Master Recipe (page 53), European Peasant (page 94), Light Whole Wheat (page 131), or Italian Semolina (page 143) dough

Flour, for the pizza peel

1. **Preheat a baking stone to 500°F (20 to 30 minutes).** You won't be using a broiler tray and shelf placement of the stone is not crucial.

2. Dust the surface of the refrigerated dough with flour and cut off a ½-pound (orange-size) piece. Dust the piece with more flour and

quickly shape it into a ball by stretching the surface of the dough around to the bottom on all four sides, rotating the ball a quarter-turn as you go. Place the dough on a flour-dusted pizza peel.

3. Using your hands and a rolling pin, roll the dough into a round with a uniform thickness of ⅛ inch throughout. This is crucial, because if it's too thick, it may not puff. You'll need to sprinkle the peel lightly with white flour as you work, occasionally flipping the bread to prevent sticking to the rolling pin or to the board. Use a dough scraper to remove the round of dough from the peel if it sticks. Do not slash the pita or it will not puff. No rest/rise time is needed. (If you are making individual pitas, form, roll, and shape the rest.)

4. Place the tip of the peel near the back of the stone, close to where you want the far edge of the pita to land. Give the peel a few quick forward-and-back jiggles and pull it sharply out from under the pita. Bake for about 6 to 8 minutes, until lightly browned and puffed. You may need to transfer the pita to a higher shelf (without the stone) to achieve browning.

5. For the most authentic, soft-crusted pitas, wrap in clean cotton dish towels and set on a cooling rack when baking is complete. The pitas will deflate slightly as they cool. The space between crusts will still be there, but may have to be nudged apart with a fork.

6. Serve the pita as sandwich pockets, or with Jim's Spicy Kebabs (page 251). Once the pitas are cool, store in plastic bags. Unlike hard-crusted breads, pita is not harmed by airtight storage.

**VARIATION: PITA BREAD BAKED UNDER THE BROILER**

If you don't have time to heat up a baking stone, just use the broiler. Prepare a heavy-gauge baking sheet, pizza pan, or cast-iron skillet with oil (if your pan is well-seasoned and the dough is well-dusted, you can use minimal oil, or even none at all). Stretch your pita as above, put it into the pan, and broil 4 to 5 inches from the heat source for about 3 minutes, or until puffy and browned. Turn over and continue for about 3 more minutes. The pita will slightly collapse with turning and may singe in places.

**TROUBLESHOOTING PITA THAT WON'T PUFF**

The two likeliest solutions: Roll it thinner, making sure to get it to ⅛-inch thickness. And, make sure your oven's up to temperature, checking with an oven thermometer (see page 23). A longer oven preheat of the stone may help, so consider trying 45 or 60 minutes if you're not getting the puffing you'd like.

# Jim's Spicy Kebabs

Jim re-created the flavors he fondly remembered from the Middle East. The meat combination yields succulent morsels, which are a perfect fit with oven-fresh pita.

***Makes 4 to 6 servings***

1½ pounds ground meat (half lamb and half veal, or all lamb)
2 teaspoons cayenne pepper (decrease or omit for milder kebabs)
2 teaspoons ground cumin seeds
2 teaspoons ground coriander seeds
2 teaspoons freshly ground black pepper
1 teaspoon koshet salt
Ground sumac or mixed za'atar spice (see headnote, page 246), (optional)
1 medium Vidalia, Spanish, red, or other sweet onion, thinly sliced
Fresh parsley, finely chopped
4 to 6 small pitas (or use halved or quartered larger pitas)

1. Mix together all of the ingredients except for the sumac, onions, parsley, and pitas. Cover and let the mixture rest in the refrigerator for 1 hour.

2. Prepare a charcoal fire or preheat a gas grill on medium-low for 15 minutes. Form the meat into elongated patties and grill, without overcooking and turning often, until the kebabs are springy to the touch, about 20 minutes.

3. Fill the pita halves with the patties and sprinkle lightly with sumac. Top with the sliced onions and garnish with chopped parsley.

# Fattoush

*Fattoush* is a Lebanese bread salad that's as wonderful to look at as it is to eat, with all its rich colors and striking Middle Eastern flavors (see color photo). It's related to other Mediterranean bread salads, such as Tuscan Bread Salad (page 97), which is always made with European bread. This Lebanese specialty has some differences from the Tuscan variety. The flavor is defined by lemon juice, mint, parsley, and, if you have it, sumac or za'atar (see Za'atar Flatbread, page 246). The salad calls for Middle Eastern pita bread (page 248), which is used fresh and toasted, rather than stale as in panzanella—stale pitas turn into hockey pucks when you toast them!

***Makes 4 servings***

**The Salad**

3 medium tomatoes, cubed
1 medium cucumber, chopped
1 scallion, sliced into rings
2 large romaine lettuce leaves, torn into bite-size pieces
1/3 cup finely chopped parsley
3 tablespoons chopped fresh mint, or 1 tablespoon dried
2 pitas (page 248), about 6 to 8 inches across, toasted crisp, and cut into bite-size chunks

**The Dressing**

1/3 cup olive oil
Juice of 1/2 lemon
1 garlic clove, finely minced
1 teaspoon salt
Freshly ground black pepper
1 teaspoon ground sumac or za'atar (see headnote, page 246)

1. Prepare all of the ingredients for the salad and place in a large salad bowl.

2. Whisk together all the ingredients for the dressing until well combined.

3. Pour the dressing over the salad and allow to stand for at least 10 minutes, or until the bread has softened.

# Lavash

Armenian *lavash* is believed to be among the world's oldest breads, dating back as many as ten thousand years (see color photo). This simple flatbread is great for mopping up sauces, or to serve with soups and dips.

The small amount of dough goes a long way because it's rolled so thin. There are thicker versions from other parts of central Asia as well as super-thin cracker versions. You can pull lavash from the oven when only lightly browned and still chewy, or let it go a little longer for a crisp cracker. And try experimenting with several doughs—this a very versatile recipe.

***Makes 1 large lavash sheet***

½ pound (orange-size portion) Master Recipe (page 53), European Peasant (page 94), Light Whole Wheat (page 131), or Italian Semolina (page 143) dough

Sesame seeds, for sprinkling the top crust

Cornstarch wash (see sidebar, page 104) or water, for brushing the top crust

1. **Preheat a baking stone near the middle of the oven to 450°F (20 to 30 minutes),** with an empty metal broiler tray on any shelf that won't interfere with rising bread.

2. Dust the surface of the refrigerated dough with flour and cut off a ½-pound (orange-size) piece. Dust the piece with more flour and quickly shape it into a ball by stretching the surface of the dough around to the bottom on all four sides, rotating the ball a quarter-turn as you go.

3. Place the dough on a piece of parchment paper and shape it into a flat round, using your hands and a rolling pin. Continue rolling

out the dough until you reach a uniform 1/16-inch thickness throughout.

4. Brush the top surface with cornstarch wash or water and sprinkle with sesame seeds. Prick the surface all over with a fork to allow steam to escape and prevent puffing. There's no need for resting time.

5. Slide the lavash directly onto the hot stone. Pour 1 cup of hot water into the broiler tray and quickly close the oven door (see page 20 for steam alternatives). Bake for about 5 minutes, or longer for a crisper result. Since the lavash is so thin, be careful not to burn it.

6. Lavash cools quickly, but can be served warm.

# Ksra (Moroccan Anise-and-Barley Flatbread)

*Ksra* is a hearty and satisfying country bread that is virtually unknown in the United States. If you can't get rolled barley or barley flour, substitute whole wheat or rye flour; either will blend well with the anise. Moroccan flatbreads are thicker than lavash and pita. We make ours about the same thickness as our focaccia.

*"I first tasted ksra on a bus in 1987. The bus was 1960s vintage, and it bumped painfully over the Atlas Mountains of Morocco. The rest stops didn't include restaurants, it was freezing at high altitude, and the ride was much longer than billed, so I was starving. At a rest stop, I bought some ksra from a street vendor. If you're going to live through an adventure like this on bread and water for sixteen hours, this is the most delicious way to do it. The heartiness of the barley made it feel like a meal."*—Jeff

***Makes four loaves, slightly less than 1 pound each. The recipe is easily doubled or halved.***

| Ingredient | Volume (U.S.) | Weight (U.S.) | Weight (Metric) |
|---|---|---|---|
| Lukewarm water (100°F or below) | 3 cups | 1 pound, 8 ounces | 680 grams |
| Granulated yeast[1] | 1 tablespoon | 0.35 ounce | 10 grams |
| Kosher salt[1] | 1 to 1½ tablespoons | 0.6 to 0.9 ounce | 17 to 25 grams |
| Anise seeds, whole | 1 tablespoon | ¼ ounce | 7 grams |
| Barley flour or rolled barley | ¾ cup | Flour: 3¼ ounces<br>Rolled: 2½ ounces | Flour: 90 grams<br>Rolled: 70 grams |

[1]Can decrease (see pages 14 and 17)

| Ingredient | Volume (U.S.) | Weight (U.S.) | Weight (Metric) |
|---|---|---|---|
| All-purpose flour | 5¾ cups | 1 pound, 12¾ ounces | 815 grams |
| Cornmeal or parchment paper, for the pizza peel | | | |

1. **Mixing and storing the dough:** Mix the yeast, salt, and anise seeds with the water in a 3-quart bowl, or a lidded (not airtight) food container.

2. Mix in the remaining dry ingredients without kneading, using a spoon or a heavy-duty stand mixer (with paddle). If you're not using a machine, you may need to use wet hands to incorporate the last bit of flour.

3. Cover (not airtight) and allow to rest at room temperature until the dough rises and collapses (or flattens on top), approximately 2 hours.

4. The dough can be used immediately after the initial rise, though it is easier to handle when cold. Refrigerate the container of dough and use over the next 10 days.

5. **On baking day,** dust the surface of the refrigerated dough with flour and cut off a 1-pound (grapefruit-size) piece. Dust with more flour and quickly shape it into a ball by stretching the surface of the dough around to the bottom on all four sides, rotating the ball a quarter-turn as you go.

6. Flatten the dough into a ¾-inch-thick round and allow to rest on a pizza peel prepared with cornmeal or parchment paper for 20 minutes.

7. **Preheat a baking stone near the middle of the oven to 450°F (20 to 30 minutes),** with an empty metal broiler tray on any shelf that won't interfere with rising bread.

8. Slide the loaf directly onto the hot stone. Pour 1 cup of hot water into the broiler tray and quickly close the oven door (see page 20 for steam alternatives). Bake for about 20 to 25 minutes, or until richly browned and firm. Smaller or larger loaves will require adjustments in resting and baking time.

9. Allow to cool, cut into wedges, and serve.

# Chilled Moroccan-Style Gazpacho

Of course, one should not really try to live on Ksra (page 256) and water alone, so here's something to go with our hearty Moroccan bread. We love the light, refreshing coolness of garden-fresh gazpacho on a summer evening, but we wanted a soup that was more like a meal. We borrowed the chickpeas and spicy *harissa* paste idea from Moroccan *harira* soup. And voilà—a smooth, tangy chilled soup with a North African accent!

***Makes 4 servings***

3 ripe medium tomatoes
½ medium cucumber, peeled and roughly chopped
1 red bell pepper, seeded and roughly chopped
2 slices bread
½ small onion, roughly chopped
2 garlic cloves, roughly chopped
2 tablespoons red wine vinegar
⅓ cup olive oil
½ teaspoon ground cumin
1 teaspoon salt
Freshly ground black pepper
3 teaspoons harissa paste (available from Middle Eastern groceries)
¼ cup chopped fresh cilantro
One 15-ounce can chickpeas, well drained

1. Place all of the ingredients except for the chickpeas into the bowl of a food processor and process to the desired consistency; we like ours a bit chunky, but purists will insist it should be smooth—your choice.

2. Add the chickpeas and allow to stand for 30 minutes in the refrigerator. Taste and adjust seasonings just before eating.

# Naan

This delicious and buttery Indian flatbread is traditionally made in a huge cylindrical clay tandoor oven, with the wet dough slapped directly onto the oven's hot walls (see color photo). Our naan is done in a hot cast-iron skillet, or a heavyweight nonstick skillet. Butter or oil (or a mixture) will work in lieu of authentic Indian clarified butter (ghee), but the taste won't be as authentic. You can find ghee at South Asian or Middle Eastern markets.

This recipe also has the distinction of producing the fastest bread in the book, since it's done on the stovetop without an oven preheat (lavash and pita are close seconds). As with many of our flatbreads, there's no need to rest the dough. You can easily make one of these just before dinner, even on busy nights (so long as you have the dough in the fridge). Try it with Suvir Saran's Chilled Yogurt Soup with Cucumber and Mint (page 262).

*"Naan has become my family's favorite bread to make while camping in the woods. All we need is a 12-inch cast-iron skillet on our sturdy Coleman stove to have freshly baked bread. We always attract a crowd of curious campers drawn to the aroma wafting amid the wood smoke."*—Jeff

***Makes 1 flatbread***

¼ pound (peach-size portion) Master Recipe (page 53), European Peasant (page 94), Light Whole Wheat (page 131), or Italian Semolina (page 143) dough
1 tablespoon ghee or oil
Unsalted butter, for brushing the loaf (if ghee is unavailable)

1. Dust the surface of the refrigerated dough with flour and cut off a ¼-pound (peach-size) piece. Dust the piece with more flour and quickly shape it into a ball by stretching the surface of the dough around to the bottom on all four sides, rotating the ball a quarter-turn

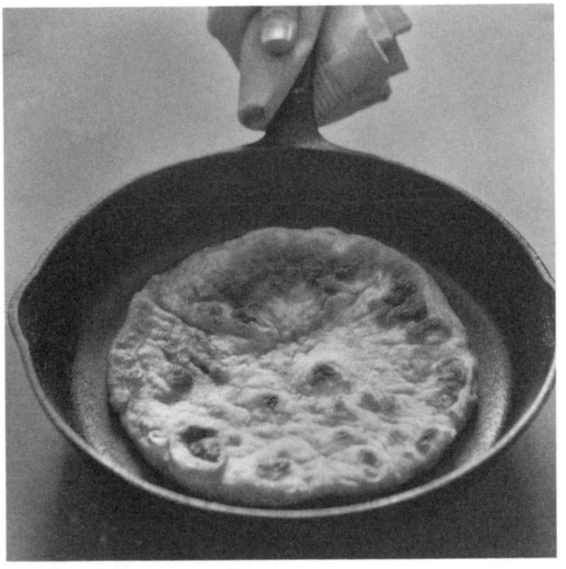

as you go. Using your hands and a rolling pin, and minimal flour, roll out to a uniform thickness of ⅛ inch throughout and to a diameter of 8 to 9 inches.

2. Heat a heavy 12-inch cast-iron skillet over high heat on the stovetop. When water droplets flicked into the pan skitter across the surface and evaporate quickly the pan is ready. Add the ghee or oil.

3. Drop the rolled dough round into the skillet, decrease the heat to medium, and cover the skillet to trap the steam and heat.

4. Check for doneness with a spatula at about 3 minutes, or sooner if you're smelling overly quick browning. Adjust the heat as needed. Flip the naan when the underside is richly browned.

5. Continue cooking another 2 to 6 minutes, or until the naan feels firm, even at the edges, and the second side is browned. If you've rolled a thicker naan, or if you're using dough with whole grains, you'll need more pan time.

6. Remove the naan from the pan, brush with butter if the dough was cooked in oil, and serve.

# Suvir Saran's Chilled Yogurt Soup with Cucumber and Mint

*"My friend, chef and cookbook author Suvir Saran, ingeniously merges very traditional Indian flavors with the most sophisticated modern cuisine. This recipe comes from his sublime book* Indian Home Cooking. *The cool and soothing yogurt, blended with bracing spices, is a provocative way to start off a summertime meal, served with fresh, soft naan, glistening with ghee (see previous recipe)."—Zoë*

***Makes 4 servings***

2 teaspoons cumin seeds
3½ cups plain yogurt
1 medium cucumber, roughly chopped
1 small fresh hot green chili, such as serrano, seeded and finely chopped
½ teaspoon garam masala
1 teaspoon salt
⅛ teaspoon freshly ground white pepper
3 tablespoons roughly chopped fresh mint leaves, plus 12 additional whole leaves for garnish

1. Toast the cumin seeds in a dry frying pan or saucepan over medium heat for 2 to 3 minutes, until lightly browned and fragrant. Grind to a powder in a spice grinder.

2. Reserving a small amount of cumin powder for the garnish, combine all of the ingredients except for the whole mint leaves in a food processor and process until smooth. Scrape the

mixture into a serving bowl. Refrigerate at least 30 minutes, until chilled.

3. To serve, garnish with whole mint leaves and sprinkle with ground cumin, if desired.

# Flatbrød

We developed this quick version of *flatbrød*, a traditional Scandinavian rye crisp bread. It is usually baked unadorned, but in an unorthodox mood we added some Mediterranean zest by topping it with olive oil and coarse salt. Unlike our lavash, it is rolled out paper thin, then baked until crisp and browned. Top with smoked fish, herring, capers, or other Scandinavian delicacies and serve.

***Makes 3 twelve-inch sheets of crisp flatbrød***

½ pound (orange-size portion) Deli-Style Rye dough (page 111), mixed without caraway seeds
Olive oil, for brushing the flatbrød
Olive oil, parchment paper, or silicone mat, for the baking sheet
Coarse salt, for sprinkling

1. **Preheat the oven to 375°F.** A baking stone is not required, and omitting it shortens the preheat. Place an empty broiler tray on any shelf that won't interfere with the flatbrød. Prepare the baking sheet.

2. Dust the surface of the refrigerated dough with flour and cut off a ½-pound (orange-size) piece. Dust the piece with more flour and quickly shape it into a ball by stretching the surface of the dough around to the bottom on all four sides, rotating the ball a quarter-turn as you go.

3. Place the dough on a pizza peel and shape the dough into a flat round, approximately 1 inch thick. Cut the dough into several small pieces and roll out on the pizza peel until it is paper thin, adding all-purpose flour as needed. You should be able to make several flatbrød from your ½-pound piece of dough.

4. Brush the crackers with olive oil and sprinkle with coarse salt. Prick the surface all over with a fork to allow steam to escape and prevent puffing. There's no need for resting time. Place them onto the prepared baking sheet.

5. Place the baking sheet in the oven and pour 1 cup of hot water into the broiler tray and quickly close the oven door (see page 20 for steam alternatives). Check for puffing at 1 minute; if you see any large bubbles popping up, prick them with a sharp fork. Bake for 2 to 5 minutes until richly browned and crisp—it will take longer if you didn't get them really thin.

6. Allow to cool on a rack and break into serving-size portions.

# 8

# GLUTEN-FREE BREADS

When we were writing the first edition of ***Artisan Bread in Five Minutes a Day*** in 2005, neither of us could have predicted the number of people who would soon be following a gluten-free diet. We've since committed to providing easy, fast, and delicious breads for the many folks who don't eat gluten. Bread is such a crucial part of our diet and culture, so we wanted to create a wide variety of gluten-free recipes that would satisfy cravings for everything from a crusty loaf of European white bread, 100 percent whole-grain, braided challah, or sweet brioche (see color photo). These doughs are just as easy to mix up as our wheat versions, but must be handled differently, since there is little of the stretch and structure you're used to. But once you've done it, you may even find that it is easier. You'll find several helpful videos on our website, BreadIn5.com.

## Gluten-Free Master Recipe

This crusty bread will become a staple of your gluten-free diet. It is ideal baked as a free-form boule to serve at dinner, or you can make it in a loaf pan to create perfect sandwich slices. You can also make this loaf egg-free by substituting ground flaxseed, which gives the loaf a nutty flavor.

***Makes four loaves, slightly less than 1 pound each. The recipe is easily doubled or halved.***

| Ingredient | Volume (U.S.) | Weight (U.S.) | Weight (Metric) |
|---|---|---|---|
| Brown rice flour | 1 cup | 5½ ounces | 155 grams |
| Tapioca flour | 3 cups | 13½ ounces | 385 grams |
| Potato flour (not starch) | ⅔ cup | 4 ounces | 115 grams |
| Sorghum flour | 1¼ cups | 5½ ounces | 155 grams |
| Granulated yeast | 2 tablespoons | ¾ ounce | 20 grams |
| Kosher salt[1] | 1 tablespoon | 0.6 ounce | 17 grams |
| Xanthan gum | 2 tablespoons | ½ ounce | 15 grams |
| Lukewarm water (100°F or below) | 3 cups | 1 pound, 8 ounces | 680 grams |
| Large eggs, lightly beaten[2] | 4 | 8 ounces | 225 grams |
| Unsalted butter, melted, or oil | ½ cup | 4 ounces | 115 grams |

[1]Can decrease to taste (see page 17)

[2]Egg substitute: 1 tablespoon finely ground flaxseed mixed with 3 tablespoons water for each egg.

1. **Mixing and storing the dough:** Whisk together the flours, yeast, salt, and xanthan gum in a 6-quart bowl or a lidded (not airtight) food container.

2. Combine the liquid ingredients and gradually mix them with the dry ingredients, using a spoon or a heavy-duty stand mixer (with paddle). **This recipe comes together more easily using the stand mixer.** If you're not using a machine, you may need to use wet hands to incorporate the last bit of flour.

3. Cover (not airtight) and allow it to rest at room temperature until the dough rises, approximately 2 hours.

**Handling the flours and doughs for gluten-free breads:** These flours tend to be very finely ground, and we've found that using volume measuring cups results in varying amounts depending on user technique. Weighing the flours takes care of that; but for bakers who want to use cup measures, just be sure to pack the flour tightly into the cup (this is different from our usual scoop-and-sweep recommendation on page 54). Also, if you find your hand-mixed dough is coming out lumpy, you can put it in a stand mixer, fitted with a paddle attachment, and let it run on high for a minute or two.

4. The dough can be used immediately after the initial rise, though it is easier to handle when cold. Refrigerate it in a lidded (not airtight) container and use over the next 5 days. Or store the dough for up to 2 weeks in the freezer in 1-pound portions. When using frozen dough, thaw it in the refrigerator overnight before use.

5. **On baking day:** Using wet hands, tear off a 1-pound (grapefruit-size) piece. Quickly shape it into a ball; this dough isn't stretched because

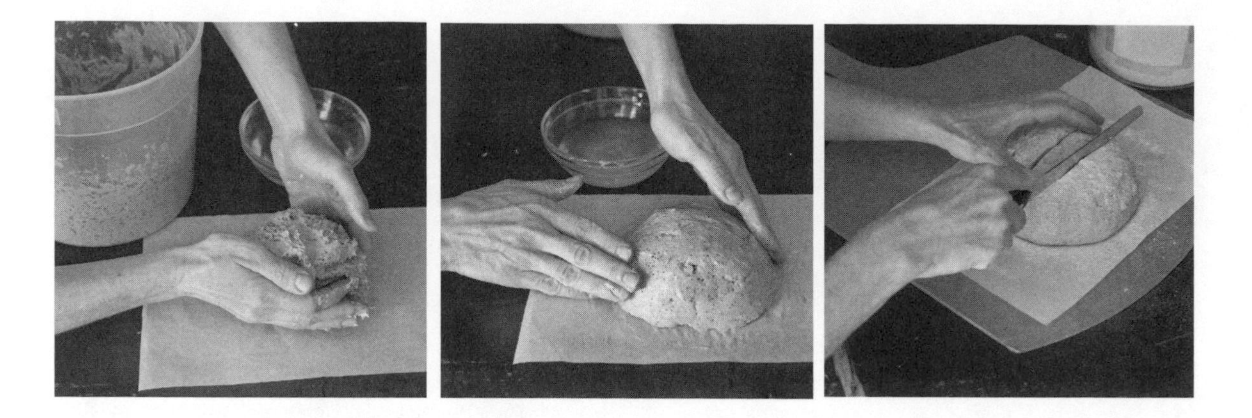

there is no gluten in it—just gently press it into shape and use wet hands to smooth the surface. Allow to rest and rise on a pizza peel prepared with cornmeal or parchment paper for 1 hour (see sidebar, page 58), loosely covered with plastic.

6. **Preheat a baking stone near the middle of the oven to 450°F (20 to 30 minutes),** with an empty metal broiler tray on any shelf that won't interfere with rising bread.

7. Dust the top with brown rice flour and slash the top, about ½-inch deep, using a serrated bread knife (see photos, page 59).

8. Slide the loaf directly onto the hot stone. Pour 1 cup of hot water into the broiler tray and quickly close the oven door (see page 20 for steam alternatives). Bake for about 40 minutes, or until richly browned and firm. Smaller or larger loaves will require adjustments in resting and baking time.

9. Allow to cool on a rack before slicing and eating.

## VARIATION: GLUTEN-FREE SANDWICH LOAF

1. **On baking day,** grease an 8½×4½-inch nonstick loaf pan. Using wet hands, tear off a 1½-pound (small cantaloupe-size) piece of dough. Quickly shape it into an oval; this dough isn't stretched because there is no gluten in it—just gently press it into the shape of an oval and use wet hands to smooth the surface. Place the dough into the prepared pan, smooth top with wet hands, and rest the dough for 90 minutes, covered with plastic wrap.

2. **Preheat the oven to 400°F**. A baking stone is not required, and omitting it shortens the preheat.

3. Using a pastry brush, paint the top of the loaf with water and bake for 55 to 60 minutes until the loaf is browned and quite firm to the touch. Smaller or larger loaves will require adjustments in resting and baking time.

4. Remove from the pan and allow to cool completely on a rack before slicing and eating.

# Gluten-Free Whole-Grain Seeded Bread

This 100 percent whole-grain, gluten-free loaf is made with coconut flour, which adds a touch of sweetness. The seeds give it substance (and crunch), and the brown rice and teff flours make it extra nutritious and delicious. We still don't recommend eating the whole loaf, but in moderation, this bread will fit into your healthy lifestyle.

***Makes four 1-pound loaves. The recipe is easily doubled or halved.***

| Ingredient | Volume (U.S.) | Weight (U.S.) | Weight (Metric) |
|---|---|---|---|
| Brown rice flour | 2 cups | 11 ounces | 310 grams |
| Teff flour | 2 cups | 10 ounces | 285 grams |
| Sorghum flour | 1 cup | 4½ ounces | 130 grams |
| Coconut flour | ½ cup | 2½ ounces | 70 grams |
| Ground flaxseeds | ¼ cup | 1¼ ounces | 35 grams |
| Sesame seeds | ¼ cup | 1¼ ounces | 35 grams |
| Poppy seeds | 2 tablespoons | ¾ ounce | 20 grams |
| Sunflower seeds | ¼ cup | 1½ ounces | 45 grams |
| Granulated yeast | 2 tablespoons | ¾ ounce | 20 grams |
| Kosher salt[1] | 1 tablespoon | 0.6 ounce | 17 grams |
| Xanthan gum | 2 tablespoons | ½ ounce | 15 grams |
| Lukewarm water | 4 cups | 2 pounds | 900 grams |

[1]Can decrease to taste (see page 17)

(continued)

*Panettone,* page 320

Judy's Board of Directors' Cinnamon-Raisin Bread, page 330

Sunny-Side-Up Apricot Pastry, page 348

Brioche à Tête, page 310

Blueberry-Lemon Curd Ring, page 352

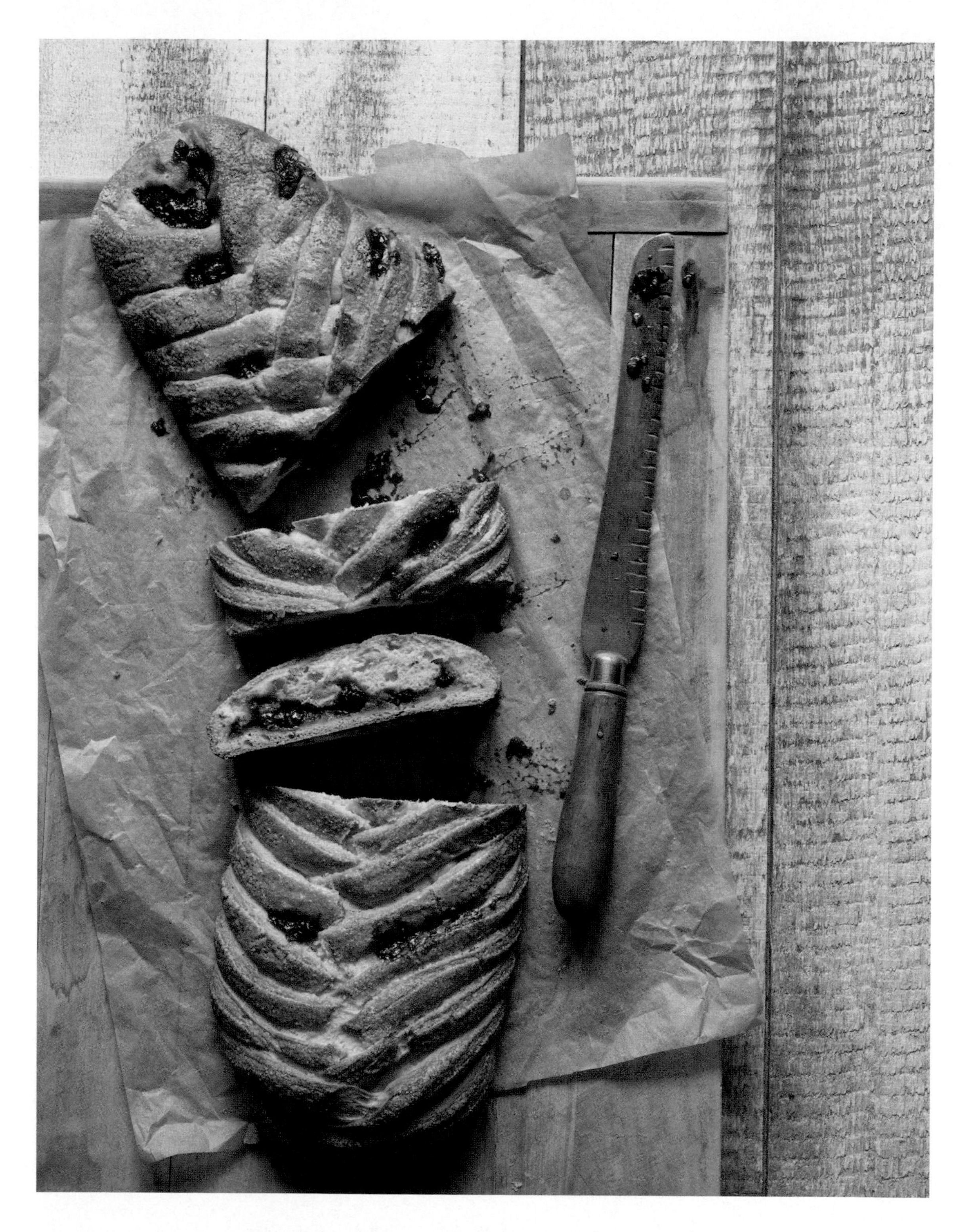

Braided Raspberry–Almond Cream Pastry, page 355

Cinnamon Twists and Turns page 358

Apple-Stuffed French Toast, page 364

| Ingredient | Volume (U.S.) | Weight (U.S.) | Weight (Metric) |
|---|---|---|---|
| Large eggs, lightly beaten[2] | 4 | 8 ounces | 225 grams |
| Oil | ½ cup | 4 ounces | 115 grams |

[2]Egg substitute: 1 tablespoon finely ground flaxseed mixed with 3 tablespoons water for each egg.

1. **Mixing and storing the dough:** Whisk together the flours, seeds, yeast, salt, and xanthan gum in a 6-quart bowl or a lidded (not airtight) food container. See sidebar on page 269 for tips on measuring and mixing gluten-free dough.

2. Combine the liquid ingredients and gradually mix them with the dry ingredients, using a spoon or a heavy-duty stand mixer (with paddle). **This recipe comes together more easily using the stand mixer.** If you're not using a machine, you may need to use wet hands to incorporate the last bit of flour.

3. Cover (not airtight) and allow it to rest at room temperature until the dough rises, approximately 2 hours.

4. The dough can be used immediately after the initial rise, though it is easier to handle when cold. Refrigerate it in a lidded (not airtight) container and use over the next 5 days. Or store the dough for up to 2 weeks in the freezer in 1-pound portions. When using frozen dough, thaw it in the refrigerator overnight before use.

5. **On baking day:** Using wet hands, tear off a 1-pound (grapefruit-size) piece of dough. Quickly shape it into a ball; this dough isn't stretched because there is no gluten in it—just gently press it into shape and use

wet hands to smooth the surface. Loosely cover with plastic wrap, and allow to rest and rise on a pizza peel prepared with cornmeal or parchment paper for 1 hour (see sidebar, page 58).

6. **Preheat a baking stone near the middle of the oven to 450°F (20 to 30 minutes),** with an empty metal broiler tray on any shelf that won't interfere with rising bread.

7. Using a pastry brush, paint the top of the loaf with water. Slash the top, about ½ inch deep, using a serrated bread knife (see photos, page 59).

8. Using a pizza peel, slide the loaf directly onto the hot stone. Pour 1 cup of hot water into the broiler tray and quickly close the oven door (see page 20 for steam alternatives). Bake for about 40 minutes, or until richly browned and firm. Smaller or larger loaves will require adjustments in resting and baking time.

9. Allow to cool on a rack before slicing and eating.

# Gluten-Free Challah

Our gluten-free challah has the delicious flavor of traditional Jewish egg bread, with a lovely texture, and the dough is easy to handle. Braiding a gluten-free challah requires a slightly different approach, but is just as simple. It is also perfect for the holidays when made with raisins and coiled into a turban (see page 304 for shaping the turban).

***Makes enough dough for at least four 1-pound or eight ½-pound challah braids. The recipe is easily doubled or halved.***

| Ingredient | Volume (U.S.) | Weight (U.S.) | Weight (Metric) |
|---|---|---|---|
| Brown rice flour | 1 cup | 5½ ounces | 155 grams |
| Tapioca flour | 3 cups | 13½ ounces | 385 grams |
| Potato flour (not starch) | ⅔ cup | 4 ounces | 115 grams |
| Sorghum flour | 1¼ cups | 5½ ounces | 155 grams |
| Sugar, plus extra for the top | ½ cup | 3½ ounces | 100 grams |
| Granulated yeast | 2 tablespoons | ¾ ounce | 20 grams |
| Kosher salt[1] | 1 tablespoon | 0.6 ounce | 17 grams |
| Xanthan gum | 2 tablespoons | ½ ounce | 15 grams |
| Lukewarm milk (100°F or below) | 3 cups | 1 pound, 10 ounces | 735 grams |

[1]Can decrease to taste (see page 17)

[2]Egg substitute: 1 tablespoon finely ground flaxseed mixed with 3 tablespoons water for each egg.

*(continued)*

| Ingredient | Volume (U.S.) | Weight (U.S.) | Weight (Metric) |
|---|---|---|---|
| Large eggs, lightly beaten[2] | 4 | 8 ounces | 225 grams |
| Unsalted butter, melted, or oil | ½ cup | 4 ounces | 115 grams |
| Rice flour, for rolling | | | |
| Egg wash (1 egg mixed with 1 tablespoon water) | | | |
| Poppy seeds, for sprinkling the top | | | |

1. **Mixing and storing the dough:** Whisk together the flours, sugar, yeast, salt, and xanthan gum in a 6-quart bowl or a lidded (not airtight) food container. See sidebar on page 269 for tips on measuring and mixing gluten-free dough.

2. Combine the liquid ingredients and gradually mix them with the dry ingredients, using a spoon or a heavy-duty stand mixer (with paddle). **This recipe comes together more easily using the stand mixer.** If you're not using a machine, you may need to use wet hands to incorporate the last bit of flour.

3. Cover (not airtight) and allow it to rest at room temperature until the dough rises, approximately 2 hours.

4. The dough can be used immediately after the initial rise, though it is easier to handle when cold. Refrigerate it in a lidded (not airtight) container and use over the next 5 days. Or store the dough for up to 2 weeks in the freezer in ½-pound portions. When using frozen dough, thaw it in the refrigerator overnight before use.

5. **On baking day,** grease a baking sheet or line with parchment paper or a silicone mat. Dust the surface of the refrigerated dough with rice flour and cut off a ½-pound (orange-size) piece. Dust the piece with more flour and quickly shape it into a ball; this dough isn't stretched because there is no gluten in it—just gently press it into the shape of a ball. You will need to use lots of rice flour to prevent the dough from sticking to your hands and the work surface, but avoid working lumps of flour into the dough.

6. **Roll out and stretch the dough:** Flatten the dough with your hands and a rolling pin on a well-floured work surface to produce a ½-inch-thick rectangle, about 8 × 4 inches. Dust with flour to keep the dough from sticking to the surface.

7. **Form the braid:** Using a pizza cutter, cut the dough into three equal strips. Gently braid them by pinching the ends of the strands together, so they are all connected. Pull the left strand over the center strand and lay it down; always pull outer strands into the middle, never moving what becomes the center strand.

8. Now pull the right strand over to the middle. Continue, alternating

outer strands but always pulling into the center. When you reach the end, pinch the strands together.

9. Place the braid on the prepared baking sheet, loosely cover with plastic wrap, and allow to rest for 45 minutes (60 minutes for 1-pound loaf).

10. **Preheat the oven to 350°F**. A baking stone is not required, and omitting it shortens the preheat.

11. Using a pastry brush, paint the top crust with egg wash, and sprinkle with the poppy seeds.

12. Bake for 35 to 40 minutes until browned and firm (50 minutes for 1-pound loaf).

13. Allow to cool on a rack before slicing and eating.

# Gluten-Free Cheesy Bread Sticks

These delicious snacks can be made with many of the gluten-free doughs in this chapter. They're quick and easy to make as a delicious treat in school lunches or as an appetizer, served with our Tuscan White Bean Dip (page 105), for a party.

***Makes eighteen 10-inch bread sticks***

½ pound (orange-size portion) Gluten-Free Master Recipe (page 268), Gluten-Free Whole-Grain Seeded Bread (page 272), or Gluten-Free Challah (page 275) dough
⅓ cup olive oil
2 ounces Parmigiano-Reggiano cheese, finely grated
Pinch of kosher salt
Rice flour, for dusting

1. Prepare a baking sheet by coating it with 2 tablespoons of the olive oil. Dust the surface of the refrigerated dough with rice flour and cut off a ½-pound (orange-size) piece. Dust the piece with more flour and quickly shape it into a ball; this dough isn't stretched because there is no gluten in it—just gently press it into shape. You will need to use lots of rice flour to prevent dough from sticking to your hands and the work surface, but avoid working lumps of flour into the dough.

2. **Roll out and stretch the dough:** Flatten the dough with your hands and a rolling pin on a well-floured work surface to produce a ¼-inch-thick rectangle, about 8 × 10 inches. Dust with flour to keep the dough from sticking to the surface.

3. **Form the bread sticks:** Using a pastry brush, paint one side of the dough with 2 tablespoons of the olive oil. Using a pizza cutter, cut the dough into 18 equal strips, each about ¼ inch wide. Gently pick up each strip and lay it on the prepared baking sheet, leaving about ½ inch between the bread sticks. Allow to rest for 15 minutes.

4. **Preheat the oven to 350°F.** A baking stone is not required, and omitting it shortens the preheat. Drizzle with the remaining 1 tablespoon olive oil, then sprinkle with the cheese and salt.

5. **Slide the bread sticks into the preheated oven:** After 10 minutes flip the bread sticks over, so they will brown evenly. Bake for another 5 minutes, or until they are golden brown.

6. Allow to cool slightly on a wire rack.

# Gluten-Free Pizza

This is the perfect last-minute meal. Just crank up the oven, roll out the dough, add your favorite toppings, and slide the pizza in the oven. In just minutes you have a hot, healthy meal that will satisfy kids and adults alike. The cornmeal and olive oil crust is so delicious, no one will ever know they are eating a gluten-free pizza.

***Makes one 10-inch pizza***

½ pound (orange-size portion) Gluten-Free Master Recipe (page 268), Gluten-Free Whole-Grain Seeded Bread (page 272), or Gluten-Free Challah (page 275) dough
2 ounces Asiago cheese, cut into ½-inch chunks
1½ ounces prosciutto ham, thinly sliced
¼ pear, cored and thinly sliced
½ ounce blue cheese, crumbled
2 tablespoons pine nuts
1 tablespoon olive oil, for drizzling over the top
Pinch of salt
1 teaspoon fresh thyme, for sprinkling on the finished pizza
1 tablespoon honey, for drizzling on the finished pizza
Cornmeal or rice flour, for the pizza peel

1. Prepare the toppings in advance.

2. **Preheat a baking stone to your oven's highest temperature (550°F or 500°F),** placing the stone near the bottom of the oven to help crisp the bottom crust without burning the cheese. Most stones will be hot enough in 20 to 30 minutes. You won't be using steam, so omit the broiler tray.

**No-fail gluten-free roll-out:** If you are having trouble rolling out the dough using rice flour, here's a no-fail trick. You can roll it out between a sheet of parchment paper and plastic wrap. Just sprinkle the parchment paper with rice flour, place the dough on it, sprinkle the dough with more flour, and place a piece of plastic wrap over the top. Roll with your pin to the desired thickness. Check once in a while to make sure the dough is not sticking to the plastic wrap. If it is, just gently lift it up and sprinkle the dough with more flour. Once the dough is the desired thickness, cover it with your toppings, and slide the pizza into the oven right on the parchment paper.

3. Dust the surface of the refrigerated dough with rice flour and cut off a ½-pound (orange-size) piece. Dust the piece with more flour and quickly shape it into a ball; the dough won't stretch—just gently press it into the shape of a ball. You will need to use lots of rice flour to prevent dough from sticking to your hands, but avoid working lumps of flour into the dough.

4. Sprinkle a pizza peel generously with cornmeal or rice flour. Flatten the dough with your hands directly on a pizza peel. Cover with plastic wrap and, using a rolling pin, roll out a 10-inch round. As you roll, shake the pizza peel gently to make sure the dough moves freely. If needed, dust with more rice flour to keep the dough from sticking to the peel. A metal dough scraper is very helpful here; use it to scrape the expanding dough round off the work surface when it sticks. Be sure that the dough is still movable before adding the toppings; if it isn't, sprinkle more rice flour under the dough.

5. **Add the toppings:** Spread the Asiago over the dough, then add the prosciutto. Lay the pear slices out like spokes of a wheel. Distribute the blue cheese, pine nuts, olive oil, and salt over the pears.

6. **Slide the pizza onto the preheated stone:** With a quick forward jerking motion of the wrist, slide the pizza off the peel and onto the preheated baking stone. Check for doneness in 8 minutes and turn the pizza around in the oven if one side is browning faster than the other. It may take a few more minutes in the oven.

7. Allow to cool slightly, preferably on a wire rack. Sprinkle with the thyme and drizzle the honey over the top, cut into wedges, and serve.

# Gluten-Free Baguette

We both love a crusty baguette, so this was an important gluten-free loaf to get just right—light enough so that it melts in your mouth, but with a crispy crust. It may not be traditional, but we like the addition of seeds to the crust. It makes a classic all that much more special.

***Makes 1 baguette***

½ pound (orange-size portion) Gluten-Free Master Recipe (page 268), Gluten-Free Whole-Grain Seeded Bread (page 272), or Gluten-Free Challah (page 275)
2 tablespoons sesame, poppy, and/or flax seeds

1. **On baking day**, using wet hands, break off a ½-pound (orange-size) piece of the refrigerated dough. Quickly shape it into a cylinder; this dough isn't stretched because there is no gluten in it—just gently press it into shape and use wet hands to smooth the surface. Allow the loaf to rest and rise on a pizza peel prepared with rice flour or lined with parchment paper for 40 minutes, loosely covered with plastic wrap (see sidebar, page 58).

2. **Preheat a baking stone near the middle of the oven to 450°F (20 to 30 minutes).** Place an empty metal broiler tray on any other rack that won't interfere with the rising bread.

3. Using a pastry brush, paint the top crust with water and sprinkle with seeds. Slash the loaf with longitudinal cuts that move diagonally across the loaf, using a serrated bread knife.

4. Slide the loaf directly onto the hot stone. Pour 1 cup of hot water into

the broiler tray and quickly close the oven door (see page 20 for steam alternatives). Bake for 25 to 30 minutes until richly browned and firm. Smaller or larger loaves will require adjustments in resting and baking time.

5. Allow the bread to cool completely on a rack before cutting and eating.

## Gluten-Free Sweet Brioche

This is the most decadent of gluten-free breads; it is lightly sweet and made rich with eggs and butter. What isn't there to love? This version of gluten-free brioche is easy to roll out and makes wonderful desserts, such as pecan rolls and apricot pastries from our Enriched Dough chapter.

***Makes enough dough for at least four 1-pound loaves. The recipe is easily doubled or halved.***

| Ingredient | Volume (U.S.) | Weight (U.S.) | Weight (Metric) |
|---|---|---|---|
| White rice flour | 1½ cups | 8½ ounces | 240 grams |
| Tapioca flour | 1 cup | 5 ounces | 140 grams |
| Cornstarch | 4 cups | 1 pound, 6 ounces | 625 grams |
| Sugar, plus extra for the top | 1 cup | 7 ounces | 200 grams |
| Granulated yeast | 2 tablespoons | ¾ ounce | 20 grams |
| Kosher salt[1] | 1 tablespoon | 0.6 ounce | 17 grams |
| Xanthan gum | 2 tablespoons | ½ ounce | 15 grams |
| Lukewarm water (100°F or below) | 2½ cups | 1 pound, 4 ounces | 570 grams |
| Large eggs, lightly beaten[2] | 4 | 8 ounces | 220 grams |
| Melted butter | 1 cup | 8 ounces | 220 grams |

[1]Can decrease to taste (see page 17)

[2]Egg substitute: 1 tablespoon finely ground flaxseed mixed with 3 tablespoons water for each egg.

| Ingredient | Volume (U.S.) | Weight (U.S.) | Weight (Metric) |
|---|---|---|---|
| Pure vanilla extract | 1 tablespoon | ½ ounce | 15 grams |
| Unsalted butter, melted, or oil, for greasing the pan | | | |

1. **Mixing and storing the dough:** Whisk together the flours, cornstarch, sugar, yeast, salt, and xanthan gum in a 6-quart bowl or a lidded (not airtight) food container. See sidebar on page 269 for tips on measuring and mixing gluten-free dough.

2. Combine the liquid ingredients and gradually mix them with the dry ingredients, using a spoon or a heavy-duty stand mixer (with paddle). **This recipe comes together more easily using the stand mixer.** If you're not using a machine, you may need to use wet hands to incorporate the last bit of flour.

3. Cover (not airtight) and allow it to rest at room temperature until the dough rises, approximately 2 hours.

4. The dough can be used immediately after the initial rise, though it is easier to handle when cold. Refrigerate it in a lidded (not airtight) container and use over the next 5 days. Or store the dough for up to 2 weeks in the freezer in 1-pound portions. When using frozen dough, thaw it in the refrigerator overnight before use.

5. **On baking day,** grease an 8½ × 4½-inch nonstick loaf pan. Using wet hands, tear off a 1-pound (grapefruit-size) piece. Quickly shape it into a ball; this dough isn't stretched because there is no gluten in it—just gently press it into shape and use wet hands to smooth the surface.

Place the ball into the prepared pan, loosely covered with plastic wrap, and rest the dough for 1 hour.

6. **Preheat the oven to 350°F.** A baking stone is not required, and omitting it shortens the preheat.

7. Dust the top of the loaf with sugar.

8. Bake for 40 to 45 minutes until the loaf is browned and quite firm to the touch. Smaller or larger loaves will require adjustments in resting and baking time.

9. Remove from the pan and allow to cool on a rack before slicing and eating.

# Gluten-Free Fruit-and-Nut Spiral Rolls

These rolls are inspired by the fruit-studded Panettone bread (page 320) that is traditionally served at Christmas. Our gluten-free brioche is rolled out and filled with dried fruit, almonds, and zest—perfect for the holidays or makes a special wonderful breakfast.

***Makes 12 rolls***

**The Rolls**

1 pound (grapefruit-size portion) Gluten-Free Sweet Brioche (page 286)
2 tablespoons unsalted butter, for greasing pan
¼ cup sugar, for rolling

**The Filling**

1 cup dried or candied fruits, finely chopped
1 tablespoon brandy or almond-flavored liqueur
½ teaspoon grated lemon zest
½ cup (about 2 ounces) almond paste, finely chopped
2 tablespoons sugar

**The Topping**

½ cup almond slices
2 tablespoons sugar
¼ teaspoon ground cinnamon
1 tablespoon unsalted butter, melted

1. **On baking day:** Grease 12 muffin cups with butter and set aside. Combine the dried fruit, brandy, and zest in a small bowl. Set aside while you roll out the dough.

2. Using wet hands, tear off a 1-pound (grapefruit-size) piece of dough. Quickly shape it into a ball; this dough isn't stretched because there is no gluten in it—just gently press it into shape.

3. Sprinkle the ¼ cup sugar on a silicone mat and place the dough on top of the sugar. Cover the dough with a piece of plastic wrap. Using a rolling pin, roll the dough between the plastic and silicone mat until you have a ¼-inch-thick rectangle. Gently peel off the plastic wrap.

4. Distribute the dried fruit and almond paste over the surface of the dough and sprinkle with the 2 tablespoons of sugar. Starting at the short end, roll the dough into a log.

5. Using kitchen shears, cut the log into 12 equal pieces and place them in the prepared muffin pan. Cover loosely with plastic wrap and allow to rest for about 45 minutes.

6. **Make the topping:** Combine the almonds, the remaining 2 tablespoons sugar, the cinnamon, and melted butter.

7. **Preheat the oven to 350°F, with the rack in the middle of the oven.**

8. Distribute the topping over the muffins. Bake for 30 to 35 minutes until the tops are lightly browned and the dough feels set when touched.

9. Allow the rolls to cool for 5 minutes, then carefully lift them out of the muffin pan.

# Gluten-Free Chocolate Bread

Cocoa powder and chopped chocolate make this gluten-free bread intensely flavored and the perfect treat to satisfy anyone with a craving for America's favorite sweet. Because we added just the right amount of sugar, this bread is perfect with a slice of sharp cheese or with a sweetened cream cheese and preserves. You can also try it in our Chocolate Cherry Bread Pudding recipe (page 362).

***Makes enough dough for at least four 1-pound loaves. The recipe is easily doubled or halved.***

| Ingredient | Volume (U.S.) | Weight (U.S.) | Weight (Metric) |
|---|---|---|---|
| White rice flour | 1½ cups | 7½ ounces | 215 grams |
| Tapioca flour | 3 cups | 13½ ounces | 385 grams |
| Unsweetened cocoa powder | 1 cup | 4 ounces | 115 grams |
| Sugar | 1 cup plus extra for top | 7 ounces | 200 grams |
| Granulated yeast | 2 tablespoons | ¾ ounce | 20 grams |
| Kosher salt[1] | 1 tablespoon | 0.6 ounce | 17 grams |
| Xanthan gum | 2 tablespoons | ½ ounce | 15 grams |
| Lukewarm water (100°F or below) | 2½ cups | 1 pound, 4 ounces | 570 grams |

[1]Can decrease to taste (see page 17)

(continued)

| Ingredient | Volume (U.S.) | Weight (U.S.) | Weight (Metric) |
|---|---|---|---|
| Large eggs, lightly beaten[2] | 4 | 8 ounces | 225 grams |
| Oil | 1 cup plus more for pan | 8 ounces | 225 grams |
| Pure vanilla extract | 1 tablespoon | ½ ounce | 15 grams |
| Bittersweet or semisweet chocolate, finely chopped | ¾ cup | 4 ounces | 115 grams |

[2]Egg substitute: 1 tablespoon finely ground flaxseed mixed with 3 tablespoons water for each egg.

1. **Mixing and storing the dough:** Whisk together the flours, cocoa powder, sugar, yeast, salt, and xanthan gum in a 6-quart bowl or a lidded (not airtight) food container.

2. Combine the liquid ingredients and gradually mix them with the dry ingredients, using a spoon or a heavy-duty stand mixer (with paddle). **This recipe comes together more easily using the stand mixer.** If you're not using a machine, you may need to use wet hands to incorporate the last bit of flour.

3. Cover (not airtight) and allow it to rest at room temperature until the dough rises, approximately 2 hours.

4. The dough can be used immediately after the initial rise, though it is easier to handle when cold. Refrigerate it in a lidded (not airtight) container and use over the next 5 days. Or store the dough for up to 2 weeks in the freezer in ½-pound portions. When using frozen dough, thaw it in the refrigerator overnight before use.

5. **On baking day,** grease an $8\frac{1}{2} \times 4\frac{1}{2}$-inch nonstick loaf pan. Using wet hands, tear off a 1-pound (grapefruit-size) piece of dough. Quickly shape it into an oval; this dough isn't stretched because there is no gluten in it—just gently press it into shape and use wet hands to smooth the surface. Place the ball into the prepared pan, loosely cover with plastic wrap, and rest the dough for 1 hour.

6. **Preheat the oven to 350°F**. A baking stone is not required, and omitting it shortens the preheat.

7. Dust the top of the loaf with the sugar.

8. Bake for 40 to 45 minutes until loaf is quite firm to the touch. Smaller or larger loaves will require adjustments in resting and baking time.

9. Remove from the pan and allow to cool on a rack before slicing and eating.

# 9

# ENRICHED BREADS AND PASTRIES

We're pleased to present great sweet enriched breads and pastries made from stored dough. If you keep enriched dough in your freezer, you'll be able to store it for weeks. Then, create terrific morning pastries, coffee cakes, holiday breads, and late-night chocolate fixes on the spur of the moment. Though some of them need a few minutes more preparation than our regular breads, they're all based on dough that will be stored, so the preparation time will be a fraction of what you've been used to with traditional pastries, and you'll have wonderful results.

# Challah

This is the bread traditionally served in Jewish households at the start of the Sabbath on Friday nights (see color photo). But variations of an egg-enriched sweet loaf appear across bread-loving cultures (the French and Italians have Brioche, page 300). The choice of melted butter versus oil definitely changes the flavor and aroma. For an intense and decadent challah, try making it with Brioche dough (page 300); the blast of butter and egg creates an incredibly rich effect.

***Makes four loaves, slightly less than 1 pound each. The recipe is easily doubled or halved.***

| Ingredient | Volume (U.S.) | Weight (U.S.) | Weight (Metric) |
|---|---|---|---|
| Lukewarm water (100°F or below) | 1¾ cups | 14 ounces | 400 grams |
| Granulated yeast[1] | 1 tablespoon | 0.35 ounce | 10 grams |
| Kosher salt[1] | 1 to 1½ tablespoons | 0.6 to 0.9 ounce | 17 to 25 grams |
| Large eggs, lightly beaten | 4 | 8 ounces | 225 grams |
| Honey | ½ cup | 6 ounces | 170 grams |
| Unsalted butter, melted (can substitute oil or melted margarine) | ½ cup | 4 ounces | 115 grams |
| All-purpose flour | 7 cups | 2 pounds, 3 ounces | 990 grams |

[1]Can decrease (see pages 14 and 17)

(continued)

| Ingredient |
|---|
| Egg wash (1 egg beaten with 1 tablespoon of water) |
| Poppy or sesame seeds, for sprinkling the top crust |
| Oil, unsalted butter, or parchment paper, for the baking sheet |

1. **Mixing and storing the dough:** Mix the yeast, salt, eggs, honey, and melted butter, margarine, or oil with the water in a 6-quart bowl or a lidded (not airtight) food container.

2. Mix in the flour without kneading, using a spoon or a heavy-duty stand mixer (with paddle). If you're not using a machine, you may need to use wet hands to incorporate the last bit of flour.

3. Cover (not airtight) and allow to rest at room temperature until the dough rises and collapses (or flattens on top), approximately 2 hours.

4. The dough can be used immediately after the initial rise, though it is easier to handle when cold. Refrigerate the container of dough and use over the next 5 days. Beyond 5 days, freeze in 1-pound portions in an airtight container for up to 3 weeks. Defrost frozen dough overnight in the refrigerator before using, then allow the usual rest and rise time.

5. **On baking day**, butter or grease a baking sheet or line it with parchment paper or a silicone mat. Dust the surface of the refrigerated dough with flour and cut off a 1-pound (grapefruit-size) piece. Dust the piece with more flour and quickly shape it into a ball by stretching

the surface of the dough around to the bottom on all four sides, rotating the ball a quarter-turn as you go.

6. Gently roll and stretch the dough, dusting with flour so your hands don't stick to it, until you have a long rope about ¾ inch thick. You may need to let the dough relax for 5 minutes so it won't resist your efforts. Using a dough scraper or knife, make angled cuts to divide the rope into 3 equal-length strands with tapering ends.

7. **Braiding the challah:** Starting from the middle of the loaf, pull the left strand over the center strand and lay it down; always pull the outer strands into the middle, never moving what becomes the center strand.

8. Now pull the right strand over the center strand. Continue, alternating outer strands but always pulling into the center. When you reach the end, pinch the strands together (see photos).

9. Flip the challah over so that the loose strands fan toward you. Start braiding again by pulling an outside strand to the middle, but this time *start with the right strand*. Braid to the end again, and pinch the strands together.

**Braiding from one end:** You can braid starting at the end of the loaf and go all the way to the other end, but starting in the middle (and flipping) makes for a more even loaf all the way along.

10. If the braid is oddly shaped, fix it by nudging and stretching. Place on the prepared baking sheet, and allow to rest and rise for 90 minutes (see sidebar, page 58).

11. **Preheat the oven to 350°F.** A baking stone is not required, and omitting it shortens the preheat.

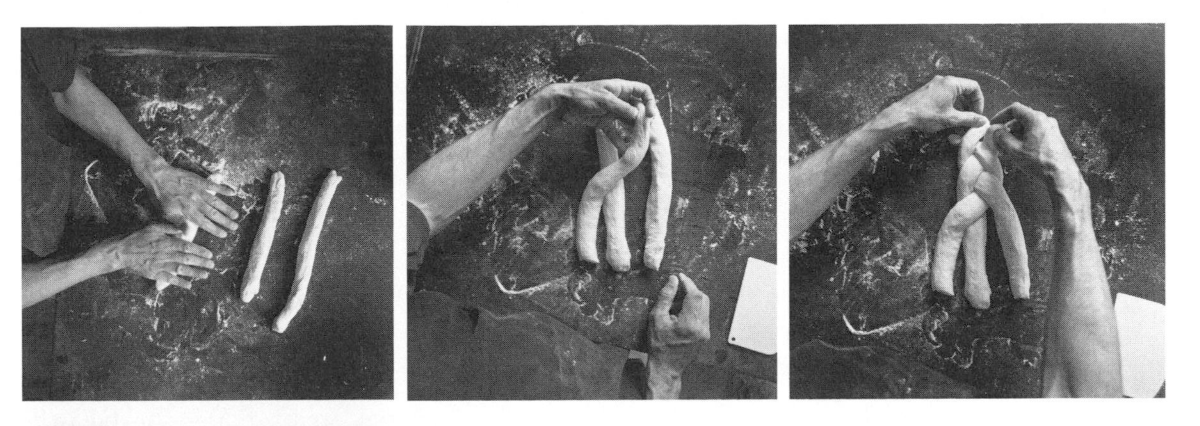

Using a pastry brush, paint the loaf with egg wash and sprinkle with the seeds.

**12.** Bake near the middle of the oven for about 30 minutes. Smaller or larger loaves will require adjustments in baking time. The challah is done when golden brown, and the braids near the center of the loaf offer resistance to pressure. Due to the fat in the dough, challah will not form a hard, crackling crust.

**13.** Allow to cool on a rack before slicing and eating.

# Brioche

The doomed Marie Antoinette is often quoted as saying *"qu'ils mangent de la brioche,"* which means "let them eat brioche," not "let them eat cake—*gâteau*!" Historians have doubts about the true author of this quote, but in any case it was brioche on their minds and not cake.

Brioche can be enjoyed as a sweet bread with tea, as a breakfast pastry, or even as a flatbread base for savory toppings. Brioche is rich with butter, eggs, and a touch of honey. It is perfect no matter its shape—baked in a simple loaf pan or as a Brioche à Tête (page 310)—and it is the inspiration for many of our pastry recipes.

***Makes enough dough for at least three 1½-pound loaves. The recipe is easily doubled or halved.***

| Ingredient | Volume (U.S.) | Weight (U.S.) | Weight (Metric) |
|---|---|---|---|
| Lukewarm water (100°F or below) | 1½ cups | 12 ounces | 340 grams |
| Granulated yeast[1] | 1 tablespoon | 0.35 ounce | 10 grams |
| Kosher salt[1] | 1 to 1½ tablespoons | 0.6 to 0.9 ounce | 17 to 25 grams |
| Large eggs, lightly beaten | 8 | 1 pound | 455 grams |
| Honey | ½ cup | 6 ounces | 170 grams |
| Unsalted butter, melted, plus butter for greasing the pan | 1½ cups (3 sticks) | 12 ounces | 340 grams |

[1]Can decrease (see pages 14 and 17)

| Ingredient | Volume (U.S.) | Weight (U.S.) | Weight (Metric) |
|---|---|---|---|
| All-purpose flour | 7½ cups | 2 pounds, 5½ ounces | 1,065 grams |
| Egg wash (1 egg beaten with 1 tablespoon of water) | | | |

1. Mix the yeast, salt, eggs, honey, and melted butter with the water in a 6-quart bowl or a lidded (not airtight) food container.

2. Mix in the flour without kneading, using a spoon or a heavy-duty stand mixer (with paddle). If you're not using a machine, you may need to use wet hands to incorporate the last bit of flour. The dough will be loose but will firm up when chilled; don't try to work with it before chilling. (You may notice lumps in the dough but they will disappear in the finished products.)

3. Cover (not airtight) and allow to rest at room temperature for 2 hours, then refrigerate.

4. The dough can be used as soon as it's thoroughly chilled, at least 3 hours. Refrigerate the container of dough and use over the next 5 days. Beyond 5 days, freeze the dough in 1-pound portions in an airtight container for up to 2 weeks. When using frozen dough, thaw in the refrigerator for 24 hours before using, then allow the usual rest and rise times.

5. **On baking day,** grease an 8½ × 4½-inch nonstick loaf pan. Dust the surface of the refrigerated dough with flour and cut off a 1½-pound (small cantaloupe-size) piece. Dust the piece with more flour and quickly shape it into a ball by stretching the surface of the dough

around to the bottom on all four sides, rotating the ball a quarter-turn as you go.

6. Elongate into an oval and place in the prepared pan. Allow to rest for 90 minutes, loosely covered with plastic wrap.

7. **Preheat the oven to 350°F.** A baking stone is not required, and omitting it shortens the preheat.

8. Using a pastry brush, glaze the top of the loaf with egg wash.

9. Place the pan near the center of the oven and bake for 45 to 50 minutes until medium golden brown and well set. Brioche will not form a hard, crackling crust.

10. Allow to cool on a rack before slicing.

**Dare we suggest kneading?** Yes, we said the dreaded ***K*** word. Because brioche is intended to have a tighter crumb than regular breads, a little kneading won't harm things. To get a bit more stretch in this dough, you can knead for as little as 30 seconds to really improve the texture. Just take the ball of dough and fold it over on itself several times on a floured surface, using the ball of your hand. The dough may need to rest for 10 minutes before you can roll it out easily.

# Turban-Shaped Challah with Raisins

Turban-Shaped Raisin Challah (see color photo) is served at the Jewish New Year, but similar enriched and fruited egg breads are part of holiday traditions all over the Western world, calling to mind the richer Italian Panettone, served at Christmas (page 320).

We've assumed in this recipe that you're using stored challah dough and rolling the raisins into it. If you're starting a batch of dough just for raisin challah, add a cup of raisins to the yeasted water when mixing.

***Makes 1 raisin challah***

1 pound (grapefruit-size portion) of Challah (page 296) or Brioche (page 300) dough, defrosted overnight in refrigerator if frozen
Unsalted butter, for greasing baking sheet
¼ cup raisins
Egg wash (1 egg beaten with 1 tablespoon of water)
Sesame seeds, for sprinkling the top

1. Defrost the dough overnight in the refrigerator if frozen.

2. **On baking day,** grease a baking sheet or line with parchment paper or a silicone mat. Dust the surface of the refrigerated dough with flour and cut off a 1-pound (grapefruit-size) piece. Dust the piece with more flour and quickly shape it into a ball by stretching the surface of the dough around to the bottom on all four sides, rotating the ball a quarter-turn as you go.

3. Using a rolling pin and minimal dusting flour, roll out the dough to a thickness of ½ inch. Sprinkle with the raisins and roll into a log.

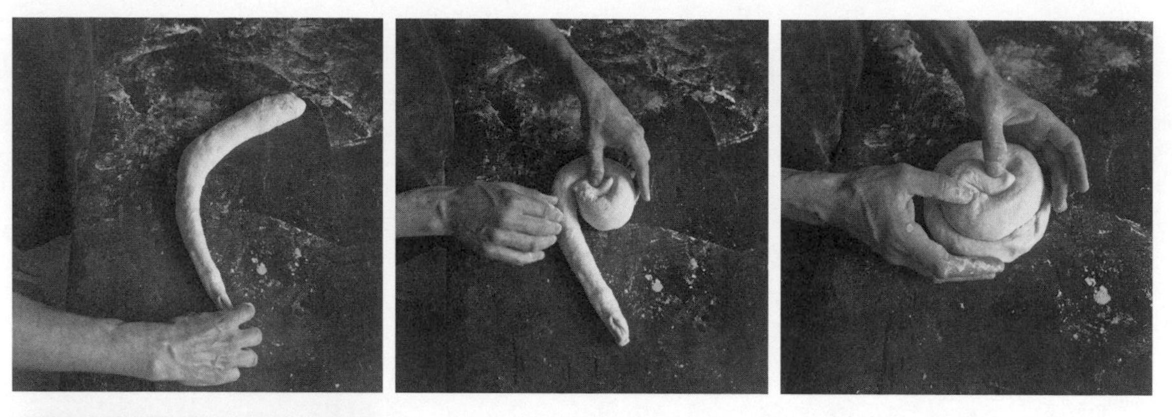

4. Rolling the dough between your hands and stretching it, form a single long, thin rope, tapering it at one end. If the dough resists shaping, let it rest for 5 minutes and try again.

5. Starting with the thick end of the rope, begin forming a coil on the prepared baking sheet. When you have finished coiling, pinch the thin end under the loaf. Allow to rest and rise for 90 minutes (see sidebar, page 58) loosely covered with plastic.

6. **Preheat the oven to 350°F.** A baking stone is not required, and omitting it shortens the preheat.

7. Using a pastry brush, paint the loaf with egg wash and sprinkle with seeds, and place in the center of the oven. Bake for about 30 minutes. The challah is done when golden brown and the center of the loaf offers resistance to pressure. Smaller or larger loaves will require adjustments in baking time. Due to the fat in the dough, challah will not form a hard, crackling crust.

8. Allow to cool on a rack before slicing and eating.

# John Barrymore Onion Pletzel

*"Pletzel"* or *"pletzl"* is a Yiddish word meaning "board." It was a savory flatbread widely available in Jewish bakeries until about thirty years ago. The pletzel flavors are a unique blend of onions and poppy seeds baked onto enriched and slightly sweetened dough. It is an Eastern European savory treat that is unforgettable when served with pot-roasted meats. Pletzel is perfect for mopping up that home-style gravy. Use the optional egg wash if you want to achieve a rich yellow color under the onions (see color photo).

*"For reasons that are to this day unknown, my grandfather called this bread 'John Barrymore Pletzel.' It's too bad I didn't ask him about it during his lifetime. I can't find any connection between the actor John Barrymore and any bread, let alone pletzel. This is one of my most vivid flavor memories from childhood. Twenty years elapsed between the last time I ate it and the first time I baked it, but the flavor is exactly what I recalled."*—Jeff

***Makes 2 pletzels***

1 pound (grapefruit-size portion) of Challah (page 296) or Brioche (page 300) dough, defrosted overnight in refrigerator if frozen
1½ tablespoons oil or unsalted butter, plus more for greasing the pan
1 small onion, thinly sliced
2 teaspoons poppy seeds
¼ teaspoon kosher salt
Optional: Egg wash (1 egg beaten with 1 tablespoon of water)

1. **On baking day,** grease a baking sheet or line with parchment paper or a silicone mat. Set aside. Dust the surface of the refrigerated dough with flour and cut off a 1-pound (grapefruit-size) piece. Dust the piece with more flour and quickly shape it into a ball by stretching the surface of

the dough around to the bottom on all four sides, rotating the ball a quarter-turn as you go.

2. Using a rolling pin or your hands, flatten the dough to a thickness of ½ inch and place on the prepared baking sheet. (Alternatively, press the unrolled dough into a well-greased, 9 × 9-inch square, nonstick baking pan.) Allow to rest and rise 20 minutes.

3. **Preheat the oven to 350°F.** A baking stone is not required, and omitting it shortens the preheat.

4. Meanwhile, in a skillet over medium heat, sauté the onion slices in the oil or butter until they just begin to color; do not overbrown, or they will burn when in the oven.

5. If you're using the egg wash, paint it onto the surface of the dough with a pastry brush.

6. Strew the onions onto the pletzel and drizzle oil or butter over them (don't completely cover the surface with onions or the pletzel won't brown well). Finish by sprinkling the poppy seeds and salt over the onions.

7. After the pletzel has rested, place the baking sheet in the center of the oven. Bake for 15 to 20 minutes, until the pletzel has browned but the onions are not burned.

8. Allow to cool, then cut into pieces and serve.

# Sticky Pecan Caramel Rolls

This crowd-pleaser was our first attempt to make dessert from stored bread dough (see color photos). Stored bread dough? For dessert? We were skeptical, but our first attempt with sweet enriched dough, caramel, toasted nuts, and spices was so successful that it reshaped our view of what this cookbook would be. We've even used the Master Recipe (page 53) for this recipe, and it works beautifully. The butter and sugar spiraled into the dough make even the non-enriched doughs taste like dessert.

***Makes 6 to 8 large caramel rolls***

**The Dough**

1½ pounds (small cantaloupe-size portion) Challah (page 296), Brioche (page 300), or Master Recipe (page 53) dough, defrosted overnight in the refrigerator if frozen

**The Caramel Topping and Filling**

¾ cup (1½ sticks) unsalted butter, melted, plus more for sides of pan
1¼ cup brown sugar, well packed
⅓ cup honey
1 teaspoon ground cinnamon
¼ teaspoon freshly grated nutmeg
½ teaspoon salt
Pinch of freshly ground black pepper
2 cups whole toasted pecans

1. **On baking day,** mix together the butter, brown sugar, honey, cinnamon, nutmeg, salt, and pepper. Grease a 9-inch cake pan with butter, then spread half the caramel mixture evenly over the bottom. Scatter half the whole pecans over the caramel mixture and set aside.

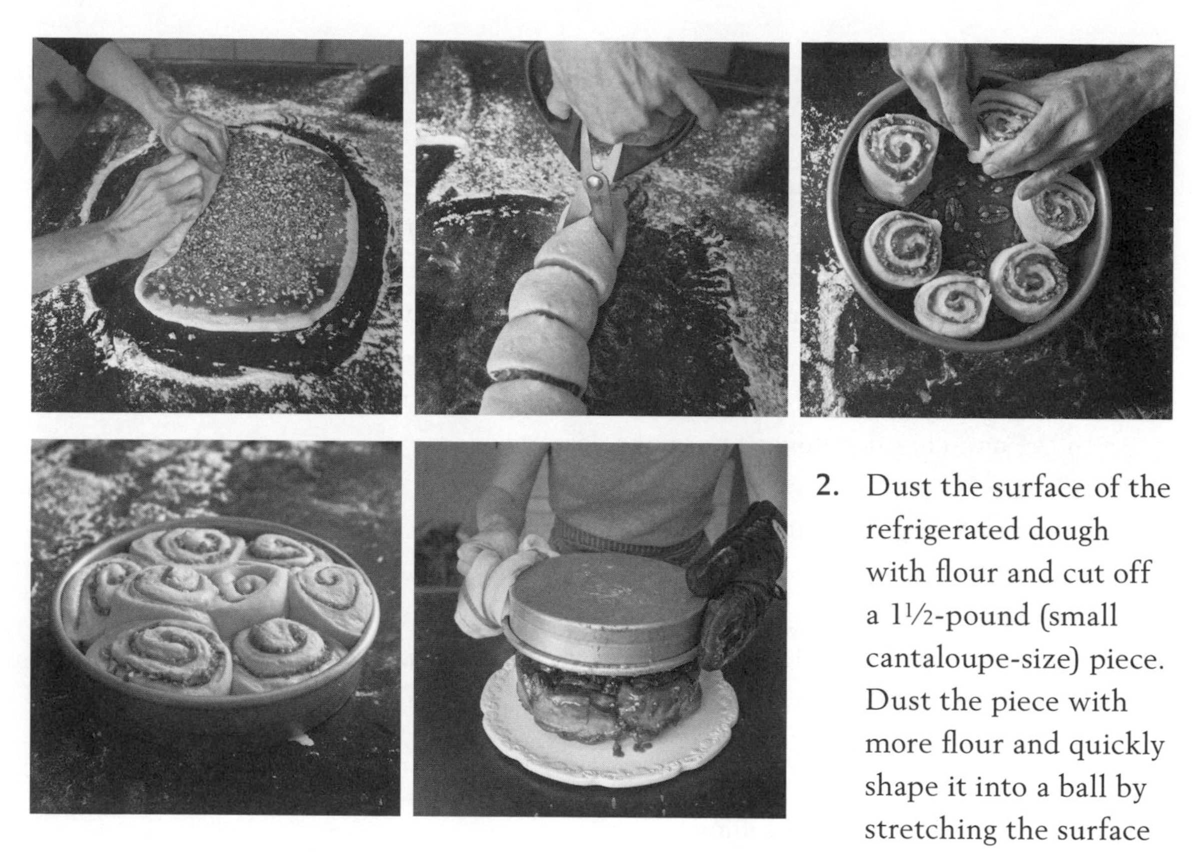

2. Dust the surface of the refrigerated dough with flour and cut off a 1½-pound (small cantaloupe-size) piece. Dust the piece with more flour and quickly shape it into a ball by stretching the surface of the dough around to the bottom on all four sides, rotating the ball a quarter-turn as you go.

3. Roll out the dough to an ⅛-inch-thick rectangle. As you roll out the dough, use enough flour to prevent it from sticking to the work surface but not so much as to make the dough dry.

4. Spread the remaining caramel mixture evenly over the rolled-out dough, then finely chop the remaining nuts and sprinkle them over the top. Starting with the long side, roll the dough into a log and pinch the seam closed.

5. Using a very sharp serrated knife or kitchen shears, cut the log into 8

equal pieces and arrange over the pecans in the prepared pan, so that the swirled cut edge is facing upward. Allow to rest for 1 hour, loosely covered with plastic wrap.

6. **Preheat the oven to 350°F.** A baking stone is not required, and omitting it shortens the preheat.

7. Place the pan on a baking sheet, in case the caramel bubbles over, and bake about 40 minutes, or until golden brown and well set in center. While still hot, run a knife around the outer edge of the pan to release the caramel rolls, and invert immediately onto a serving dish. If you let them set too long they will stick to the pan and will be difficult to turn out.

# Brioche à Tête

*Brioche à tête* is a traditional French bread, baked in a beautifully fluted pan and sporting an extra little ball of dough at the top (the *tête,* or head—see color photo). Your guests will think you slaved over this one. The shape is ubiquitous in Parisian shops but quite rare elsewhere.

***Makes 1 loaf***

1 pound (grapefruit-size portion) Brioche dough (page 300), defrosted overnight in the refrigerator if frozen
Unsalted butter or oil, for greasing the pan
Egg wash (1 egg beaten with 1 tablespoon of water)

1. Grease an 8-inch fluted brioche pan.

2. Dust the surface of the refrigerated dough with flour and cut off a 1-pound (grapefruit-size) piece. Break off about an eighth of the dough to form the tête (head) and set it aside. Dust the large piece with more flour and quickly shape it into a ball by stretching the surface of the dough around to the bottom on all four sides, rotating the ball a quarter-turn as you go.

3. Place the larger ball into the prepared pan, seam side down; the pan should be about half full. Poke a fairly deep indentation in the top of this ball of dough. This is where you will attach the tête.

4. Quickly shape the small piece into a teardrop shape by rounding one end and tapering the other. Place the teardrop, pointed side down, into the indentation of the dough in the pan and pinch the two together gently but firmly to ensure the tête stays attached during baking.

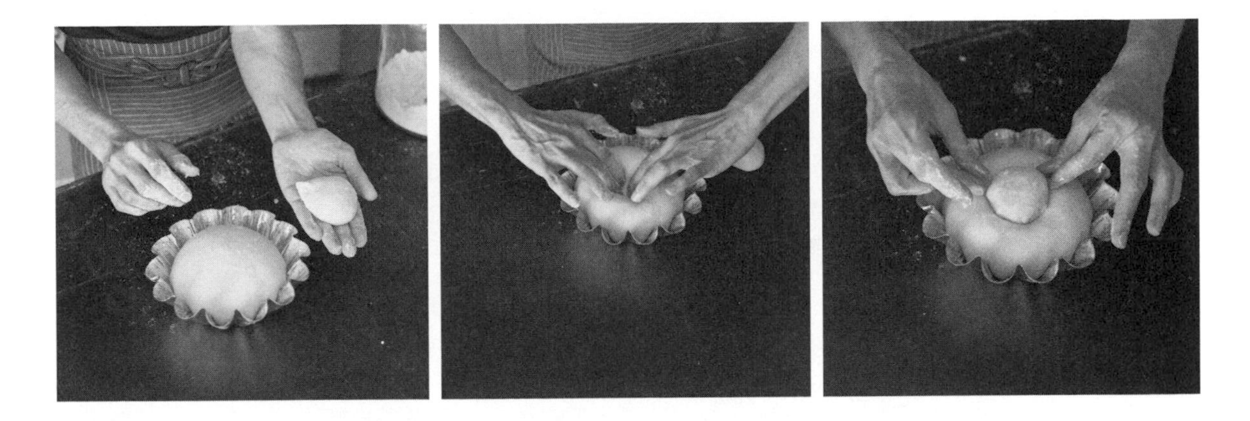

5. Allow to rest at room temperature for 90 minutes, loosely covered with plastic wrap.

6. **Preheat the oven to 350°F.** A baking stone is not required, and omitting it shortens the preheat.

7. Using a pastry brush, glaze the loaf with egg wash and place it in the center of the oven. Bake for about 45 minutes, or until golden brown and well set. Smaller or larger loaves will require adjustments in resting and baking times.

8. Immediately remove from mold and cool on a rack.

# Almond Brioche (Bostock)

We adore *Bostock* with its combination of buttery brioche, almond cream, and orange zest–infused sugar (see color photo). The traditional method involves baking brioche, slicing it, topping the slices with almond cream and re-baking it. But that's just too much work for our five-minutes-a-day philosophy. We wanted the flavors without the extra work, so we rolled the filling into the dough and baked it just once.

***Makes 1 loaf***

**The Dough**

1½ pounds (small cantaloupe-size portion) Brioche (page 300) or Challah (page 296) dough, defrosted overnight in the refrigerator if frozen

**Almond Cream**

4 tablespoons (½ stick) unsalted butter, at room temperature
½ cup almond paste
¼ cup all-purpose flour
1 large egg
¼ teaspoon orange-flower water (optional)
¼ teaspoon almond extract

¼ cup sugar, plus more for dusting the greased pan
Grated zest of half an orange
½ cup sliced natural (raw and unsalted) almonds
Butter or oil for greasing the pan

1. **Make the almond cream:** Cream together the butter, almond paste, flour, egg, orange-flower water, and almond extract in a food processor until smooth and well combined. Set aside.

2. **Assemble the brioche:** Dust the surface of the refrigerated dough with flour and cut off a 1½-pound (small cantaloupe-size) piece. Dust the piece with more flour and quickly shape it into a ball by stretching the surface of the dough around to the bottom on all four sides, rotating the ball a quarter-turn as you go.

3. Roll out the ball into a ¼-inch-thick rectangle. As you roll out the dough, use enough flour to prevent it from sticking to the work surface but not so much as to make the dough dry.

4. Spread the almond cream evenly over the rectangle, leaving a 1-inch border all around. Roll up the dough, jelly-roll style, starting at the long end, and being sure to seal the seam and the ends.

5. Generously grease a 9-inch round springform pan with butter. Sprinkle the greased pan with a dusting of granulated sugar.

6. Cut the dough into 8 equal pieces with kitchen shears. Place them evenly in the prepared cake pan so that the swirled cut edge is facing upward. Allow the dough to rest for 1 hour, loosely covered with plastic wrap.

7. **Preheat the oven to 350°F.** A baking stone is not required, and omitting it shortens the preheat.

8. Mix together sugar, orange zest, and almonds and sprinkle over the brioche. Place the springform pan on a baking sheet, to catch any drips, and bake without steam until golden brown and well set in the center, about 40 minutes.

9. Run a knife around the edge of the pan to release the brioche while it is still hot and transfer to a serving dish. If you let it set too long it will stick to the pan and will be difficult to turn out. Eat warm.

# Brioche Filled with Chocolate Ganache

This is the closest you'll ever get to the aroma of a Paris pastry shop in your own kitchen. The rich brioche and smooth ganache is like eating a *pain au chocolat,* without all the fuss and time. It makes a great treat for after meals or as a decadent breakfast with a cup of coffee.

***Makes 1 loaf***

1 pound (grapefruit-size portion) Brioche dough (page 300), defrosted overnight in the refrigerator if frozen
¼ pound bittersweet chocolate, finely chopped
2 tablespoons unsalted butter, plus more for greasing the pan
4 teaspoons unsweetened cocoa powder
1 tablespoon rum
¼ cup corn syrup
Egg wash (1 egg beaten with 1 tablespoon water)
Granulated sugar, for sprinkling the top

1. **Make the ganache:** Melt the chocolate over a double boiler or in the microwave on low. Remove from heat, add the butter, and stir until smooth. Add the cocoa powder, rum, and corn syrup to the chocolate mixture and whisk until smooth.

2. **Assemble the brioche:** Grease an 8½ × 4½-inch nonstick loaf pan. Dust the surface of the refrigerated dough with flour and cut off a 1-pound (grapefruit-size) piece. Dust the piece with more flour and quickly shape it into a ball by stretching the surface of the dough around to the bottom on all four sides, rotating the ball a quarter-turn as you go.

3. Roll out the ball into a ¼-inch-thick rectangle, dusting with flour as needed. Spread ⅓ cup of the ganache evenly over the rectangle, leaving a 1-inch border all around. Starting at the long end, roll up the dough and pinch the seam to seal.

4. Tuck the ends underneath the loaf and drop into the prepared pan. Allow to rest 90 minutes, loosely covered with plastic wrap.

5. **Preheat the oven to 350°F.** A baking stone is not required, and omitting it shortens the preheat. Using a pastry brush, paint the top crust with egg wash. Sprinkle lightly with granulated sugar.

6. Bake the brioche for about 45 minutes, or until the top is golden brown and the sugar caramelizes.

7. Remove from the pan and cool completely; then drizzle the remaining ganache over the top crust.

# Beignets

*Beignet* is French for "fritter," or as we Americans like to call them, doughnuts. They're made from rich, yeasted dough, fried in oil, and then covered generously in confectioners' sugar. What's not to love? Here's a re-creation, using our simple recipe, of the sweet confection made famous by Café Du Monde in New Orleans.

*"A while ago, my husband and I went to New Orleans for a long weekend. Our first stop in town was Café Du Monde. After two orders of fluffy hot beignets and plenty of café au lait, we were covered in confectioners' sugar and ready to find some jazz. We managed to return to Café Du Monde at least once every day during our stay."*—Zoë

***Makes 5 or 6 beignets***

1 pound (grapefruit-size portion) Challah (page 296) or Brioche (page 300) dough, defrosted overnight in the refrigerator if frozen
Vegetable oil, for deep-frying
Confectioners' sugar, for dusting

**Equipment**
Deep saucepan for deep-frying, or an electric deep fryer
Slotted spoon
Paper towels
Candy thermometer

1. Dust the surface of the refrigerated dough with flour and cut off a 1-pound (grapefruit-size) piece. Dust the piece with more flour and quickly shape it into a ball by stretching the surface of the dough around to the bottom on all four sides, rotating the ball a quarter-turn as you go.

2. Roll the dough into a ½-inch-thick rectangle on a lightly floured surface. Using a pizza cutter or knife, cut the dough into 2-inch squares. Allow the dough to rest for 15 minutes.

3. Meanwhile, fill the saucepan (or electric deep-fryer) with at least 3 inches of oil. Bring the oil to 360° to 370°F as determined by the candy thermometer.

4. Carefully drop the beignets in the hot oil, two or three at a time, so they have plenty of room to float to the surface. Do not overcrowd, or they will not rise nicely.

5. After about 2 minutes, gently flip the beignets over with a slotted spoon and deep-fry for another minute or until golden brown on both sides.

6. Using the slotted spoon, remove the beignets from the oil and transfer to paper towels to drain.

7. Repeat with the remaining dough until all the beignets are fried.

8. Dust generously with confectioners' sugar and eat with a cup of café au lait.

# Chocolate- or Jam-Filled Beignets

As if the traditional beignets weren't decadent enough, we felt compelled to fill them with chocolate or jam (see color photo). They are quite simple to make and everyone who eats them becomes a little bit happier.

***Makes 5 or 6 beignets***

1 pound (grapefruit-size portion) Challah (page 296) or Brioche (page 300) dough, defrosted overnight in the refrigerator if frozen
Vegetable oil, for deep-frying
4 ounces semisweet chocolate, cut into ½-ounce pieces, or 4 tablespoons of your favorite jam
Confectioners' sugar, for dusting

**Equipment**
Deep saucepan for deep-frying, or an electric deep fryer
Slotted spoon
Paper towels
Candy thermometer

1. Dust the surface of the refrigerated dough with flour and cut off a 1-pound (grapefruit-size) piece. Dust the piece with more flour and quickly shape it into a ball by stretching the surface of the dough around to the bottom on all four sides, rotating the ball a quarter-turn as you go.

2. Roll the dough into a ¼-inch-thick rectangle on a lightly floured surface. Using a pizza cutter or knife, cut the dough into 2-inch squares, then place a half-ounce of chocolate or a teaspoon of jam in the center of each square. Gather the edges of the dough around the

filling, pinching at the center to form a seal. If you are not able to seal the edges *very* well, use a small amount of water to help stick them together.

3. Allow the beignets to rest for 15 minutes.

4. Meanwhile, fill the saucepan (or electric deep-fryer) with at least 3 inches of oil and bring to 360° to 370°F as determined by the candy thermometer.

5. Carefully drop the beignets in the hot oil, two or three at a time, so they have plenty of room to rise to the surface. Do not overcrowd or they will not rise nicely.

6. After about 2 minutes, gently flip the beignets over with a slotted spoon and deep-fry for another minute or until golden brown on both sides.

7. Using the slotted spoon, remove the beignets from the oil and transfer to paper towels to drain.

8. Repeat with the remaining dough until all the beignets are fried.

9. Dust generously with confectioners' sugar and eat with a cup of café au lait.

## Panettone

Panettone is the classic Christmas bread sold all over Italy during the holidays (see color photo). It originated in Milan around the fifteenth century, and has been the subject of much lore. The most commonly told story of how this bejeweled bread came to be goes something like this: A young nobleman falls in love with a baker's daughter named Toni. He disguises himself as a pastry chef's apprentice and creates the tall fruit-studded bread to present to Toni, calling it *"Pan de Toni."* The bread is a success in the bakery and the father blesses the marriage.

The story is as rich and fanciful as the bread, made with dried fruit and the essence of lemons and vanilla. There are traditional panettone molds that are very high sided and come either straight or fluted. They can be found at cooking stores or on the Web. You can use a brioche mold, but the bread won't have the classic high sides. Paper panettone molds are available from baking supply stores.

***Makes at least three loaves slightly larger than 1½ pounds each. The recipe is easily doubled or halved.***

| Ingredient | Volume (U.S.) | Weight (U.S.) | Weight (Metric) |
|---|---|---|---|
| Lukewarm water (100°F or below) | 1½ cups | 12 ounces | 340 grams |
| Granulated yeast[1] | 1 tablespoon | 0.35 ounce | 10 grams |
| Kosher salt[1] | 1 to 1½ tablespoons | 0.6 to 0.9 ounce | 17 to 25 grams |
| Honey | ½ cup | 6 ounces | 170 grams |

[1]Can decrease (see pages 14 and 17)

*(continued)*

| Ingredient | Volume (U.S.) | Weight (U.S.) | Weight (Metric) |
|---|---|---|---|
| Large eggs, lightly beaten | 8 | 1 pound | 455 grams |
| Unsalted butter, melted and slightly cooled | 1 cup | 8 ounces | 225 grams |
| Lemon extract | 1 teaspoon | 0.2 ounce | 5 grams |
| Pure vanilla extract | 2 teaspoons | 0.4 ounce | 10 grams |
| Lemon zest, grated | 2 teaspoons | 0.2 ounce | 5 grams |
| Mixed dried and/or candied fruit[2] | 2 cups | 12 ounces | 340 grams |
| All-purpose flour | 7½ cups | 2 pounds, 5½ ounces | 1,065 grams |
| Egg wash (1 egg beaten with 1 tablespoon water) | | | |
| Butter for greasing pan | | | |
| Sugar, for the top | | | |

[2]Golden raisins, dried pineapple, dried apricots, dried cherries, and candied citrus, just to name a few that we've tried and loved in this bread

1. **Mixing and storing the dough:** Mix the yeast, salt, honey, eggs, melted butter, extracts, and zest with the water in a 6-quart bowl or a lidded (not airtight) food container.

2. Mix in the flour and dried fruit without kneading, using a spoon or a heavy-duty stand mixer (with paddle). If you're not using a machine, you may need to use wet hands to incorporate the last bit of flour. The

dough will be loose, but will firm up when chilled (don't try to use it without chilling).

3. Cover (not airtight) and allow to rest at room temperature until the dough rises and collapses (or flattens on top), approximately 2 hours.

4. The dough can be used as soon as it's chilled after the initial rise, or frozen for later use. Refrigerate the container of dough and use over the next 5 days. Beyond that, freeze the dough in 1-pound portions in an airtight container for up to 2 weeks. When using frozen dough, thaw in the refrigerator for 24 hours before using, then allow the usual rest and rise time.

5. **On baking day,** grease a 6-inch panettone or brioche pan with a small amount of butter.

6. Dust the surface of the refrigerated dough with flour and cut off a 1½-pound (small cantaloupe-size) piece. Dust the piece with more flour and quickly shape it into a ball by stretching the surface of the dough around to the bottom on all four sides, rotating the ball a quarter-turn as you go. Place the ball into the prepared pan, seam side down.

7. Allow to rest at room temperature for 90 minutes, loosely covered with plastic wrap.

8. **Preheat the oven to 350°F**. A baking stone is not required, and omitting it shortens the preheat.

9. Remove the plastic wrap, brush the panettone with egg wash, and sprinkle top generously with sugar. Bake near the center of the oven

for 50 to 55 minutes until golden brown and well set. The amount of dough and baking times will vary depending on the pan size.

**10.** Allow to cool on a rack before slicing and eating.

# Soft American-Style White Bread

American-style sliced white bread doesn't get a lot of respect from serious bread lovers. Most of our experience with it is based on plastic-wrapped products, often chemically preserved to sit on the shelf for long periods of time. But it doesn't have to be this way. Homemade white bread is a completely different creation.

While many people will be happy with the Crusty White Sandwich Loaf in chapter 5, some (especially kids) will want a bread with a softer crust. What keeps crust so soft is adding a bit of shortening, either plain old creamery butter or oil, and a little sugar for tenderness. Try it with our grilled French ham and cheese sandwich, the Croque Monsieur (page 80).

***Makes enough dough for two 2-pound loaves. The recipe is easily doubled or halved.***

| Ingredient | Volume (U.S.) | Weight (U.S.) | Weight (Metric) |
|---|---|---|---|
| Lukewarm water (100°F or below) | 3 cups | 1 pound, 8 ounces | 680 grams |
| Granulated yeast[1] | 1 tablespoon | 0.35 ounce | 10 grams |
| Kosher salt[1] | 1 to 1½ tablespoons | 0.6 to 0.9 ounce | 17 to 25 grams |
| Sugar | 2 tablespoons | 1 ounce | 30 grams |
| Unsalted butter,[2] melted, plus additional for brushing the top crust | ½ cup (1 stick) | 4 ounces | 115 grams |
| All-purpose flour | 7 cups | 2 pounds, 3 ounces | 990 grams |

[1]Can decrease (see pages 14 and 17)
[2]Can substitute oil or melted margarine

1. **Mixing and storing the dough:** Mix the yeast, salt, sugar, and melted butter with the water in a 6-quart bowl or a lidded (not airtight) food container.

2. Mix in the flour without kneading, using a spoon or a heavy-duty stand mixer (with paddle). If you're not using a machine, you may need to use wet hands to incorporate the last bit of flour.

3. Cover (not airtight) and allow to rest at room temperature until the dough rises and collapses (or flattens on top), approximately 2 hours.

4. The dough can be used immediately after the initial rise, though it is easier to handle when cold. Refrigerate the container of dough and use over the next 7 days, or freeze for up to 3 weeks.

5. **On baking day,** grease an 8½ × 4½-inch nonstick loaf pan. Dust the surface of the refrigerated dough with flour and cut off a 2-pound (large cantaloupe-size) piece. Dust the piece with more flour and quickly shape it into a ball by stretching the surface of the dough around to the bottom on all four sides, rotating the ball a quarter turn as you go. Elongate the ball into an oval.

6. Drop the dough into the prepared pan.

7. Allow the dough to rest for 90 minutes, loosely covered with plastic wrap.

8. **Preheat the oven to 350°F.** A baking stone is not required, and omitting it shortens the preheat.

9. Using a pastry brush, paint the top surface with melted butter. Bake the bread near the center of the oven for about 45 minutes, or until

golden brown. Brush the top crust with more butter or oil right when the loaf comes out of the oven.

10. Allow to cool completely before slicing; otherwise you won't get well-cut sandwich slices.

# Buttermilk Bread

Many traditional American and British breads use buttermilk, which tenderizes the bread, creating a lovely soft crust and crumb, and a terrific flavor. It makes an ideal sandwich loaf, and it's heavenly in Judy's Board of Directors Cinnamon-Raisin Bread (page 330). You can also use this dough in any of the basic recipes in chapter 5, lowering the baking temperature to 375°F and increasing the baking time.

***Makes two loaves, slightly less than 2 pounds each. The recipe is easily doubled or halved.***

| Ingredient | Volume (U.S.) | Weight (U.S.) | Weight (Metric) |
|---|---|---|---|
| Lukewarm water (100°F or below) | 2 cups | 16 ounces | 455 grams |
| Buttermilk | 1 cup | 8½ ounces | 240 grams |
| Granulated yeast[1] | 1 tablespoon | 0.35 ounce | 10 grams |
| Kosher salt[1] | 1 to 1½ tablespoons | 0.6 to 0.9 ounce | 17 to 25 grams |
| Sugar | 1½ tablespoons | 0.75 ounce | 20 grams |
| All-purpose flour | 6½ cups | 2 pounds, ½ ounce | 920 grams |
| Unsalted butter, melted, for greasing the pan and brushing the top of loaf | | | |

[1]Can decrease (see pages 14 and 17)

1. **Mixing and storing the dough:** Mix the yeast, salt, and sugar with the water and buttermilk in a 6-quart bowl or a lidded (not airtight) food container.

2. Mix in the flour without kneading, using a spoon or a heavy-duty stand mixer (with paddle). If you're not using a machine, you may need to use wet hands to incorporate the last bit of flour.

3. Cover (not airtight) and allow to rest at room temperature until the dough rises and collapses (or flattens on top), approximately 2 hours.

4. The dough can be used immediately after the initial rise, though it is easier to handle when cold. Refrigerate the container of dough and use over the next 5 days, or freeze for up to 3 weeks.

5. **On baking day,** lightly grease an 8½ × 4½-inch nonstick loaf pan. Dust the surface of the refrigerated dough with flour and cut off a 2-pound (large cantaloupe-size) piece. Dust the piece with more flour and quickly shape it into a ball by stretching the surface of the dough around to the bottom on all four sides, rotating the ball a quarter-turn as you go. Elongate the ball into an oval.

6. Drop the dough into the prepared pan.

7. Allow the dough to rest for 90 minutes, loosely covered with plastic wrap.

8. **Preheat the oven to 350°F.** A baking stone is not required, and omitting it shortens the preheat.

9. Using a pastry brush, paint the top surface with melted butter. Bake the bread near the center of the oven for about 45 minutes, or until golden brown. Brush the top crust with more butter right when the loaf comes out of the oven.

10. Remove the bread from the pan. Allow to cool completely before slicing, or it will be nearly impossible to slice.

# Judy's Board of Directors' Cinnamon-Raisin Bread

*"My friend Judy is the C.E.O. of a successful company. She has a passion for bread that she brings into the boardroom. At one tense meeting with her board of directors, she used the simple magic of shaping loaves to win over skeptical board members. She slammed the dough onto the conference table.*

*"Growing a company," Judy told them, "is like baking bread. Sometimes you have to be patient, and wait for the dough to rise. You can't rush it. Things need to develop spontaneously, on their own." She shaped a loaf, pushing and prodding. A cinnamon-raisin bread was formed! And the board gave its blessing to the company's next stage. She's continued to serve this bread, with butter and jam, at all kinds of business meetings, tense or otherwise."*—Jeff

We adapted Judy's recipe for our quick method—and the result was beautiful (see color photo). As always with our dough, don't bother kneading (unless you're trying to intimidate your board).

***Makes one 2-pound loaf***

1½ pounds (small cantaloupe-size portion) Buttermilk Bread dough (page 327)
Unsalted butter or oil, for greasing the pan
⅓ cup sugar
1½ teaspoons ground cinnamon
¾ cup raisins
Egg wash (1 egg beaten with 1 tablespoon water)

1. Lightly grease an 8½ × 4½-inch nonstick loaf pan. Set aside. Dust the surface of the refrigerated dough with flour and cut off a 1½-pound (small cantaloupe-size) piece. Dust the piece with more flour and quickly shape it into a ball by stretching the surface of the dough around to the bottom on all four sides, rotating the ball a quarter-turn as you go.

2. With a rolling pin, roll out the dough to an 8×16-inch rectangle about ¼ inch thick, dusting the board and rolling pin with flour as needed. You may need to use a metal dough scraper to loosen rolled dough from the board as you work.

3. Mix together the sugar and cinnamon and sprinkle the mixture evenly over the dough. Evenly distribute the raisins.

4. Starting from the short side, roll it up jelly-roll style. Pinch the edges and ends together, and tuck the ends under to form an oval loaf.

5. Place the loaf, seam side down. in the prepared pan. Allow to rest for 90 minutes, loosely covered with plastic wrap.

6. **Preheat the oven to 375°F**. A baking stone is not required, and omitting it shortens the preheat.

7. Using a pastry brush, paint the top lightly with egg wash. Bake for 40 minutes until golden brown.

8. Remove the bread from the pan and allow to cool before slicing.

## Chocolate Chocolate-Chip Bread

Chocolate bread is found in artisan bakeries all over the country. Its origin is unknown, but we'd like to thank the chocophile who found yet another way to satisfy our chocolate cravings. The texture says bread, but chocolate cake lovers won't be disappointed. Door County Sour Cherry Preserves (page 335) are a perfect, not-too-sweet counterpoint here.

***Makes two 2-pound loaves. The recipe is easily doubled or halved.***

| Ingredient | Volume (U.S.) | Weight (U.S.) | Weight (Metric) |
|---|---|---|---|
| Lukewarm water (100°F or below) | 2½ cups | 1 pound, 4 ounces | 565 grams |
| Vegetable oil | ¾ cup | 6 ounces | 170 grams |
| Granulated yeast[1] | 1 tablespoon | 0.35 ounce | 10 grams |
| Kosher salt[1] | 1 to 1½ tablespoons | 0.6 to 0.9 ounce | 17 to 25 grams |
| Sugar | 1 cup | 7 ounces | 200 grams |
| All-purpose flour | 5½ cups | 1 pound, 11½ ounces | 780 grams |
| Unsweetened cocoa powder, preferably dark | ¾ cup | 3 ounces | 85 grams |
| Bittersweet or semisweet chocolate chips | 1½ cups | 6 ounces | 170 grams |

*(continued)*

| Ingredient |
| --- |
| Unsalted butter, melted, for greasing loaf pan and brushing top of loaf |
| Sugar, for sprinkling over top of loaf |

[1]Can decrease (see pages 14 and 17)

1. **Mixing and storing the dough:** Mix the oil, yeast, salt, and sugar with the water in a 6-quart bowl or a lidded (not airtight) food container.

2. Mix in the flour, cocoa powder, and the chocolate chips without kneading, using a spoon or a heavy-duty stand mixer (with paddle). If you're not using a machine, you may need to use wet hands to incorporate the last bit of flour.

3. Cover (not airtight) and allow to rest at room temperature until the dough rises and collapses (or flattens on top), approximately 2 hours.

4. The dough can be used immediately after the initial rise, though it is easier to handle when cold. Refrigerate the container of dough and use over the next 5 days. Beyond 5 days, freeze the dough in 1-pound portions in an airtight container for up to 4 weeks. When using frozen dough, thaw in the refrigerator for 24 hours before using, then allow the usual rest and rise time.

5. **On baking day,** grease an 8½ × 4½-inch nonstick loaf pan. Dust the surface of the refrigerated dough with flour and cut off a 2-pound (large cantaloupe-size) piece. Dust the piece with more flour and quickly shape it into a ball by stretching the surface of the dough around to the bottom on all four sides, rotating the ball a quarter-turn as you go. Elongate the ball into an oval. Drop the dough into the prepared pan.

6. Allow the dough to rest for 90 minutes, loosely covered with plastic wrap.

7. **Preheat the oven to 350°F.** A baking stone is not required, and omitting it shortens the preheat.

8. Using a pastry brush, paint the top surface with melted butter, and sprinkle with sugar. Bake the bread in the center of the oven for about 50 to 60 minutes, or until set firm when you press on the top of the loaf.

9. Remove the bread from the pan and allow to cool completely before slicing.

# Door County Sour Cherry Preserves

Door County in Wisconsin produces some of the world's most flavorful sour cherries. If you can get there in late July or early August you'll find them at their peak of perfection. Pick them yourself, or buy fresh from a farm stand—choose the phenomenal Montmorency variety if they're available. They are quite tart, but their explosive and spicy fruit flavor is brought out by the sugar in the preserve. This is a fantastic combination with Chocolate Chocolate-Chip Bread (page 332). As in Laura's Three-Citrus Marmalade (page 165), the Sure-Jell box was the culinary inspiration.

If you're intimidated by canning, make a smaller quantity and simply skip the sterilization procedure in the final step, then refrigerate the preserves for up to 2 months or freeze them for up to a year.

***Makes 6 cups preserves***

4¾ cups sugar
3 pounds ripe sour cherries (Montmorency variety if available), or enough to make 4 cups when pitted and finely chopped
One 1.75-ounce box Sure-Jell fruit pectin

1. Measure the sugar and set aside. Do not be tempted to reduce the amount of sugar, or the preserves may not set properly.

2. Remove the stems from the cherries and pit them (a cherry pitter is helpful here). Chop the cherries finely, and measure exactly 4 cups.

3. Place the measured cherries and their juice into a 6- to 8-quart saucepan. Stir in the box of fruit pectin and bring the mixture to a full rolling boil.

4. Stir in the sugar quickly, return to a full rolling boil, and cook for 1 minute. Remove from heat and skim off any foam.

5. Pour the preserves into clean canning jars. Process according to the canner's and U.S. Department of Agriculture (USDA) recommendations or refrigerate and use within 2 months. The preserves also can be frozen, without canning, for up to 1 year.

# Sunflower Seed Breakfast Loaf

*"Thomas Gumpel, my bread instructor and friend from the Culinary Institute of America, inspired this recipe. The first time I made the bread in his class was under some duress. I'd been a bit impertinent during a lecture and he decided to make an example of my kitchen misdemeanor. He had me mix the sunflower bread in an old-fashioned 'bread bucket' (circa 1900) in the dining hall as public humiliation. The process took the better part of the class period, and my pride, albeit strong, took some abuse. But the bread was sublime. As harrowing as my first experience with this bread was, I've always loved to make it, but now it takes only a fraction of the time to prepare."*—Zoë

***Makes two loaves, slightly smaller than 2 pounds each. The recipe is easily doubled or halved.***

| Ingredient | Volume (U.S.) | Weight (U.S.) | Weight (Metric) |
|---|---|---|---|
| Lukewarm milk (100°F or below) | 2 cups | 1 pound | 450 grams |
| Honey | ½ cup | 6 ounces | 170 grams |
| Sugar | 2 tablespoons | 1 ounce | 30 grams |
| Granulated yeast[1] | 1 tablespoon | 0.35 ounce | 10 grams |
| Kosher salt[1] | 1 to 1½ tablespoons | 0.6 to 0.9 ounce | 17 to 25 grams |
| Sunflower oil (or canola oil), plus more for greasing the pan | ¼ cup | 2 ounces | 55 grams |
| Large eggs | 3 | 6 ounces | 170 grams |

(continued)

| Ingredient | Volume (U.S.) | Weight (U.S.) | Weight (Metric) |
|---|---|---|---|
| Bread flour | 6 cups | 1 pound, 14 ounces | 850 grams |
| Sunflower seeds | 1 cup, plus 2 tablespoons for top of the loaf | 4¾ ounces | 135 grams |
| Egg wash (1 egg beaten with 1 tablespoon water) | | | |

[1]Can decrease (see pages 14 and 17)

1. **Mixing and storing the dough:** Mix the honey, sugar, yeast, salt, sunflower oil, and eggs with the milk in a 6-quart bowl or a lidded (not airtight) food container.

2. Mix in the flour and sunflower seeds without kneading, using a spoon or a heavy-duty stand mixer (with paddle). If you're not using a machine, you may need to use wet hands to incorporate the last bit of flour. Add the sunflower seeds to the dough.

3. Cover (not airtight) and allow to rest at room temperature until the dough rises and collapses (or flattens on top), approximately 2 hours.

4. Dough will be loose, but will firm up when chilled. Don't try to use it without chilling for at least 3 hours. Refrigerate the container of dough and use over the next 5 days. Or store the dough for up to 2 weeks in the freezer in 1-pound portions. When using frozen dough, thaw it in the refrigerator overnight before use.

5. **On baking day,** grease an 8½ × 4½-inch nonstick loaf pan. Dust the surface of the refrigerated dough with flour and cut off a 2-pound (large cantaloupe-size) piece. Dust with more flour and quickly shape

it into a ball by stretching the surface of the dough around to the bottom on all four sides, rotating the ball a quarter-turn as you go. Elongate the ball into an oval and place into the prepared pan.

6. Allow the dough to rest for 90 minutes, loosely covered with plastic wrap.

7. **Preheat the oven to 350°F.** A baking stone is not required, and omitting it shortens the preheat.

8. Using a pastry brush, paint the top surface with egg wash, and sprinkle with the remaining seeds. Place the bread in the center of the oven and bake for 50 to 60 minutes, or until golden brown.

9. Remove the bread from the pan and allow to cool on a rack before slicing and eating.

# Chocolate-Prune Bread

This bread is a great combination of flavors; it is rich and powerfully chocolatey (especially if you use chocolate dough as the base) without being too sweet. We like to use bittersweet chocolate, but semisweet will work beautifully as well.

Some years ago, marketers decided that prunes had a public relations problem, so these days the fruit is known as "dried plums" rather than prunes. We're sticking with "prunes," but whatever the name, they're delicious, nutritious, and have a marvelous concentrated flavor that says, well, prunes. This bread pairs well with a glass of Armagnac (or a glass of milk!).

***Makes one 1½-pound loaf***

1½ pounds (small cantaloupe-size portion) Challah (page 296), Brioche (page 300), or Chocolate Chocolate-Chip Bread (page 332) dough
Softened unsalted butter, for greasing the pan
6 ounces (170 grams) high-quality bittersweet chocolate (2 ounces/55 grams if using Chocolate Chocolate-Chip Bread dough), chopped
¾ cup chopped prunes
Egg wash (1 egg beaten with 1 tablespoon water)
¼ cup sugar, for sprinkling over the top of the bread and preparing the pan

1. **On baking day,** generously grease an 8½ × 4½-inch nonstick loaf pan with butter, sprinkle some sugar evenly over the butter, and shake the pan to distribute.

2. Dust the surface of the refrigerated dough with flour and cut off a 1½-pound (small cantaloupe-size) piece. Dust the piece with more flour and quickly shape it into a ball by stretching the surface of the dough around to the bottom on all four sides, rotating the ball a

quarter-turn as you go. Using a rolling pin, roll out the dough into a ½-inch-thick rectangle. As you roll out the dough, use enough flour to prevent it from sticking to the work surface but not so much as to make the dough dry.

3. Sprinkle the chocolate and chopped prunes over the dough and roll up the dough, jelly-roll style, to enclose them. Fold the dough over itself several times, turning and pressing it down with the heel of your hand after each turn. This will work the chocolate and prunes into the dough; some may poke through.

4. With very wet hands, form the dough into a loaf shape and place it in the prepared pan. Allow to rest and rise for 90 minutes, loosely covered with plastic wrap.

5. **Preheat the oven to 350°F.** A baking stone is not required, and omitting it shortens the preheat.

6. Using a pastry brush, paint the top with egg wash, and sprinkle with sugar. Bake the loaf in the center of the oven for 50 to 60 minutes until firm. Smaller or larger loaves will require adjustments in baking time.

7. Remove the bread from the pan and allow to cool on a rack before slicing and eating.

## Chocolate-Raisin Babka

In our *babka*, based on a Ukrainian recipe, we call for sixteen egg yolks, which make it extremely rich and velvety. In the traditional method, the milk and flour are cooked together, and the egg yolks are added one by one—sometimes up to thirty of them. We've simplified the recipe without losing any of the old-fashioned charm. You can freeze the leftover egg whites and use them later to make meringue.

***Makes at least three 1½-pound loaves. The recipe is easily doubled or halved.***

| Ingredient | Volume (U.S.) | Weight (U.S.) | Weight (Metric) |
|---|---|---|---|
| Lukewarm milk (100°F or below) | 3 cups | 1 pound, 9½ ounces | 725 grams |
| Egg yolks | 16 | 1 pound | 455 grams |
| Granulated yeast[1] | 1½ tablespoons | 0.55 ounce | 15 grams |
| Sugar | ½ cup | 3½ ounces | 100 grams |
| Kosher salt[1] | 1 to 1½ tablespoons | 0.6 to 0.9 ounce | 17 to 25 grams |
| Unsalted butter, melted, plus more for greasing the pan | ¾ cup (1½ sticks) | 6 ounces | 170 grams |
| All-purpose flour | 7½ cups | 2 pounds, 5½ ounces | 1,065 grams |
| Raisins | ¾ cup | 4½ ounces | 130 grams |

[1]Can decrease (see pages 14 and 17)

| Ingredient | Volume (U.S.) | Weight (U.S.) | Weight (Metric) |
|---|---|---|---|
| Bittersweet chocolate, finely chopped or shaved | ¾ cup | 4½ ounces | 130 grams |
| Rum, for soaking the baked loaf | ¼ cup | 2 ounces | 55 grams |

1. **Mixing and storing the dough:** Mix the egg yolks, yeast, sugar, salt, and melted butter with the milk in a 6-quart bowl or a lidded (not airtight) food container.

2. Mix in the flour without kneading, using a spoon or a heavy-duty stand mixer (with paddle). The mixture will be quite loose because of all the egg yolks.

3. Cover (not airtight) and allow to rest at room temperature until the dough rises and collapses (or flattens on top), approximately 2 hours.

4. Dough will be loose, but will firm up when chilled. Do not try to use it without chilling for at least 3 hours. Refrigerate the container of dough and use over the next 5 days. Beyond five days, freeze the dough in 1½-pound portions in an airtight container for up to 2 weeks. When using frozen dough, thaw in refrigerator for 24 hours before use, then allow the usual rest and rise times.

5. **On baking day,** grease an 8½ × 4½-inch nonstick loaf pan. Dust the surface of the refrigerated dough with flour and cut off a 1½-pound (small cantaloupe-size) piece. Dust the piece with more flour and quickly shape it into a ball by stretching the surface of the dough around to the bottom on all four sides, rotating the ball a quarter-turn as you go.

6. Roll the dough into a ¼-inch-thick rectangle. Sprinkle the raisins and chocolate evenly over the dough. Roll the dough into a log, starting at the short end. Tuck the two ends under and form it into a ball.

7. Fill the prepared pan with dough. Allow to rest and rise 90 minutes, loosely covered with plastic.

8. **Preheat the oven to 350°F**. A baking stone is not required, and omitting it shortens the preheat.

9. Place the pan in the center of the oven. Bake for about 45 minutes, or until golden brown and firm. Brush with rum immediately.

10. Allow to cool on a rack before slicing and eating.

# Apple and Pear Coffee Cake

*"Every year my family goes to the orchards to pick apples. Here in Minnesota we are blessed with the finest apples I've ever experienced. I like to bake with a combination: some sweet and some tart, some that keep their shape and others that will break down and get saucy. No matter what apple you pick, this recipe will be a favorite. I like to include the pear for the variety of flavor—it adds an almost perfumey quality."*—Zoë

***Makes 1 coffee cake***

**The Streusel Topping**

1 cup oats
1 cup all-purpose flour
1 cup brown sugar, well packed
1 cup chopped nuts (optional)
½ cup melted unsalted butter
Pinch of ground cinnamon

**The Cake**

1 pound (grapefruit-size portion) Brioche dough (page 300)
Unsalted butter, for greasing the pan
Flour, for dusting the pan
2 small apples (1 tart and 1 sweet), cored, quartered, and thinly sliced
1 pear, cored, quartered, and thinly sliced
3 tablespoons brown sugar
Grated zest of half an orange
1½ cups streusel topping (above)
Whipped cream, for serving (optional)

1. **Prepare the topping:** Combine all streusel ingredients in a bowl and mix until the butter is roughly incorporated. Do not overmix—you want a crumbly texture. Set aside.

2. **Assemble the cake:** Grease an 8-inch springform pan with butter and dust with flour. Set aside.

3. Toss the apples, pear, brown sugar, and zest together in a small bowl and set aside.

4. Dust the surface of the refrigerated dough with flour and cut off a 1-pound (grapefruit-size) piece. Divide the piece in two, dust with more flour and quickly shape them into rough balls by stretching the surface of the dough around to the bottom on all four sides, rotating the ball a quarter-turn as you go.

5. Roll out the dough balls into two ¼-inch-thick rounds, each about 9 inches in diameter. As you roll out the dough, add flour as needed to prevent sticking.

6. Place one of the dough rounds in the bottom of the prepared pan. Top with half of the apple and pear mixture, then sprinkle half of the streusel topping over it. Repeat with the next layer of dough, apple and pear mixture, and streusel.

7. Allow the cake to rest for 90 minutes.

8. **Preheat the oven to 350°F.** A baking stone is not required, and omitting it shortens the preheat.

9. Bake the cake in the center of the oven 55 to 60 minutes.

10. Allow to cool for 10 to 15 minutes. While the cake is still warm remove it from the springform pan.

11. Serve warm or at room temperature with whipped cream, or just on its own.

# Sunny-Side-Up Apricot Pastry

It's as fun to make and look at as it is to eat (see color photo). This combination of buttery brioche dough, sweet vanilla pastry cream, and tart apricots masquerading as a sunny-side-up egg was made popular in Julia Child's book *Baking with Julia*.

Pastry cream is a staple in the pastry kitchen. To flavor this silky custard, you can use pure vanilla extract, or try a vanilla bean, which gives the most intense flavor. To use the bean, just slice it lengthwise with a paring knife to expose the seeds. Scrape the seeds out of the pod and throw the seeds and the pod into your saucepan. The pod will get strained out at the end, leaving the fragrant aroma and the flecks of real vanilla behind.

***Makes eight 4-inch pastries***

**The Pastry Cream (makes 3 cups)**

2 cups whole milk
½ cup sugar
2 tablespoons unsalted butter
Pinch of salt
½ vanilla bean, split lengthwise and seeds scraped out, or 1 teaspoon pure vanilla extract
2 tablespoons cornstarch
1 large egg
3 large egg yolks

**The Pastries**

1½ pounds (small cantaloupe-size portion) Brioche dough (page 300)
1 cup pastry cream (above)
8 ripe apricots, halved (fresh, canned, or substitute 8 tablespoons apricot preserves)

½ cup apricot jam, melted
2 cups sugar

1. **Make the pastry cream:** Bring the milk, ¼ cup of the sugar, butter, salt, and vanilla bean to a gentle boil in a medium to large saucepan. Remove from the heat and set aside to infuse.

2. Whisk together the cornstarch and the remaining ¼ cup sugar. Add the egg and egg yolks to the cornstarch and mix into a smooth paste.

3. Slowly, and in small amounts, whisk a little of the hot milk into the egg mixture to temper the eggs. Once the egg mixture is warm to the touch, pour it back into the milk in the pan.

4. Return the custard to the stovetop and bring to a boil, whisking continuously for 2 to 3 minutes until thickened and cornstarch is well cooked.

5. Strain the pastry cream into a shallow container and cover with plastic wrap, pressed directly on the surface to keep a skin from forming.

6. Set the container in the freezer for 15 minutes, just until chilled, then refrigerate.

7. **Make the pastries:** Line a baking sheet with parchment paper or a silicone mat.

8. Dust the surface of the refrigerated dough with flour and cut off a 1½-pound (small cantaloupe-size) piece. Dust the piece with more flour and quickly shape it into a rough ball by stretching the surface of

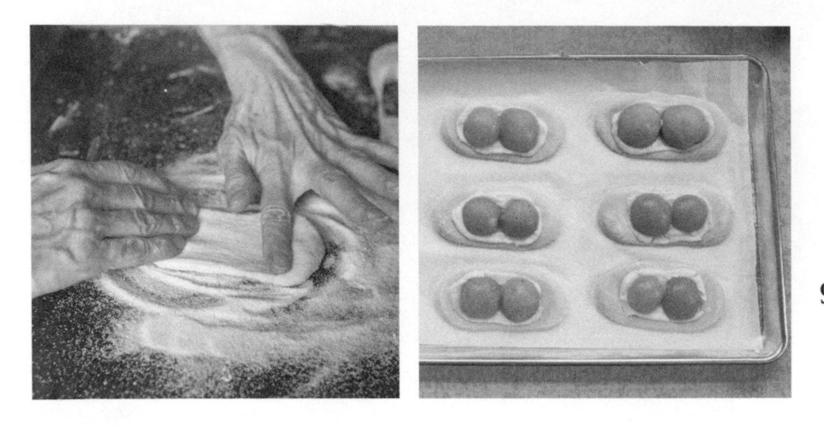

the dough around to the bottom on all four sides, rotating the ball a quarter-turn as you go.

9. Roll the dough to a ¼-inch-thick rectangle, adding flour as needed to prevent sticking.

10. Using a round baking cutter, cut out eight 4-inch circles. Save the dough scraps to use in Cinnamon Twists and Turns (page 358).

11. Cover the work surface with a generous coating of the sugar. Take one of the rounds and lay it in the sugar. Using a rolling pin, roll back and forth over the center, stopping ½ inch from the two ends to create an oval. If the dough sticks to the rolling pin, dust the pin with a bit of flour. Lay the oval, sugar side up, on the lined baking sheet. Repeat with the rest of the dough, spacing the ovals at least 1 inch apart on the sheet.

12. Spread 2 tablespoons of the pastry cream in the center of each sugared oval. Place 2 apricots over the pastry cream so they resemble sunny-side-up eggs. Allow the pastry to rest for 45 minutes.

13. **Preheat the oven to 350°F.** A baking stone is not required, and omitting it shortens the preheat.

14. Bake the pastries in the center of the oven for about 30 to 35 minutes, or until the dough is golden brown and the sugar is nicely caramelized.

15. As soon as the pastries come out of the oven, brush the apricot jam over the pastries to give them a nice shine. Serve warm or cooled.

# Blueberry–Lemon Curd Ring

This wreath-shaped pastry showcases the bright flavors of fresh lemon and the sweetness of in-season blueberries (see color photo). The delicious lemon curd is perfect for slathering on a hot piece of toast as well as for the filling of this pastry recipe.

***Makes 8 servings***

**The Lemon Curd (makes 1 cup)**
6 large egg yolks
1 cup sugar
½ cup freshly squeezed lemon juice
1 tablespoon grated lemon zest
8 tablespoons (1 stick) unsalted butter, cut into ½-inch slices

**The Ring**
1 pound (grapefruit-size portion) Brioche (page 300) or Challah dough (page 296)
½ cup lemon curd
1½ cups fresh blueberries
Egg wash (1 egg beaten with 1 tablespoon of water)
Sugar, for dusting the top

1. **Make the lemon curd:** In a double boiler, whisk together all of the ingredients except for the butter.

2. Stir constantly over gently simmering water with a rubber spatula until the lemon curd begins to thicken, about 10 minutes.

3. Add the butter and continue to stir until it is completely melted and the curd is quite thick; it will be the consistency of smooth pudding.

4. If there are any lumps, strain the curd into a container. Cover with plastic wrap and place in the freezer until cool, then refrigerate.

5. **Make the ring:** Line a baking sheet with parchment paper or a silicone mat.

6. Dust the surface of the refrigerated dough with flour and cut off a 1-pound (grapefruit-size) piece. Dust the piece with more flour and quickly shape it into a rough ball by stretching the surface of the dough around to the bottom on all four sides, rotating the ball a quarter-turn as you go.

7. Roll out the ball to a ⅛-inch-thick rectangle. As you roll out the dough, add flour as needed to prevent sticking.

8. Spread the lemon curd evenly over the dough. Sprinkle the berries over the lemon curd.

9. Starting with the long side of the dough, roll it up into a log. Pinch the seam closed. Stretch the log until it is about 2 inches thick. Join the two ends together to form a wreath shape; pinch together to seal. Place on the prepared baking sheet. Stretch the dough to make sure you have a nice wide opening in the middle of your wreath.

10. Allow to rest and rise for 40 minutes.

11. **Preheat the oven to 350°F.** A baking stone is not required, and omitting it shortens the preheat.

12. Using a pastry brush, paint the wreath lightly with egg wash, then generously dust with sugar. Make evenly spaced cuts all the way around the wreath, about 1½ inches apart. The cuts should be about ½ inch deep.

13. Bake the ring in the center of the oven for 35 to 40 minutes until golden brown and well set.

14. Allow to cool for about 15 minutes before cutting. This pastry can be served warm or cool.

# Braided Raspberry–Almond Cream Pastry

Although this is easy to put together, the end result is dramatic and impressive for a special brunch or potluck (see color photo). If fresh raspberries are unavailable, feel free to show off seasonal fruits, such as apples, pears, peaches, and cherries.

***Makes 1 braid***

1 pound (grapefruit-size portion) Brioche (page 300) or Challah (page 296) dough
½ cup almond cream (page 312)
½ cup raspberry jam
1 cup fresh raspberries
Egg wash (1 egg beaten with 1 tablespoon of water)
Sugar, for dusting the top

1. Line a baking sheet with parchment paper or a silicone mat.

2. Dust the surface of the refrigerated dough with flour and cut off a 1-pound (grapefruit-size) piece. Dust the piece with more flour and quickly shape it into a rough ball by stretching the surface of the dough around to the bottom on all four sides, rotating the ball a quarter-turn as you go.

3. Roll out the dough into a ⅛-inch-thick rectangle. As you roll out the dough, add flour as needed to prevent sticking.

4. Lift the dough onto the lined baking sheet. Cover the center third of the dough with the almond cream, the jam, and the berries.

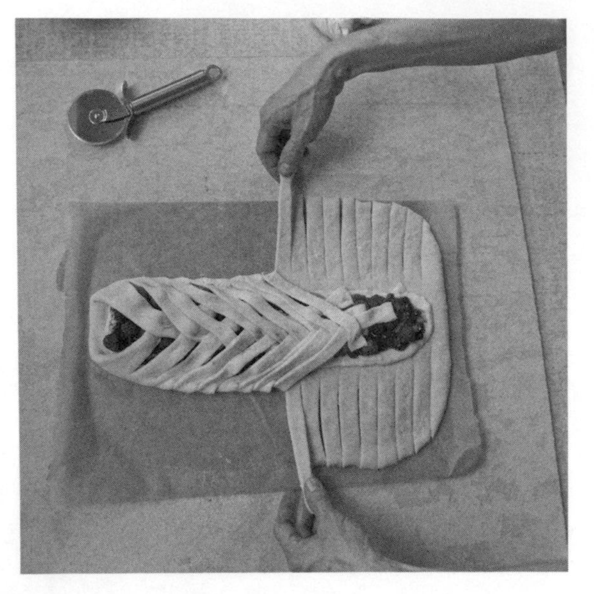

5. Using a pizza cutter, cut about twelve ½-inch-wide strips down each side. Fold the strips, left over right, crisscrossing over the filling (see photo). Lightly press the strips together as you move down the pastry, creating a braid. Allow the braid to rest for 40 minutes.

6. **Preheat the oven to 350°F**. A baking stone is not required, and omitting it shortens the preheat.

7. Brush lightly with egg wash, then generously sprinkle with sugar.

8. Place the baking sheet in the center of the oven. Bake the braid for 35 to 45 minutes until golden brown and bubbling. Serve warm.

SAVORY VARIATION: GREEK- OR TURKISH-STYLE SPINACH PIE WITH FETA AND PINE NUTS

Omit the almond cream, jam, raspberries, and sugar. Instead. . . .

1. In a skillet over medium heat, sauté 1 pound of **fresh chopped spinach** in 1 tablespoon of **olive oil,** until it's wilted and has given up a good amount of liquid, which you must drain to prevent a soggy bottom crust.

2. Prepare and roll out the dough as above, and distribute ½ pound of crumbled **feta cheese** down the center of the dough rectangle. Layer the drained spinach over the cheese.

3. Sprinkle ⅓ cup of **pine nuts** over the spinach, then complete the braid as above. Finish by brushing with **egg wash,** but omit the sugar topping

and sprinkle with **black sesame seeds** (white seeds are fine but the black ones are traditional in Greece and Turkey).

4. Allow to rest and bake as above.

This variation also works with non-enriched doughs, which can be baked at 450°F for 20 to 25 minutes. Use cornstarch wash (see page 104) or water instead of egg wash, which would burn at this temperature.

## Cinnamon Twists and Turns

This is a great recipe for leftover scraps of rolled-out Brioche dough (page 300). The end result may look a bit like modern art, but the flavor will be a real treat—wonderful with a cup of coffee (see color photo).

½ cup sugar
1 tablespoon ground cinnamon
Brioche dough or scraps
Egg wash (1 egg beaten with 1 tablespoon of water)

1. Line a baking sheet with parchment paper or a silicone mat.

2. **Preheat the oven to 350°F.** A baking stone is not required, and omitting it shortens the preheat.

3. Mix the sugar and cinnamon together in a small bowl. Set aside.

4. Using a pastry brush, paint the surface of the brioche scraps very lightly with egg wash, and sprinkle generously with the cinnamon-sugar. Flip the dough over and repeat on the opposite side.

5. Using a pizza cutter, cut the dough into ¾-inch strips or leave the scraps in odd shapes. Twist the strips into spirals and space evenly on the baking sheet. Let rest for 15 minutes. Depending on the size of the twists, they may turn in the oven and take on their own shape.

6. Bake for 15 to 20 minutes until golden brown. Serve warm.

# Bread Pudding

Bread pudding is the ultimate comfort food. It is also the perfect use for the day-old bread you will have left over when making all the recipes in this book. We like to use slightly stale bread because it absorbs the custard so well. This is wonderful served with Kumquat Champagne Confit (page 361) when you want something decadent for brunch.

***Makes 8 servings***

8 large egg yolks
1 cup sugar
1 quart half-and-half
¼ cup rum or brandy (optional)
1 teaspoon pure vanilla extract
¼ teaspoon freshly grated nutmeg
¼ teaspoon ground cinnamon
½ teaspoon grated orange zest
12 slices day-old bread, cut ½ inch thick
¾ cup raisins (optional)
Vanilla ice cream, for serving (optional)

1. **Preheat the oven to 325°F.**

2. In a large mixing bowl, whisk together the egg yolks, sugar, half-and-half, rum, vanilla, nutmeg, cinnamon, and zest until well combined.

3. Arrange the bread slices to fit in an 8 × 12 × 2-inch baking dish. Sprinkle the raisins over the bread, if using. Pour the custard slowly over the bread; let sit about 10 minutes. You may have to push the bread into the custard to guarantee no bread remains dry.

4. Cover loosely with aluminum foil, and poke a few holes in the top to allow steam to escape. Place on the center rack. Bake the pudding for about 1 hour, or until the center is just firm.

5. Remove from the oven and allow to stand for 10 minutes. Serve warm with Kumquat Champagne Confit (page 361), and vanilla ice cream, if desired.

# Kumquat Champagne Confit

This is a quick and tasty alternative to the more traditional marmalade recipe (page 165), and isn't meant to be canned. It comes together very quickly and packs an incredible flavor. We love this on fresh baguettes with a nice soft cheese like Brie or chèvre. It is also marvelous as a topping for the Bread Pudding (page 359); just add a scoop of vanilla ice cream.

***Makes 3 cups confit***

1 cup sugar
2 cups champagne
1 cup water
1 star anise
25 kumquats, thinly sliced

1. In a medium saucepan, bring the sugar, champagne, water, and star anise to a simmer. Cook, stirring, until the sugar has dissolved.

2. Add the kumquats and gently simmer over medium-low heat until they are tender and the liquid is the consistency of thick maple syrup, about 45 minutes.

3. Refrigerate and use within 1 week.

# Chocolate Cherry Bread Pudding

*"There is no end to the combinations of flavors you can use to make bread pudding. This recipe was inspired by my family's annual vacation in Door County, Wisconsin, where we pick a bounty of fresh cherries. I first made this pudding with the Chocolate Chocolate-Chip Bread (page 332). The intensity of the chocolate mixed with the tart cherries is a classic. It is also wonderful made with Brioche or Challah doughs, and dried cherries can be substituted when fresh are not available. Served with a premium-quality vanilla ice cream, this dessert will satisfy any chocolate craving."*—Jeff

***Makes 8 servings***

3 cups half-and-half
3/4 cup brown sugar, well packed
1/2 pound finely chopped bittersweet chocolate
1/4 cup unsalted butter, cut in 1/2-inch slices
3 whole large eggs
2 large egg yolks
6 cups cubed day-old baked Chocolate Chocolate-Chip Bread (page 332), Brioche (page 300), or Challah (page 296)
1 1/2 cups pitted sour cherries, fresh or frozen
Vanilla ice cream, for serving

1. **Preheat the oven to 325°F.**

2. **In a small saucepan,** bring the half-and-half and brown sugar to a simmer. Remove from heat and add the chocolate and butter, stirring until the chocolate is completely melted and smooth. Allow the mixture to cool slightly, about 5 minutes.

3. In a medium bowl, whisk together the eggs and egg yolks and add to the cooled chocolate mixture.

4. Arrange the cubed bread and cherries in an 8 × 12 × 2-inch baking dish. Pour the chocolate custard over the bread and allow it to sit for 15 minutes. You may have to push the bread down into the custard to make sure it is well soaked.

5. Cover loosely with aluminum foil, and poke a few holes in the top to allow steam to escape. Bake for about 50 minutes, or until the center is firm to the touch.

6. Allow to sit for 10 minutes before serving with vanilla ice cream.

# Apple-Stuffed French Toast

French toast is a staple in kitchens all over because it is a simple and decadent crowd-pleaser. This version takes the standard and makes it sensational (see color photo). Start with a thick slice of your favorite enriched five-minute bread and stuff it with caramelized apples, bananas, or peaches, soak it in custard, and then fry the toast in a touch of butter.

***Makes 8 servings***

4 firm tart apples, peeled, cored, and chopped into small dice
2 tablespoons granulated sugar
6 tablespoons (3/4 stick) unsalted butter
8 slices of baked Challah (page 296), Brioche (page 300), or Buttermilk Bread (page 327), cut 1 inch thick
8 large egg yolks
1 quart half-and-half
1/4 cup rum or brandy (optional)
2 teaspoons pure vanilla extract
1/4 cup sugar, plus more for sprinkling the top
1 teaspoon ground cinnamon
Maple syrup or confectioners' sugar, for serving

1. In a skillet over medium-low heat, sauté the apples, sugar, and 4 tablespoons (1/2 stick) of the butter. Cook until the apples are tender and the juices have thickened slightly, about 10 minutes. Set aside.

2. In a large mixing bowl, whisk together the egg yolks, half-and-half, rum, vanilla, sugar, and cinnamon until well combined.

3. Using a small serrated knife, cut a pocket into each slice of bread from the top crust edge. Be careful not to cut all the way through to the other edges. Divide the apple filling and stuff the 8 bread pockets. Very carefully dip the stuffed bread into the custard; let sit for a couple of minutes. You may have to push the bread into the custard to guarantee no bread remains dry.

4. In a large skillet over medium heat or on a griddle, melt the remaining 2 tablespoons butter. Sprinkle the top of the soaked bread with sugar, and cook the stuffed French toast until the bottom is golden brown and the custard is set. Flip it over and continue to cook on the other side. Cook as many as will fit in the pan comfortably and then repeat with the remaining slices.

5. Serve with maple syrup or a sprinkle of confectioners' sugar.

# SOURCES FOR BREAD-BAKING PRODUCTS

**BreadIn5.com store:** www.BreadIn5.com
**Bob's Red Mill:** BobsRedMill.com, 800.349.2173
**Cooks of Crocus Hill (St. Paul, Edina, and Stillwater, Minnesota):** CooksOfCrocusHill.com, 651.228.1333, 952.285.1903, or 651.351.1144
**Emile Henry cookware:** EmileHenryUSA.com, 888.346.8853
**Gold Medal Flour:** GoldMedalFlour.com
**Hodgson Mill:** HodgsonMill.com, 800.347.0105
**King Arthur Flour:** KingArthurFlour.com/shop, 800.827.6836
**Le Creuset cookware:** LeCreuset.com, 877.418.5547
**Lodge Cast Iron cookware:** LodgeMfg.com, 423.837.7181
**Penzeys Spices:** Penzeys.com, 800.741.7787
**Red Star Yeast:** RedStarYeast.com, 800.445.5746
**Tupperware:** Tupperware.com, 800.366.3800

# INDEX

# Index